Political Policing

Political Policing

The United States and Latin America

Martha K. Huggins

Duke University Press Durham and London 1998

© 1998 Duke University Press   All rights reserved

Printed in the United States of America on acid-free paper ∞

Typeset in Weiss by Keystone Typesetting, Inc.

Library of Congress Cataloging-in-Publication Data appear on the

last printed page of this book.

Portuguese edition by Cortez Editora, SãoPaulo, Brazil, 1998

Frontispiece: Leon Golub's *White Squad V*, 1984, acrylic on canvas.

The Eli Broad Family Foundation. © *Leon Golub*

to Malcolm Willison
for his lifelong struggle to democratize power
and secure justice and peace

Contents

Preface   ix

Acknowledgments   xix

1   Policing International Politics: Theory and Practice   1

2   "Gunboat" Policing: The First Twenty-five Years   25

3   "Good Neighbor" Policing   41

4   From Policing Espionage to Supressing "Communism":
    World War II and Its Aftermath   58

5   Policing Containment   79

6   Counterinsurgency Policing: Internationalization and
    Professionalization   99

7   Policing Brazil's "Cleanup," 1964–1968   119

8   Repression and the Brazilian Police, 1968–1969   141

9   Fortifying Security and Privatizing Repression: Torture and Death
    Squads in Authoritarian Devolution, 1969–1970   161

10   Closing the Circle: Devolution Abroad and at Home   187

Conclusion   Police Assistance as a "Protection Racket"   197

Appendixes   205
Notes   209
References   213
Index   237

Preface

This book is a study of how internationalizing U.S. security through foreign police training affected countries within Latin America and in particular Brazil. Examining U.S. assistance to police elsewhere brings together issues of international relations with those of internal security and human rights, as well as of criminal justice and the sociology of policing. Such intellectual intersections, however, were not the initial intention of this study, begun almost ten years ago as a straightforward examination of U.S. police training in Latin America. Yet the data made clear that what appeared to be a simple U.S. criminal justice initiative in foreign police assistance had in fact much wider significance. The once-classified records of the U.S. Departments of State, War, and Defense, of the Agency for International Development, and of the Federal Bureau of Investigation and the Central Intelligence Agency demonstrated that the apparent criminal justice function and purposes of foreign police training programs masked more fundamental domestic and foreign, internal and external security objectives of U.S. assistance to foreign police. These documents helped reveal the real relationship of U.S. policy to foreign police violations of international human rights, including the evolution of death squads in Brazil.

Thus, although this study was not launched to focus on internal security issues or international relations, not to have done so would have ignored clear patterns in the data. By carefully examining data from more than six hundred sources—most of them original primary materials (almost a thousand pages of previously classified U.S. and Brazilian government documents)—*Political Policing* begins to reconstruct more than eighty years of U.S. involvement with Latin American internal security, with particular emphasis on Brazil. This reconstructed picture has suggested that this study focus on the links among—and their consequences for—criminal justice in Latin America, relations with the United States, and U.S. definitions of "national security" at home and abroad.

Theoretical Background

When I began this research, there were no clear theoretical guidelines for uncovering and explaining patterns in the data. Only now can

Ethan Nadelmann's *Cops Across Borders* (1993), a masterful study of cross-border drug policing, provide important insights into the possible international relations intentions and consequences of cross-national policing; however, Nadelmann himself did not fully consider these implications. Gary Marx's ongoing comparative analysis of police systems in Europe provides a model for analyzing cross-national policing, but this too does not seem to link such policing theoretically to internal security planning. More recently, two theoretically informed studies by Elizabeth Cancelli (1993) and Laura Fleischman Kalmanowiecki (1994) have examined more systematically the international politics of policing in Brazil and Argentina, respectively. However, these studies focus only on the 1920s and 1930s. Peter Gill's *Policing Politics: Security Intelligence and the Liberal Democratic State* (1994) examines, primarily for Great Britain, the domestic and international politics of internal security. Yet like almost all of the other scholarship, Gill's insightful analysis was not available ten years ago when I began this study.

Hypotheses

Thus, in the early stages of this research, it was simplest to posit that U.S. assistance to foreign police was aimed at promoting more effective criminal justice in host nations, taking conventional criminology's premise that improvements in criminal justice foster fairer, more rational, and more apolitical maintenance of public order. Yet the archival data on U.S. programs to assist foreign police soon consistently demonstrated that even though such assistance had indeed been outwardly promoted as a nonpolitical and legal-rational instrument for democratizing and putting the restraints of law on recipient countries' justice systems, the impact and sometimes even the internally expressed intention of such assistance had often been just the opposite.

On the one hand, this raised the possibility that a well-intentioned program had simply gone awry for one or several reasons or, on the other hand, suggested that the implicit but real goals of U.S. foreign police training were indeed something other than its explicitly stated objectives. In fact, according to the latter explanation, the actual intent of U.S. training of foreign police has been above all U.S. political control over recipient countries' internal security. This proposition is hardly surprising after everything that has come out about the United States' involvement in Vietnam, El Salvador and Guatemala, and a host of other countries. But it is not suggested by the ordinary criminological or internal security literatures.

A conventional mainstream hypothesis might go so far as to posit that training foreign police in "modern" techniques had an international relations objective. But this goal would be simply to depoliticize foreign police and make recipient countries' internal security systems more just and bound by law. Such a hypothesis has certainly been supported by public U.S. foreign policy statements and official papers.

However, one alternative hypothesis can be derived from the world-systems view of center-and-periphery relations, which would propose that foreign police training offered by a powerful modern state would be primarily politically motivated to foster the offering country's own international security agenda—whether or not recipient governments became more just and legalistic in the process. This hypothesis seems clearly substantiated by the secret and top secret classified U.S. government documents examined for this book.

But this study will in fact demonstrate that rather than one of these seemingly competing hypotheses being correct and the other false, both motives appear to be true, depending on which evidence one relies on. The public pronouncements of U.S. government officials have indeed proposed foreign police assistance as an apolitical means of fostering democracy and justice, whereas the covert plans and programs of U.S. internal security specialists have been expressly aimed at making foreign police into a political extension and servant of U.S. military and CIA internal security concerns. In any case, rather than U.S. foreign police assistance making recipient country police more humane and respectful of citizen rights, such assistance has most frequently fostered the opposite development. This study thus shows that "modernization" and "professionalization" have unintended (or sometimes intended) consequences that contradict the assumption that these processes always lead to greater constraint on police toward legality and justice.

Secrets in International Security

Thus a study that had begun as an examination of an international criminal justice initiative and its consequences for host countries became also an analysis of the U.S. domestic politics of international internal security efforts. However, seeking guidance from the academic international relations and internal security literatures, I found no significant analyses of past U.S. foreign police assistance programs, despite the evidence that was turning up on their unsavory outcomes. This surprising gap deepened my suspicion that there were unexamined objectives behind U.S. assistance to foreign police, which could help to explain acceptance of outcomes unacceptable for a democratic society—as the covert-motives hypothesis suggested. In fact, one is led to suspect that it is precisely because U.S. foreign police training programs were so closely linked to U.S. international security planning and operations that scholarly research on their significance had been so little encouraged or successfully pursued. This possibility naturally whetted my desire to find out what seemed to be the hidden U.S. agenda.

Researching under Secrecy

It does not help our understanding of these programs that so much archival data about U.S. foreign police assistance has been classified "secret," "top secret," or "for eyes only." Fear of unsavory revelations undoubtedly also explains why it was so difficult to secure interviews with former U.S. internal security officials and foreign recipient police. Yet although the greatest stumbling block to this research was—and still is—U.S. government secrecy, I myself was uneasy about examining a subject that so many present and former U.S. and Latin American government officials considered off-limits. Indeed, the long association of U.S. post–World War II foreign police training with the CIA could not help but intimidate almost any researcher.

In any case, no matter how often U.S. government agencies were petitioned through the Freedom of Information Act (FOIA), much information was blacked out or could not be secured at all for a variety of countries, particularly covering the 1960s and 1970s. Thus, because of these gaps in information about U.S. programs to assist foreign police, the analysis here relies not on a continuous historical narrative but on a series of episodes treated as test cases.

Among the Latin American countries receiving foreign police assistance, the most complete records are on Brazil, the largest country in Latin America, and in any event a very important case of U.S. assistance to Latin American police. In the first place, Brazil holds great geopolitical significance for the United States—as Latin America's largest and most populous country, with the biggest gross national product per

capita in Latin America. Second, because of Brazil's geopolitical importance to the United States, it was a model for U.S. rural and urban anti-
insurgency planning in Latin America. Third, among Latin American
countries, Brazil received the largest amount of U.S. internal security
assistance (Abourezk 1974b). Fourth, as a result of investigations into
the U.S.-Brazilian police assistance program, along with mounting evidence of other assisted countries' abuses of human rights, the United
States Congress in 1974 banned most further U.S. assistance to foreign
police. Finally, the relative visibility in congressional hearings of the
U.S. police training program in Brazil made these data somewhat easier
to obtain.

Yet it is not possible to develop broad theoretical propositions about
U.S. internal security objectives abroad, nor about the social control
consequences of U.S. assistance to foreign police, by examining only
Brazil after 1959, when the U.S. police program began there. In order
to chart the changing U.S. rationales for, procedures in, and impacts
from U.S. foreign police assistance, and to illustrate both overt and
covert motives for changing impacts of internal security initiatives, it
was necessary to take a longer time frame for Brazil and use this also to
examine a variety of other Latin American countries.

Research Process and Data

The research for *Political Policing* took ten years, as already indicated.
Between bouts of writing, I went periodically to the field, whether to
conduct interviews or to consult archives in the United States or Brazil.
I traveled to eight U.S. states and Washington, D.C., and to four of the
largest state capitals in Brazil, as well as Brasília, the federal capital. Well
over half the data have never been used by other social scientists. Much
of the data were obtained by persuading officials to be interviewed, by
the long, drawn-out application process through the FOIA and Mandatory Review legislation, and by negotiating with Brazilian authorities
and police. But although a great deal of "national security" secrecy
surrounded the data for this study, the research process follows the
standard mode for empirical studies in the social sciences.

The first step was to locate appropriate archival data and interviewees
through the secondary literature about the various aspects of my subject and by initial research at the National Archives. These sources then
pointed to appropriate archival records and suggested possible inter-

viewees as I more carefully defined the scope of my research project. After each research trip to a U.S. government archive, I submitted new sets of Mandatory Review or FOIA requests. Over the course of eight years, I became quite experienced and persistent in submitting FOIA requests to the various U.S. government agencies. Such petitioning required time and patience, as the waiting period on any FOIA or Mandatory Review request was between one and five years and involved many request denials and resubmissions. In the end, about 30 percent of my FOIA and Mandatory Review requests were denied because the data were still defined as too closely linked to "national security." And in some cases when documents were actually received, they were so heavily blacked out ("sanitized") that they were only marginally useful.

A good portion of the written materials for this study was obtained from presidential libraries—in particular, those of Franklin Roosevelt, Dwight Eisenhower, John Kennedy, and Lyndon Johnson. Many of the presidential documents had not yet been seen by other scholars and had to be secured through Mandatory Review legislation.

Another source of data was the U.S. National Archives itself, in particular, its holdings in Old and New Military Affairs, Old and New State Department, and the Legislative Archives. Many of these documents, too, were classified top secret or secret and could be obtained only under Mandatory Review legislation. The majority of these requests were granted, although again not without some "sanitizing" of the texts. A great many of these materials, too, had not been used by other researchers.

Among the most useful documents on U.S. assistance to foreign police were those of the U.S. Agency for International Development Office of Public Safety (OPS), which had administered foreign police training under John Kennedy and Lyndon Johnson. A particularly rich source of OPS information was its monthly police training reports (TOAID) from Brazil; they were submitted to AID each month by U.S. police advisors in the field. These reports contain information about police advisors' Brazilian police contacts, the advisors' projects and accomplishments, and their observations. These richly informative and never-before-consulted reports were obtained from AID through the Freedom of Information Act.

But despite my using the FOIA to secure documents from the Central Intelligence Agency, the National Security Council, and the Federal

Bureau of Investigation, only about 20 percent of these were released by the agencies. In fact, it was the CIA's reluctance to declassify information about their 1950s and 1960s police programs that confirmed the strategic importance of foreign police assistance to U.S. international security planning and operations.

The records of two former FBI agents who had worked in Brazil during the 1930s and 1940s were requested from the FBI, including information about these FBI agents' Brazilian contacts and informants. The names of the FBI agents and their informants had been secured from records at the Franklin D. Roosevelt Library and the National Archives; to obtain their records, I had to supply proof that the former FBI agents and their informants were deceased. A Brazilian senator helped me get proof-of-death information on the FBI's former Brazilian informants; the FBI verified that its former agents had died. Yet even with such information, I was able to secure only about 20 percent of my FOIA requests to the FBI, and some of the documents obtained were thoroughly blacked out.

The senatorial papers of James Abourezk (D-S.Dak.), Frank Church (D-Idaho), and J. William Fulbright (D-Ark.) also provided important insights into U.S. internal security programs. Of these, Abourezk's papers at the University of South Dakota provided the richest picture of U.S. foreign police training, given the senator's vigorous efforts to abolish the program in the 1960s and early 1970s. Archival research in the Abourezk papers was conducted by Mary Helgevold at my request and following my suggested leads. I traveled to Boise, Idaho, to consult Senator Frank Church's papers, only to discover that the CIA had withdrawn and classified as top secret much of the rich documentation from the Church hearings. The papers of J. William Fulbright at Fayetteville, Arkansas, cover the senator's long tenure in Congress, providing useful background on the period of this study. But Senator Fulbright's papers in fact contained little material on police training, even though other archival records show that Fulbright had reviewed funding for the police program and had heard testimony from CIA director Richard Helms about Brazil's police training program. None of this material was among Fulbright's papers.

A complementary source of information about U.S. foreign police training was the archives of the International Association of Chiefs of Police (IACP) at Gaithersburg, Maryland. This private association of police chiefs was involved in some phases of U.S. foreign police training under Eisenhower—usually in collaboration with the CIA. Yet the IACP archives provided relatively little information about this organization's involvement in foreign police training. This was probably because, according to an IACP official who supervised the CIA's removal of IACP documents from this facility, most of these materials were "warehoused" and thus beyond my reach. One suspects they contained too much about the CIA's involvement with IACP foreign police training.

Unlike the IACP documents, the records of Michigan State University, providing U.S. police training in South Vietnam during Eisenhower's presidency, still contain evidence of the CIA's involvement with foreign police training. But the MSU documents were not useful to this study of Latin America because almost all apply to South Vietnam, where MSU had its principal program.

In São Paulo, I surveyed the newly opened state civil police (DOPS) records at the Archives of the State of São Paulo (Arquivo do Estado de São Paulo); I also went through the daily *Estado de São Paulo* newspaper morgue. In Niterói, near Rio de Janeiro, I obtained data from the newly opened records of the Rio de Janeiro DOPS, consulted historical papers at the Getúlio Vargas Foundation, and examined *O Globo*'s newspaper archives. The Rio de Janeiro DOPS records had not been catalogued or organized; they were stacked on shelves, without alphabetical, chronological, or subject order. It was necessary to sort through stacks of record books and read almost every police voucher from the 1950s and 1960s just to locate relevant information.

Interviews with Participants

An even greater challenge, however, was to secure oral history interviews with U.S. and Brazilian government police and other officials who had been associated with police assistance efforts. Many of these people were reluctant to give away their own or their organization's secrets. Their unwillingness to participate in my study was fueled by the negative publicity about their operations surrounding Congress's abolishing U.S. foreign police training in 1974. The resentment and anger of people who had been involved in foreign police training meant that many of them did not trust anyone examining their programs. Indeed, the response of Loren "Jack" Goin, former head of AID's police assistance program, to my writing a *Los Angeles Times* op-ed article—"U.S. Assistance to Foreign Police Backfires" (1987)—was to turn my name over to the Accuracy in the Media organization (AIM) and recommend that his AID colleagues not grant me any interviews. But even such tactics could be overcome through persistence and by better interviewing skills.

In the United States, a number of officials were interviewed who had been involved with U.S. foreign police training programs. Among them were former Under Secretary of State U. Alexis Johnson—over the telephone; former CIA Deputy Director of Intelligence Robert Amory—at his house and then in his old Ford Pinto in the parking lot of the First American Bank in Roswell, Virginia; Byron Engle, first director of the USAID Office of Public Safety—over buffalo hamburgers at his Bethesda, Maryland, apartment; Goin, Engle's replacement as head of OPS—in the basement office of his house in Virginia; Robert Komer, national security advisor to John Kennedy and former head of the Phoenix Program in Vietnam—over the telephone; and former OPS police advisors Nicholas Yantsen, Ralph Turner, and Stanley Sheldon—at their homes. Sheldon, besides having been a police advisor in Brazil, had been a consultant for the police show *Dragnet*.

Some of the most important primary material for this study came from oral histories taken from Brazilians who had been in police service during the military period (1964–1985). Initially, when I could not get police who had been in the police torture and death squad apparatus to grant me interviews, I sought out police who had been in units associated with political repression in general (Huggins and Haritos-Fatouros 1996a, 1996b). Ironically, the prospective interviewees who had been involved directly in torture and death squads were reluctant to grant an interview, even though Brazil had granted amnesty from prosecution to those who had tortured and murdered. But from the perspective of such potential interviewees, they had nothing to gain and everything to lose from letting me dig into their pasts: besides having to remember things that they had worked hard to deny and forget, experience had taught them that they might be pursued by human rights activists for their past police activities (Huggins and Haritos-Fatouros 1996a, 1996b).

Nonetheless, after several months of interviewing policemen who had been in service during Brazil's military period, I finally located a police official who had commanded a police squad infamous for torture and murder. This official then recommended me to one of his colleagues, and that official to one of his colleagues, and so on. The interviews progressed thereafter by referral, from one police colleague to another.

In all, a total of twenty-seven oral histories were conducted with former police in São Paulo, Rio de Janeiro, Rio Grande do Sul, Pernambuco, and Brasília. About a third of these oral history interviews—which are part of a study with Mika Haritos-Fatouros on Brazilian police torturers—involved former police who had been directly involved in torture and death squads.[1] Following the interviewees' stipulation, their names will not be cited in this manuscript, only their initials, the date, and the interview location.

Analytical Framework

The patchy record from U.S. assistance to foreign police led me to devise an analytical strategy for developing and testing theoretical assertions with these only partially available data. My technique was to pinpoint available episodes in the history of U.S. assistance to Latin American police and then place such data in their international and national sociopolitical contexts. It was from the process of archival research, interviews, analysis, and writing up of patterns in these episodes—each representing different moments in the politics of Latin American police assistance—that I have derived the four principal theoretical theses on the relationship of foreign police assistance to the internationalization, bureaucratization, and devolution of internal security.

Overall, these theses assert that U.S. assistance to Latin American police contributed to internationalizing the U.S. internal security concerns by helping to centralize recipient countries' internal security services and become more militarized and authoritarian. This process, in turn, gave rise over time to a partial devolution of such states' internal security systems, as the central government gave up some control over the operations that U.S. police training had helped to create. These theses are elaborated in Chapter 1 and then demonstrated in sociological analyses of the episodes presented throughout the book.

Acknowledgments

I learned quickly that research involving people guarding personal and institutional secrets cannot be accomplished without assistance from a variety of scholars, journalists, and writers. The most helpful were those who had already conducted research on U.S. foreign police training programs. Taylor Branch, author of *Parting the Waters* (1988), supplied information from his earlier research about a CIA proprietary front that had been part of the Eisenhower and Kennedy police training programs. Joseph Spear, of the news-gathering Jack Anderson Organization, gave me his old investigative reports and field notes on U.S. police training programs. Senator Thomas Daschell (D-S.Dak.), a former aide to Senator James Abourezk (D-S.Dak.) during Abourezk's campaign to abolish U.S. training of foreign police, helped me obtain data on past police training programs. James Abourezk himself granted me an interview and gave generous and invaluable assistance with locating information for this study. They all deserve my thanks.

Several others also provided direction for this study. Philip Agee read a final version of the manuscript and made valuable criticisms. Also most helpful was A. J. Langguth, whose *Hidden Terrors* (1978) is a classic in the study of police training and terror in Brazil and Uruguay. Jan Black's scholarly account of U.S. assistance to Brazilian police, "Redefining Law and Order: The Public Safety Assistance Program," a chapter in her *United States Penetration of Brazil* (1977), is another early model for scholarship on this highly sensitive subject, as is Michael Klare and Cynthia Arnson's *Supplying Repression* (1981). Roger Morris's court records from a lawsuit brought against him by former police trainer Adolph Saenz for Morris's *Playboy* article about Saenz's role as warden at the time of the New Mexico Prison massacre also provided data on the torture and violence committed by U.S.-affiliated foreign police.

To all who assisted me in this way, I owe a tremendous debt. But in particular I want to thank Jack Langguth for taking time to discuss his research with me; he provided a great deal of intellectual and moral support early in the research when I most needed it. Two other writers, Taylor Branch and Roger Morris, were also especially instrumental in getting this project launched. The two anonymous referees selected by Duke University Press provided feedback on the completed manuscript to make it more polished.

Among Brazilianists, I owe thanks especially to Robert Levine, who read and critiqued an early version of this manuscript. Frank McCann provided numerous analytical comments on my presentations of this project. Police sociologist David Bayley provided generous guidance at various points in my writing on policing in general. Charles Call carefully read a final version of the manuscript and provided useful feedback and additional information about a new U.S. government police training initiative. Attending conferences and meeting in the field with human rights activist and police specialist Paul Chevigny was inspiring; his guidance on studying the police has been vital to my education. My colleagues at the Columbia University Brazil Seminar asked hard questions and provided valuable insights about the politics of U.S. police assistance to Brazil.

Elizabeth Cancelli of the University of Brasília and Myriam Mesquita, formerly at the University of São Paulo's Núcleo de Estudos da Violência and now with UNICEF in São Paulo, provided constant guidance and encouragement. Ester Kosovski of the Federal University of Rio de Janeiro, besides encouraging me to complete this project, also provided moral support and a place to stay in Rio de Janeiro. Several Brazilian police informants and my Brazilian colleague and police specialist, Guaracy Mingardi, were very helpful in clarifying the structure of Brazilian policing.

Two old friends, Nancy Sharlet and Charley Tidmarch, both of whom have died, were always enthusiastic and encouraging about my work. Four friends, Elizabeth Griffen and Andrew Feffer, and Eshtagh Motahar and Lana Cable, listened carefully to my ideas and helped guide them. William Bristol, an old friend and colleague, was always ready with historical facts, figures, and orientation.

My students, Tamara Albury, Amy Herf, Dena Mahar, Ahnya Mendes, Erika Migliaccio, and Monét Warren, carried out valuable tasks, from locating and checking references to verifying quotes, locating and listing agency names, and helping assemble the final manuscript. Especially for the latter, Erika is due very special thanks. In São Paulo, Caryn Howell Pellegrino worked with me on the *Estado de São Paulo* archives and acted as a sounding board for ideas. I owe a debt of gratitude to all of these and other scholars, friends, and students for assisting this project. For typing drafts of various chapters, I thank Carolyn Micklas, Janet McQuade, and Marianne Moore, without whose care and close attention this manuscript could not have reached its final form. I will be forever indebted to Valerie Millholland of Duke University for accepting *Political Policing* into her Latin America series and, along with her able assistant, Laura Barnebey, guiding the study skillfully to its final form.

None of this research would have been possible without the capable assistance of archivists at the Roosevelt, Eisenhower, Kennedy, and Johnson Presidential Libraries, and at the National Archives, Federal Bureau of Investigation, International Association of Chiefs of Police, and Agency for International Development. Over the eight years of researching and writing this book, Union College's reference librarians, especially Donna Burton, Mary Cahill, Bruce Connolly, and David Gerhan, helped me assiduously in locating obscure sources, always with gracious and enthusiastic encouragement and expert assistance. Special thanks are also due to Robert Parks of the Franklin D. Roosevelt Library and Willette Smith of USAID for their last-minute research on missing facts. All these librarians and archivists deserve my heartfelt thanks.

Of course, my research at widely scattered locations required funding. Yet although I wrote innumerable grant proposals to appropriate foundations, they never seemed convinced that sufficient information could be obtained on programs that had been affiliated with U.S. military intelligence and the CIA. Consequently, the majority of the support for this research came from my endowed Roger Thayer Stone Chair in Sociology at Union College, for which I am most grateful to the late Dr. Doris Zemurray Stone and her son, Dr. Samuel Z. Stone. For the research on former Brazilian police who had been in Brazil's national security apparatus, the Hamburger Stiftung zur Förderung von Wissenschaft und Kultur gave funding; Mika Haritos-Fatouros, my colleague in that research, suggested the police torture study in the first place and encouraged me to use some of our data in this project.

Even more than with my other two books, this difficult study could not have been accomplished without the support, encouragement, and editorial guidance of my husband, Malcolm Willison—to whom *Political Policing* is dedicated for his own lifelong struggle to democratize power and secure justice and peace.

\

1 Policing International Politics: Theory and Practice

In the early 1990s, more than fifteen years after Congress had abolished programs to assist foreign police, the United States had 125 police assistance programs abroad. Such initiatives were justified as legitimately exempted from the 1973 and 1974 laws abolishing U.S. assistance to foreign police. The new police assistance programs aim at a range of problems from combating common and organized crime and "gangsterism" to "terrorism" and drugs. A broad array of U.S. government agencies and civilian police specialists carry out such assistance today (GAO 1992).

In Russia, Eastern Europe, and Asia, the Federal Bureau of Investigation oversees police programs on the "rule of law" to control petty crime, "organized crime," and "gangsterism." In the process, the FBI hopes to develop "speaking partners" among its police trainees— nationals who will become "trustworthy enough to help the FBI . . . [obtain foreign offenders'] bank records, [and] other materials and [who will become reliable] witnesses" in FBI investigations of crime in the host country (Pincus 1994).

The United States is completely reorganizing indigenous police forces in a number of foreign countries, mostly through the Department of Defense Program to Assist National Police Forces, including those of Bolivia, Peru, Ecuador, Colombia, Panama, and Mexico (GAO 1992). In Bosnia, the U.S. Justice Department has civilian police specialists working with local police forces; in the early 1990s, the U.S. military was creating a new police system in Somalia. In Haiti, U.S. military and civilian police specialists, assisted by United Nations forces and the Central Intelligence Agency—all headed by former New York City Police Commissioner Raymond W. Kelly—have been reorganizing the national police constabulary there.

Throughout the Caribbean—particularly in the republics of the Leeward and Windward Islands—U.S. military and civilian police specialists are carrying out "antiterrorist" police training, funded in part through the U.S. State Department's $12 million Anti-Terrorism Assistance Program (ATA) (GAO 1992). The ATA's goal is "to enhance the skills of experienced police officials in the unique context of fighting terrorism" (Andersen 1993, 99). The U.S. Drug Enforcement Administration (DEA) is also sponsoring police training programs, these in South America, with a mix of purposes—anticrime, counterterrorism, counterinsurgency, and drug interdiction.

Within this overlapping set of U.S. agencies and individuals assisting foreign police, the Justice Department's International Criminal Investigative Training Assistance Program (ICITAP) has emerged in the 1990s as a primary coordinator of U.S. assistance to foreign police. Established in 1986 under the administration of the Department of Justice, ICITAP operates with policy guidance from the Department of State. ICITAP funding comes from the United States Agency for International Development, channeled through the State Department.[1] ICITAP's objective is to train foreign police, prosecutors, judges, and other criminal justice personnel to further the "rule of law" in their countries (GAO 1992). Promoting an ideology different from its Cold War predecessor, which was the Agency for International Development's Office of Public Safety (OPS) (1962–1974), ICITAP aims at promoting peaceful respect for the "rule of law." AID had focused on counterinsurgency as a means of blocking the spread of international Communism. Yet, in fact, both of these foreign police assistance initiatives share a common foreign policy objective: developing, enhancing, and protecting U.S. interests abroad and promoting abroad and at home U.S. images of "national security."

As powerfully as the "rule of law" might now ideologically guide and justify foreign police assistance, in fact, today, no single all-powerful ideology explains U.S. assistance to foreign police and military systems, as did the Cold War containment doctrine from the 1950s through the 1980s. Thus—as the ideological underpinnings of foreign police assistance have shifted with geopolitical changes in the world system, and as the centralizing hegemonies of the Cold War are replaced by post–Cold War decentralization, and counterinsurgency with the "rule of law"—the objective of assisting foreign police remains to transform such police into "transmission belts" (see Arendt 1951) for U.S. foreign policy and U.S. economic and political interests abroad. In the process, such programs provide a mechanism for the United States to penetrate foreign states through their police systems, turning foreign police into appendages of U.S. foreign policy—a process whose political roots and foreign policy objectives reach deep into the last century.

Purposes of Foreign Police Assistance

For example, looking just at Latin America, we notice that in the first third of the twentieth century, the United States established police constabularies in its dependencies in the Greater Antilles and Central America. These constabularies helped secure the U.S. hold over Cuba, Puerto Rico, and the Virgin Islands and guard U.S. construction and operation of the Panama Canal. Just before and during World War II, fear of threats to U.S. interests in Latin America turned U.S. involvement with Latin American police into a means for gathering information that would help protect the Western Hemisphere against Communist organizing and fascist espionage activities.

In the years after World War II, U.S. training of Latin American police was explicitly designed to combat the perceived threat of left-wing subversion and armed guerrilla insurgency; the United States feared that local police would not be organizationally or ideologically prepared to confront these perceived threats to the United States—a frame of mind promoted by a Cold War national security ideology. Helping to create a climate of crisis and fear justifying the need for U.S. internal security assistance, Cold War containment ideologies remained strong into the 1990s, even as Cold War counterinsurgency ideology was increasingly replaced by discourse about counterterrorism, narcotics control, and suppression of organized crime.

Policing International Relations

As we have already suggested, foreign police assistance has had an important place in United States foreign policy, even though it is seldom included in foreign policy analyses. Most important, as a foreign policy instrument, police assistance has the advantage of appearing to be a relatively benign and low-key form of U.S. intervention. Indeed, when Washington ties foreign police assistance to the rationale that it will make recipient police forces more democratic, less violent, less corrupt, and more professional—as Washington has argued most recently for Somalia and Haiti—the U.S. image abroad and at home can be (at least initially) bolstered by such relatively invisible intervention. In contrast, military incursions (with takeover by force of a foreign government and reorganization of its military and police systems) are highly visible forms of U.S. intervention, often very unpopular at home and abroad, and have potentially serious consequences for U.S. politics and its image in the world. Police assistance can accomplish many of the same U.S. foreign policy objectives as military intervention while appearing less political in the process.

As Arendt (1951, 421) has argued, having foreign police penetrate another country acts as a "transmission belt . . . which . . . transform[s one country's foreign policy] into the . . . domestic business of [another country]." In other words, as the United States trains foreign police, it can establish intelligence and other social control infrastructure for protecting and strengthening its position vis-à-vis the recipient country and maximize its position within the international world system. This makes foreign police assistance—whether publicly recognized or not— fundamentally political, although of course this has not usually been a publicized motive behind U.S. assistance to foreign police.

Consequences of Foreign Police Assistance

Although Washington's public motive for offering assistance to foreign police has been to increase "public security" and make police practices more humane, there is no evidence that earlier foreign police training has made recipient countries safer, less crime ridden, or more free of drugs (Huggins 1987). Nor is there any evidence that long-term assistance to foreign police has made the practices of recipient police more democratic or their countries' populations more secure from arbitrary treatment by state agents, as evidenced by the impact of almost a century of U.S. assistance to Latin American police. Indeed, two well-publicized Senate hearings, one by Frank Church (D-Ind.) (1972) and the other by James Abourezk (D-S.Dak.) (1973), uncovered persistent and mounting evidence of torture, disappearances, and killings by police trained and equipped by the United States.

Take Guatemala, where in the 1960s the Spanish passive verb *desaparecido* (to be disappeared) originated: the nation had had U.S. police training programs since the 1954 U.S.-orchestrated overthrow of democratically elected president Jacobo Arbenz Guzmán. Since then, the police have participated with the Guatemalan army in torturing and killing or "disappearing" at least 130,000 civilians (Americas Watch 1988, 5–6).

As a warning of how foreign police assistance programs could violate fundamental American values, the 1971 U.S. Senate Subcommittee

Hearings on Western Hemisphere Affairs (CFR 1971a) particularly focused on U.S. assistance to Brazil. The subcommittee questioned whether—rather than increasing Brazil's internal security—police assistance had simply bolstered Brazil's authoritarian military government by fostering police militarization and death squads while damaging the U.S. image abroad and undermining Brazil's social peace.

Thus, in spite of the long-standing political importance of foreign police to U.S. internal security planning, in 1974 Congress in bipartisan action banned most further U.S. assistance to foreign police. But, as we have seen, this ban on U.S. training of foreign police did not put an end to such assistance. Congress immediately exempted narcotics control and then in the 1980s further expanded foreign police assistance to cover antinarcotics training abroad (see GAO 1992; Nadelmann 1993). In 1985 the Reagan administration officially reinstated foreign police training to counter what the president labeled Nicaraguan and Cuban "terrorism." In the Eastern Caribbean, a newly created Regional Security System included police "counterterrorism" training, particularly after the U.S. invasion of tiny Grenada against supposedly Cuban-backed insurgents (Treaster 1985, A2). In 1986 the CIA announced its borrowing of U.S. police for temporary duty abroad in its "war against terrorism" (Raab 1986). U.S. military and CIA advisors began training police "counterterrorism" units in Costa Rica, El Salvador, Honduras, and Guatemala (Lugar 1985).

Yet in most countries, even the more recent decades of such U.S. assistance have not brought recipients closer to respecting the "rule of law." Consider El Salvador, where the United States has trained police since the 1940s. By the late 1980s—a period of renewed U.S. police aid to El Salvador—that country had one of the worst human rights records in the hemisphere. Between 1987 and 1988 alone, killings by Salvadoran security forces were up 28 percent; death squad murders had increased by 135 percent (*NYT* 1988b). The 1992 United Nations "Truth Commission" Report on El Salvador (U.N. 1993) confirmed that the U.S.-trained police and military forces had acted with widespread brutality throughout the 1980s.

In early 1988, reports surfaced in Honduras that a U.S.-trained Honduran Special Investigations Directorate—already notorious as "Battalion 316"—had been operating as a death squad responsible for the murder of at least 130 Hondurans by that time (*New Yorker* 1988, 23). And in 1988 and 1989, while the United States was providing antiterrorism training to the Honduran police—following thirty years of al-most continuous U.S. police assistance—the torture and beatings of civilians by police and security forces tripled, with at least seventy-eight killed in just the first seven months of 1989 (Gruson 1989, 14).

Today, as the United States attempts to reform the historically brutal and corrupt U.S.-trained Haitian police, the police demonstrate few positive benefits from past U.S. assistance. In fact, decades of U.S. training of Haitians have been associated, especially over the last thirty years, with well-documented human rights abuses. Just as the newest round of police assistance was getting under way, it was disclosed that the leader of one of Haiti's most infamous and violent paramilitary groups, FRAPH—allegedly established with CIA support and encour-agement—was still on the CIA's payroll (Engelberg 1994, 1, 4; Nairn 1994). While linked to the CIA, Emmanuel "Toto" Constant, a sup-porter of the military dictatorship, organized a violent demonstration to prevent the docking of a U.S. Navy ship that was bringing troops to support the reinstatement by the United States and its allies of Jean Bertrand Aristide, Haiti's democratically elected president. In other words, decades of U.S. assistance had guaranteed neither nonviolence nor loyalty to U.S. policy.

Police Assistance in International Relations:
Some Alternative Hypotheses

Clearly, this review of some past and present recipients of U.S. police assistance calls into question U.S. public foreign policy documents, official government memoranda, and other discourse that has proposed that training foreign police would make these police more neutrally professional, positively humanitarian, and democratically responsive to civilian control. The data to be presented here suggest the contrary—that the more foreign police aid given, the more brutal and less demo-cratic the police institutions and their governments become. Several alternative hypotheses will be needed to explain both these effects of and the international relations motives revealed behind U.S. training of foreign police.

Before presenting the evidence for these counterhypotheses in subse-quent chapters, it would be useful to introduce briefly the explanations to be proposed on how U.S. training might have allowed greater police repression in recipient countries. One answer might be that the U.S.

government was unaware of these results or powerless to do anything about them. But we shall see that the data will not support such an explanation. An alternative hypothesis is that this outcome has been the result of deliberate U.S. policy—the data at least indirectly substantiate this. An associated hypothesis is that greater police repression in countries that are recipients of U.S. assistance results from "professionalization"—in particular, the kind of "professional" police assistance the United States has most often offered, namely, militarizing the police and inculcating a war model of social control—suggesting a hypothesis that the data will support. Where this model meant providing foreign police with military arms and equipment and promoting militarized modes of social control, then violence and violent repression could be expected, leading to even more harm to citizens. This is certainly suggested by Jerome Skolnick and James Fyfe's *Above the Law* (1993), a parallel examination of the effects of police militarization on the Los Angeles Police Department in California, and by Paul Chevigny's *Edge of the Knife: Police Violence in the Americas* (1995), a comparative study of municipal police violence in Buenos Aires, São Paulo, Mexico City, Jamaica, Los Angeles, and New York City. If such a hypothesis about the effects of U.S. militarizing of Latin American police is supported by the evidence, it would suggest the naïveté of any assumption—and the inauthenticity of any claim—that U.S. training of Latin American police was intended to make those police more neutral in enforcement, humanitarian in goals and outlook, democratic in public behavior, and responsive to civilian government.

Indeed, another of this study's countertheses is that the real objective of foreign police assistance has been quite uninterested in such goals, but rather to gain political control over recipient countries' internal security by increasing the information available to the training country—the United States—and expanding its influence over host governments' internal security systems. So this study of political policing therefore also hypothesizes that rather than an apolitical means for international technology and values transfer—as U.S. assistance to foreign police has often been described—foreign police training has been used almost exclusively to promote specific U.S. national security political interests and objectives.

In turn, if this hypothesis is supported by the study's finding a lack of U.S. concern for democratizing police, then this in turn reinforces the claim that foreign police training resulted in just the opposite of democratic control. By increasing the recipient state's efficiency in stifling citizen participation and political dissent, such a consequence could promote authoritarian government by militarizing internal control—whether or not this was the explicit objective of U.S. police training.

In fact, in theory, and in official statements, U.S. assistance to foreign police and constabulary forces has been guided by a legal-rational model involving U.S. civil police professionals' providing knowledge and skills about police work to foreign host country police officials and their rank and file. The expressed mission of civil police trainers has been to "professionalize" recipient police and improve the administration and practice of routine police work. However, as we shall see, U.S. training of Latin American police has seldom adhered to such an apolitical model of police professionalization, nor has it been directed at improving the policing skills of an officer walking the beat.

In fact, between 1898 and 1974, U.S. training of Latin American police usually deviated profoundly from this theoretical model. Symptomatically, U.S. personnel who were training Latin American police most often and increasingly came from the U.S. military or national security agencies, and not from civil police organizations. Accordingly, the policing and social control techniques taught were oriented toward military, not civilian, models of control.

In any case, we shall show that the primary objective of such foreign police training was to monitor the host country's internal political threats to U.S. interests or to the host country's own regime or to whatever faction was allied with the United States. And, of course, a Cold War ideology was used to justify such international relations thinking and practice as necessary for U.S. national security interests.

The Police and Politics

Paul Chevigny (1995, 119) has argued that "politics, in the most direct sense, has been part of the police as the police have been part of politics" (see also Bayley 1977; Tilly 1975). When police work is carried out in a highly politicized social climate, as has often been the case in much of Latin America, the politics of such policing are fairly obvious. Likewise, in the United States, when police "red squads" and other police intelligence units have spied on, raided, and arrested alleged political subversives, the politics of this policing are extremely visible. But the politics of policing are more opaque, and often denied, in "normal" policing in the United States and Europe. In such cases, good police work is assumed to be insulated from political motives and objectives. Yet this study assumes that all policing is political, ranging on a continuum from police being very visible handmaids of organized power, as historically in much of Latin America, to their relationship to power being obscured by ideologies of democracy and social control that claim to make police merely extensions of a class-neutral state and "the people."

In fact, however, even this latter version of policing is political, because it involves an official agency backed by state power using force, or threats of force, to control individuals, groups, and classes considered inimical to the social, economic, and political order of the state, and thus to the interests of its dominant classes. Therefore, the role of the police—any police—is to prevent, arrest, or manage regime-threatening conflicts in order to create and maintain a class-structured state monopoly over the use of coercive force. To demonstrate the universal politics of policing, we need to start not with Latin America but with the history of policing in the United States and Europe, where ideologies about democracy and professionalism now project an image of class-neutral policing that often runs counter to the politics of "normal" police practice.

Political Policing in Democracies

Permanent police forces were established in major U.S. cities in the 1840s during a period of intense industrial, social, and political turmoil, when immigration was increasing rapidly, when class, ethnic, and racial riots were exploding in the bigger U.S. cities, and when labor strife was constantly on the rise. According to Harring (1983, 34), urban turmoil led "local commercial elites, concerned about the threat to property and wary of the problem of controlling a growing working class, to brace up local police forces."

Born of political motives, U.S. urban police moved quickly and easily into the politics of their cities. In fact, policemen's job tenure depended on loyal service to local politicians. For example, in New York City in the mid-1850s, "if a Democrat's term expired when the Whigs or later the Republicans [came to] . . . power, [a policeman] could be reasonably sure of having to find a new job" (Richardson 1974, 28). It was a fact of life that U.S. big-city policemen could not afford to be politically neutral (Chevigny 1995, 120).

Indeed, according to Fogelson (1977, 17), "what set the American police apart from . . . [the more centralized] French, German, and British police [was the] relationship [of American police to] the [local] political machine," which benefited from dispensing police jobs as patronage and from using loyal police to maintain its power over the opposition and the unruly. The policemen in turn received not only job security but also the machine's protection and other political favors as long as it was in power (Chevigny 1995, 119–20).

Thus we can see that, from their inception, U.S. urban police forces were "a significant resource at the command of local political organizations" (Haller 1976, 304). In mid-nineteenth-century New York City,

Whoever governed the police had a major source of patronage, could control entry into and operation of illegal businesses . . . [had control over] legitimate businesses subject to public regulation, such as saloons, and had a major advantage in elections. (Richardson 1974, 46)

Police, Professionalization, and Power

Rather than being atypical, New York City's extreme politicizing of the police, in fact, can be considered only one end of a continuum of policing. One way of looking at these policing poles is to label the most visibly political forms of policing as "high" policing, where the police are explicitly used to control any opposition to government. In contrast, at the other pole is "low" policing—ordinary, daily policing that is supposedly without political content (Chevigny 1995, 5). At the low pole, the positioning of modern police within an apparently legal-rational bureaucracy helps generate the general impression of "rule by nobody" (Arendt 1951; see also Ferguson 1984, 16). This leads the larger society—and the police themselves—to consider policing as simply enforcing the impersonal rules of the polity.

But Bourdieu's (1977) view can be used to argue that this analysis of low policing "misrecognizes" the political relationship of police and their work to a class-structured state. A police apparently neutral with respect to politics and class helps disguise and mystify the actually unequal power relations embedded in a social class hierarchy of which police are a part and a support. Professionalization of policing perpetuates the power and privileging of the few through an ideological reorientation of the police toward their work. Through technological and organizational changes in the tools of policing, police carry out their work in support of sociostructural inequality while seeming to do no such thing.

Obscuring Political Policing through Professionalization

But how have modern police been transformed from visible servants of personalistic economic and political interests—where the powerful directly control private gangs and security forces, militias, civil guards, state troops, or urban police—to being seen as an apolitical institution attached to a class-neutral state, while in fact remaining heavily political? The primary mechanism for accomplishing this shift in public and police perception has been this police professionalization. This involves developing and applying a specialized body of knowledge and training, a self-imposed occupational standard of operation, and impersonal and universalistic rules for police appointments, promotion, demotion, and remuneration (Reiss 1971; Chevigny 1995). Whether intended or not, the significant by-product of these changes has been to neutralize the connections between the police and organized power, making these links less visible while diluting the self-identification of rank-and-file police with those whom they control.

To understand this process, we need first to look at why, according to historians of the police, modern police forces were established in the first place, and why in Europe and the United States local and regional power holders did not just continue using their own militias to settle disputes or make greater use of the national military. Robinson's (1978) research on early-twentieth-century Chicago police shows that the elite preferred to use a seemingly apolitical police, over which they had indirect control, rather than continue using more direct control over their own armed groups and the states' National Guard and the U.S. military. At the very least, the less-visible nature of leaders' relationship to the police made possible their disclaiming responsibility for any police repression and malpractice that raised public protest.

Military officers, too, have recognized that using their armed forces to maintain internal security can undermine the public's belief in the military as a patriotic nationalist symbol and even in the legitimacy of the government it serves. Furthermore, the use of the military in maintaining domestic order can create military factions, sometimes splitting the officers' ranks (Bayley 1990; Silver 1967). In any case, the deployment of armies and militias for domestic control tends "to exacerbate [political] problems, making law enforcement transparently political" (Bayley 1990, 43).

Thus, in the nineteenth century, many European governments "faced with reluctant but too forceful armies and enthusiastic but unreliable militias . . . withdrew armies from domestic riot duty, abolished militias, and developed a specialized, public police" (Bayley 1990, 43). In England, for example, during the trade union struggles of the 1830s, the police were apparently more reliable than military recruits because "the soldiers originally shared the economic and social circumstances of many of the discontented persons who went into the riotous mobs, [making] it possible [for the soldiers to] feel sympathetic or even share political views that would impair their performance" (Hamburger 1963, 214). A paid professional police could insulate the power structure "from popular violence . . . [and draw] attack and animosity upon itself" (Silver 1967, 11). Where an "independent police . . . fights the mob, . . . antagonism is directed toward the police, not the power structure" (Cain 1979, 156). In other words, enmeshing police institutions within a complicated civil bureaucracy—including positioning civil police between the state and the military, on the one side, and the people on the other—makes state repression much less obvious in protecting social class and state prerogatives.

Shaping Police Allegiances

But although political leaders have recognized that the police can serve their interests more dependably than military recruits, the predictability of police response to such leaders has not been perfect. The lesson from much research on European and U.S. policing is that the allegiance of rank-and-file police to organized state power has been far from automatic. Gutman's research (1961, 1962, 1968) on riots and strikes in the United States during the late 1870s suggests that the police were also sometimes unwilling to act against striking workers. However, Harring (1983) found, in his research on 100 working-class strikes between 1885 and 1915 in major U.S. cities of the Great Lakes and Ohio Valley, that by then there were relatively few police defections to the side of strikers. In fact, Harring (1983, 102) argues that there is no inconsistency between his and Gutman's findings because by the end of the nineteenth century, many U.S. municipal police had undergone thirty to forty years of preparation for anti-working-class activity. As a result, the "individual police . . . who may have had some sympathy toward striking workers were [more] controlled in . . . anti-working class activity" (Harring 1983, 104). U.S. police were being shaped and molded by police occupational professionalization, a powerful mechanism for nurturing police loyalty to organized government (Fogelson 1977; see also Hays 1964, 1965).

Police professionalization involved cutting the self-identifications of rank-and-file police with the similar class and ethnicity of those they must control. An important step in this process made policing into a full-time public service occupation and turned the rank and file into state-paid employees, providing the police uniforms to visually separate them from common citizens, and encouraging occupational self-identification rather than ethnic and class identities. Regular salaries and relatively long-term appointments elevated police earnings somewhat above the working class as a whole, allowing lifestyle differences to develop between sets of people within an essentially similar social class (Fogelson 1977; ISLE 1975; Johnson 1976; Richardson 1970, 1974).

Police professionalization has also meant bureaucratic restructuring of the police as an institution, including reorganizing job hierarchies, creating a more elaborate chain of command, and setting standards for promotion and merit: in other words, bringing policing under bureaucratic regulation and control. Such professionalized nationwide bureaucratizing has given higher state-linked officials greater control over police by making police more accountable to the officials who control the hierarchy, their performance assessments, and the awarding of occupational rewards (see Fogelson 1977; Hays 1965).

Societal Consequences of Professionalization

Police professionalization has had several consequences for the larger social system. First, molding police organizations into a complex legal-rational bureaucratic institution has helped to create, as already indicated, a general impression throughout the society of the "rule of law"— with its corollary, "rule by no one"—where those who actually wield power in society come to be shielded by a police institution that does not explicitly seem to promote and protect their interests.

Second, it is often assumed that bureaucratizing police makes them more just and less prone to violence. Apparently, the presumption is that legal-rational bureaucratic organization eliminates the source and rationale for police violence, making social control more rational and less violent. The larger system thus benefits from the reduction in violence by bureaucratized social control. The assumption that bureaucratizing social control—even under a war ideology—will reduce violence is made questionable by the example of the Prussian Army. It was the first European army to be bureaucratized fully and it served as a model for Prussia's civil bureaucracy, yet this military social control bureaucracy was expected to carry out state violence, as it did under the Nazis.

Finally, within an opaque hierarchy of power, the position of professional police—with their specialized knowledge and skills for fighting crime—encourages dependence of citizen "clients" on the crime-fighting professional. Those who must rely on the trained expert's specialized knowledge are simply expected to trust that person's professional judgment and guidance (Bledstein 1976, 90). In turn, according to Bledstein, the culture of professionalism promotes itself by

cultivat[ing] an atmosphere of constant crisis—emergency—in which [professional] practitioners both create . . . work for themselves and reinforce . . . their authority [engendering the image of] an irrational world, an amoral one in the sense of constant crisis, ma[king] the professional . . . who possesse[s] . . . special knowledge indispensable to the victimized client . . . [the latter] reduced to a condition of desperate trust. (Bledstein 1976, 102)

This image of crisis helps to promote what Tilly (1985) identifies as a government-organized "protection racket," in which threats—whether really intrinsic to social conditions, or merely the result of government action itself—call up the need for protection by the government's own "professionalized" police forces. The internationalization of foreign police assistance results in the United States—through its technical assistance to foreign police—running a foreign assistance "protection racket" that promotes the U.S. security agenda in other countries and, through this, U.S. economic and political interests there.

Ideologies and Technologies for Professional Policing

Not surprisingly, therefore, along with professionalization of policing have come new ideologies about crime, criminals, and police work. Such ideologies identify the trained police professional as practicing the best means to eradicate these "evils." The crime-control orientation associated with professional policing transforms local rule violators into "outsiders" to be managed through heavy and generalized police repression. Violence against such "outsiders" is seen as necessary and legitimate for protecting "good citizens." This image of the world, in turn, justifies creating an ever more hierarchical professional police, including technical crime-fighting squads and the matériel to combat an increasingly specialized, yet generalized, "enemy." This was particularly the case in Latin America during the Cold War.

Such a crime-control ideology further alienates professionalized crime-fighting police from local communities and neutralizes police self-identification with others of similar class and ethnic backgrounds (see Chevigny 1995, chap. 4; Richardson 1974, 149). As Chevigny (1995, 124) has argued,

when the "war on crime" analogy is combined with the professionalized, anti-crime approach to police work, the results distort and poison police relations with citizens. The police think of themselves as an occupying army, and the public comes to think the same. The police lose the connection with the public.

In contrast, when police have assumed a primarily public-service role—more characteristic of earlier "preprofessional" police systems—rank-and-file police are pulled closer to their ethnic and class communities (Richardson 1974, 149) and kept more loyal to local, rather than state, interests and more open to "corruption" by such interests.

The technologies associated with a professionalized crime-control orientation have further separated police from their own class and ethnic origins. For example, the increasing use of motorized police over foot patrols has placed greater spatial distance between police and public. Where the public comes to be known by the police only through a passing patrol car's windshield, citizens are easily transformed into objects to be managed. Likewise, where the division of labor in policing is finely delineated, such that many police activities are strictly separated from each other and defined by their instrumental relationships to alleged deviants, the "clients" are likely to be treated in terms of their narrow relationship to police agents' demands and objectified and dehumanized in the process.

Social Consequences of Police Professionalization

Increased specialization and division of labor within policing—characterized by the early motorized "flying squads," modern specialized detective units, police intelligence "Red Squads," "criminalistics" units, and riot control and SWAT teams (Donner 1990; Fogelson 1977)—have created greater social distance not only between the specialized police units and the people they control but also among the units themselves and between specialized colleagues and the larger unspecialized police organization (see Chevigny 1995, chap. 4; Richardson 1974; Skolnick and Fyfe 1993). This "scientific Taylorization" of policing (i.e., increased rationalization and segmentation of police work) subdivides police action so narrowly that this division also contributes to obscuring the relationship of the police to political power. In other words, police professionalization and specialization has had consequences for the police system itself, for police behavior toward the public, and for the larger relationship of police to the communities they patrol—even though such consequences have not usually been an explicitly articulated part of the discourse on professionalization.

Therefore, within a single country, as we can see for the United States, police professionalization carried out by a country's own nationals usually occurs within an unequal internal distribution of political power, where one region or political party or faction or class or ethnic group has used police professionalization to wrest or keep control of the police from political rivals. And where police professionalization has succeeded, the political power of the winning side over and through the police has been augmented, and the political autonomy of the police has been reduced, although this process has also insulated the police from popular contacts and control, making them less accountable to immediate local community pressures and regulation. But of course such manipulation has often produced political tension among factions struggling to control the police and has thus in fact exacerbated conflict among and within police forces, as we shall demonstrate (see Gutman 1961, 1962, 1968; Robinson 1978; Harring 1983).

Intercountry Policing: Theory and Practice

As we have seen in a variety of sociocultural settings, police forces have been studied in terms of their development and changes in response to internal political and social crises. But what about situations where changes in police systems have been influenced by the political motives of extranationals? In such cases, whose internal security interests are promoted, and with what consequences for the recipient police system and its state and citizens? Since the United States has been training and equipping Latin American police for almost one hundred years, these are relevant questions.

In fact, whereas in every sense all policing is political, the quintessential example of politicized policing may very well be one country's training another country's police. Although both intra- and intercountry police training and professionalization have taken place within systems of unequal distribution of power, it is intercountry police training that occurs in a world system of nation-states where the recipient country holds a subordinate position relative to the training nation: in effect, such police training reduces the political autonomy of the country receiving it and can be a tool for shaping the host nation's politics and its political processes and outcomes. Of course, foreign police training can also be expected to have return effects on the training country and its police practices as lessons learned abroad are brought home.

Where another country trains a nation's police, the recipient police institutions come to be linked to that other state beyond their own nation's borders. This connection can transform recipient country police into subordinate actors in global politics and, in the process, further strengthen a foreign state's control over the recipient state.

Ironically, perhaps, professionalization of host country policing has been one mechanism for accomplishing such control. The ideology of professionalism—that professionals know best how to help clients eliminate, stabilize, or improve a control problem or situation—transforms the foreign recipients of professional police assistance into dependent clients who must "respect the moral authority of those whose claim to power lay in [their specialized knowledge and skills]" (Bledstein 1976, 90). This deference grants autonomy to the foreign professional within the host country's internal security system, because professionalism "emancipate[s the] . . . sovereign person as he perform[s] organized activities within comprehensive spaces" (Bledstein 1976, 87). This ethos of professionalism therefore reduces the recipient government and state to a position of relative vulnerability and less power with respect to its foreign police advisors: "By pointing to and even describing a potential disaster, the professional often reduce[s] the client to a state of desperation in which the victim would pay generously, cooperate fully, and express undying loyalty to the knowledgeable patron who might save him from a threatening universe" (Bledstein 1976, 100). Such a dependent-subordinate relationship, founded as it is on a sense of emergency, perhaps illuminates one of the functions of Cold War national security ideology: it generated and explained a social threat and, for eliminating it, established a role for professionalized police. We shall see that the United States certainly pushed U.S. foreign police training to combat Communism and did so in the name of professionalizing Latin American police.

Although intracountry police training is governed, at least theoretically, by the host country's legal structures and organizational rules—more or less equally binding on police and their trainers—police trainers on foreign soil can be much less restricted in what they are allowed to promote and in the consequences of their police training and action. In any case, the United States, in creating social-control institutions favorable to U.S. political and economic interests abroad, has often benefited from a recipient country's lack of legal guarantees of civic rights and liberties, and from ignoring more informal constraints on local police action.

However, at the same time, the professional training of one country's police by another has almost inevitably led to popular and political resistance in both donor and recipient nations, thus increasing both national and international political conflict and tensions and exposing recipient police to charges of being political, the very problem that professionalization is meant to counteract. Even more ironically, as this study will demonstrate, police centralization, professionalization, and specialization has led to increasing conflict among the various specialized police divisions and units in a country and also between its newly centralized and its previously decentralized police units and divisions. Professionalization's insistence on centralized and specialized police activities seems also to lead to devolution (e.g., debureaucratization), as the activities of professionalized, specialized, and autonomous national police agencies increasingly diverge from the centers of authority that have produced them. This process then produces still further devolution and even privatization as public opinion at home and abroad turns out not to approve of the new quasi-official police activities. In a world system of modern armies and nuclear-strike capabilities, these realities of cross-national policing must be seriously addressed.

Working Theses

Indeed, the basis for this study's concluding empirical theses about the consequences of U.S. foreign police training in Latin America is that the fundamental purpose for U.S. assistance to Latin American police was to serve as a mechanism for gaining political control over recipient countries' internal security systems rather than to further the spread of democracy. Such a conclusion is suggested by four interrelated propositions derived inductively from the data to be presented on U.S. assistance to Latin American police.

The *internationalization* proposition maintains that one mechanism for a country to gain political control over another state is to penetrate the other country's police system, although reaching large numbers of rank-and-file police is not necessary. Indeed, U.S. officials clearly considered that the most certain way of internationalizing U.S. security through assistance to Latin American police was to shape the political attitudes and technological preferences of key police officials, making sure that U.S.-trained police headed and otherwise participated in their country's most important internal security organizations.

The *centralization* proposition suggests that a country, to internationalize its own security, attempts to foster the development of other dependent states' internal security systems, including setting up new police and other internal security organizations and linking these to one another within each foreign country. Taking this centralizing process further still means encouraging subordination of police to the national military so that this internal security system is more closely tied to national executive power, which in turn is connected indirectly to the foreign power offering the training. Of course, in some Latin American countries, such centralization was fostered initially by Latin American nationals themselves, sometimes assisted by the United States, whereas in other Latin American countries it was largely a product of U.S. initiatives.

In the case of U.S. foreign police training, centralization was directed toward creating an internal security network under indirect U.S. tutelage, which was legitimized by a national security ideology arguing that centralization is necessary to protect against political subversives. Whether or not the United States took the lead in centralizing Latin American internal security, Washington could focus on getting U.S.-trained police into leadership positions within a country's national police organizations or internal security units and then on bringing such social-control entities under the control of indigenous central national-level executive power. Along the way, the more decentralized and politically factionalized police systems could be centralized, to be commanded by U.S.-trained nationals closely linked to the host country's executive power. Centralization would reduce the autonomous operation of local politicos' social-control entities and increase U.S. influence over recipient countries' more centralized internal-control systems, making such states still more amenable to Washington's internal security agenda.

According to the *authoritarianizing* proposition, the form and content of the centralizing initiatives would result in a top-down system of control that cuts off political participation and dissent. In the process, recipient countries' police systems and states become more militarized, as each phase of centralizing internal security becomes a foundation for new centralizing initiatives, each building incrementally on previous ones toward developing ever more militarized internal security systems. Such authoritarianizing has often meant superimposing new hybrid military and internal police security organizations on existing police bodies, all subordinated to the national military and legitimized by national security ideology.[2] This amounted to bureaucratizing, rationalizing, and routinizing secrecy, deceit, violence, and terror, all under the guise of "modernizing" social control to protect internal security against Communism. This further reduced the internal security system's public accountability, a consequence of professionalizing internal security in any case (Bledstein 1976, 87–90).

Yet although the ultimate result of authoritarianizing internal security can be subordination of police to the military, Enloe (1975) has pointed out that neither "policization" of the military nor militarization of the police should be confused with an actual equivalence between these two social-control entities. Even where these agencies' differences have been temporarily eclipsed—owing, for example, to a declaration of martial law—many structural, functional, bureaucratic, and professional distinctions still remain. There has been a tendency for the original jurisdictional differences between civil police and militaries to reemerge after the cessation of a social or political emergency, although usually without an associated demilitarization of the internal control system. This is just one aspect of the ultimate devolution of a centralized, internationalized, authoritarian system.

Indeed, the final proposition, on *devolution*, suggests that even the most oligarchically consolidated and militarily fortified bureaucratic-authoritarian state using specialization and compartmentalization, as well as secrecy, deceit, and violence, eventually experiences internal tensions, social conflicts, and public resistance. These give rise to partial debureaucratizing and decentralizing of militarized authoritarian social control, particularly among parts of the system most militarily specialized. Such devolution from bureaucratized militarization is often manifested in the emergence of social-control groups with less direct, more tenuous links to the state. These take the form of death squads related only in varying degree to police, or police-linked *justiceiro* lone-wolf killers, or parts of the internal security system that have turned against other parts—as when one internal security organization spies on, or takes action against, another (see Huggins 1991, 1997).

There has been a tendency to see such devolution as a return to traditional methods of social control—where different local power aspirants and their geographically localized militia and paramilitary forces battle with one another to control local politics. But it can be shown that modern forms of devolution are not equivalent to what existed in Latin America before this century. More recent forms of devolution can be very compatible with modernity (Huggins and Haritos-Fatouros 1996a, 1996b; Huggins 1997), representing a dialectic between bureaucratic-authoritarian states' centralizing and authoritarianizing and their debureaucratizing and privatizing of social control (Huggins 1991, 1997), a process we shall explore in much more detail (see chapter 9). Thus, at the same time as parts of the state become more bureaucratically modernized—although not necessarily consistently more efficient at internal control—they become more internally fortified and more centrally controlled. In the process, these states generate their apparent opposite—seemingly decentralized and debureaucratized forms of social control not visibly linked to the state. At first this is a deliberate state policy for reasons we can suggest here and will analyze further in chapter 9.

Once debureaucratizing gains speed, the state has difficulty controlling the process because authoritarian states in fact benefit, at least in the short run, from vigilante justice. On the one hand, vigilantism gives repressive states more social-control options than either national budgets or national or international political conditions permit, and on the other hand, such devolution lowers the political costs of repression by refocusing national and international attention away from the authoritarian state's own violence: death squads are "a less visible target for internal and international public opinion," and they "refocus . . . public attention and outrage" (Alves 1985, 258).

The thesis on devolution thus proposes that such vigilantism is a product of a consequent—if not fully intended—process of state de-construction, in which parts of the formal control system split off, debureaucratize, and increasingly carry out violence clandestinely and extralegally. Five sources of devolution are suggested in this analysis: (1) from the state's own interest in separating itself from the more egregious examples of its own violence; (2) out of the process of formal organization itself—particularly in the structural consequences of bureaucratic centralization, above all in the competition especially associated with a war model of policing; (3) an outgrowth of state-related illegalities—where devolution spawns further devolution into decentralization and loss of state control, which, in turn, encourages (4) the privatizing of policing as a response to the failure of state control over violence and to domestic and international pressures against state violence itself, so that (5) internal security becomes a monetized commodity in a free market.

Such outcomes would of course suggest more and more violence by more and more Latin American death squads. However, in Latin America, privatized justice in the long run generates a host of problems for the governments there, sometimes even threatening state hegemony over internal control, as earlier in Argentina, Uruguay, and Haiti, continuing in Guatemala and El Salvador, and now in Peru, Colombia, and Mexico (see Huggins 1991). Such states find themselves in the situation of "the sorcerer who is no longer able to control the powers of [a] nether world . . . [that] he has called up by his spells" (Marx and Engels 1985, 85–86).

As for U.S. international security planning, if pro-U.S. Latin American leaders cannot control a segment of their country's internal security apparatus, how can the United States expect these countries to offer a climate of security hospitable to U.S. interests? So U.S. assistance to Latin American police may have helped to foster the very disorder that foreign police assistance was ostensibly designed to overcome, certainly an ironic paradox.

The Working Theses in the Organization of This Book

The theoretical foundations for *Political Policing* developed in this chapter will be examined in the sociological analyses of eight subsequent chapters on episodes in U.S. assistance to Latin American police, primarily that of Brazil. These chapters illustrate, in varying degrees and in changing forms, the interrelated internationalizing, centralizing, authoritarianizing, and devolution processes just outlined.

Internationalizing U.S. security through police assistance can be seen throughout the seventy-five-year period examined, although the strategies for accomplishing internationalization change: In the first decades of the twentieth century (chapter 2), the United States used its own direct military intervention to establish new national constabularies and to promote U.S. control over Latin American internal security. In the 1930s, the United States more indirectly tried to influence Latin American police (chapter 3). During and immediately after World War II, the United States transformed its own international security machinery and developed an ideology that justified more effectively, yet invisibly, internationalizing U.S. security throughout Latin America (chapter 4). In the 1950s and 1960s, economic development programs were the mechanisms and the cover for gaining control over Latin American police and other internal security systems. The U.S. national security ideology justified internationalizing and centralizing Latin American internal security as Washington spread its newly developed internal security methods to neutralize perceived or expected insurgency threats abroad (chapters 5–9).

Centralizing of Latin American internal security assumed different forms between 1898 and 1974. The United States initially set up centralized national police systems in Central America and the Caribbean (chapter 2). Then, in the 1930s, the United States stepped back from direct intervention as its Latin American strongman allies centralized their own police institutions (chapter 3). These centralizing processes then and later usually resulted in authoritarianizing Latin American internal security (especially chapters 7–9), such that Latin American states and their social-control systems tried to integrate their military and police organizations under the national security ideology and used these agencies to penetrate and dominate their own civil society, eliminating in the process citizen participation and making political protest risky and dangerous.

Yet as chapters 7 through 9 illustrate, these highly rationalized systems of repression generated their apparent opposite—a devolution of internal control—where part of the social-control apparatus debureaucratizes—that is, breaks off formal ties to the official bureaucracy—even as it remains secretly tied to the formal control system (see also Huggins 1997). Chapter 9 further clarifies the model for understanding the roots and dynamics of this dialectic of internationalizing, centralizing, and authoritarianizing against devolution within a highly rationalized and modern system of social control. This can then be used to explain the paradoxical contrast between the theoretical expectations of traditional criminology and the actual practices and outcomes of U.S. foreign policy in professionalizing and militarizing police.

Chapter 10 closes the devolutionary cycle by bringing this process back to United States policy in the 1970s and 1980s. U.S. foreign policy reverts to the informal, personalistic decentralization that the whole police assistance program had initially been designed to supersede.

In the conclusion, U.S. assistance to Latin American police is discussed as part of a state-run international state-maintaining and state-making entrepreneurial enterprise to promote the interests of the United States, which sold police training to Latin America and other Third World client states after World War II as a "protection racket" (Tilly 1985). This, in turn, contributed to a devolution, commodification, and privatization of internal security, with policing and internal security becoming customer-defined products, "bought and sold within a market" (Shearing 1996), further fostering the devolutionary spiral, as we shall see.

2 "Gunboat" Policing:
The First Twenty-five Years

By the end of the nineteenth century, the United States had emerged as a world power and was taking steps—particularly after the Spanish-American War of 1898—to secure its newly gained political and economic advantages. The U.S. economy was growing rapidly, and U.S. foreign policy supported free international trade and investment. This "Open Door" policy began as a demand that no country have a monopoly over trade with China but was also directed at countries more directly within the new U.S. spheres of influence. To ensure its trade with these countries, the United States would work to guarantee their economic and political stability, and their independence of other world powers. One way to do this with the more problematic regimes was to create new, or to reorganize old, security forces in these countries.

Explicitly linking U.S. investment with improvements in policing, U.S. secretary of state Elihu Root argued in 1905 that U.S. trading partners in Latin America and elsewhere needed efficient professional police forces that could "repress subversive disorder and preserve the public peace" (in Lobe 1975, 21). In that same year, the United States spearheaded the move to link foreign investment with reform of the Moroccan police (Lobe 1975, 21). In a more general assertion of the security-for-trade principle, President Woodrow Wilson continued to argue between 1914 and 1917 that Latin America needed "a functioning regional system, secure from European interference, open to the expansion of trade, and capable of policing itself" (Gilderhus 1980, 422), referring of course not to the police themselves but to the concept of letting indigenous forces maintain their own national security, internal as well as external.

Several related goals were attached to this security-for-trade principle: protection of U.S. creditors and property, stability in these new areas of U.S. control, and hemispheric security. More specifically, once the United States had acquired Puerto Rico and assumed responsibility for Cuba in 1898, and, above all, started the Panama Canal in 1903, Central America and the Caribbean assumed much greater strategic importance.

An early mechanism for U.S. penetration into Latin American internal security was for Washington to establish and then direct police constabularies there. These police-military hybrids were military in structure and technology but were also vested with police functions, having both internal and external defense responsibilities. Clearly, some Washington policy makers saw such centralized police and quasi police as buffers against internal security threats. For example, in parts of the Caribbean at the dawn of the new century, and in the midst of political conflicts between local and regional *poderosos* in Central and South America, the United States imposed newly trained, centralized national constabulary forces on some Caribbean and Central American governments. This was sometimes done with, and sometimes without, their nationals' assistance or approval. Washington argued that new U.S.-funded and -officered nonpolitical professional constabularies would eliminate disorder and reduce the political turmoil created by competing elites' battling security forces. In effect, Washington was superimposing a further centralizing process on one already being fostered by local and national elites, and in the process, the United States was internationalizing its security in the region.

Constabularies Open the Door

In 1898, U.S. occupation armies in Cuba established a police constabulary to guarantee the security of U.S. investment and trade. This new national constabulary was trained, equipped, and directed by the U.S. Marines; former New York City police officers helped organize Havana's municipal police system (Birr and Curti 1954, 93). U.S. influence was also felt in Cuba's prison system: in the early 1900s, the warden of the Havana penitentiary visited U.S. federal prisons in Leavenworth, Kansas, and Joliet, Illinois, to bring their methods back to Cuba (Birr and Curti 1954, 93).

Within two decades after establishing the Cuban constabulary, the U.S. War Department had set up police constabularies in Haiti (1915), the Dominican Republic (1916), Panama (1918), and Nicaragua (1925). Washington policy makers reasoned that one way to secure U.S. interests was for the United States to strengthen these countries' internal security where they had weak, highly politicized, or even nonexistent militaries and to establish constabulary forces with primary loyalty to the United States. Sometimes this meant dismantling a country's national military and setting up a new civil police force, as in Cuba and Haiti. At other times, it meant creating a new constabulary where there was no effective unified national military—as in Nicaragua in the early 1920s.

Washington's control over these new national constabularies varied according to how they had been established in the first place. Of course, there was greater internationalizing of U.S. influence where Washington had direct control over constabulary formation. Where the United States had only indirect control, there was less U.S. penetration of a country's internal security system.

For example, the United States had direct control over constabulary development in Cuba (1898), Haiti (1915), and the Dominican Republic (1916), where it created or restructured these countries' police forces after full military intervention. U.S. officers replaced national elites in government and abolished existing military and police, and a new constabulary was trained and placed under U.S. control. In contrast, where U.S. intervention was partial or nonmilitary, as in Nicaragua in 1923 and 1925, national government institutions remained more or less intact, and traditional elites continued to hold office and direct the new constabulary that U.S. military "volunteers" or contract employees had established and trained (Goldwert 1962, 48–49).

It is possible to contrast constabulary development after direct U.S. military intervention in Haiti (1915–1920) with more indirect U.S. political intervention in Nicaragua (1923–1927). These illustrate two different models for centralizing the police and internationalizing U.S. security through police training and suggest their different impacts on recipient countries' internal security arrangements and long-term authoritarianizing.

The Haitian Constabulary

Looking back on the 1915 military intervention in Haiti, Washington analysts stated that in 1930 Haiti had been in a state of "social, economic, and political chaos" (ONR 1969, 36). Between 1886 and 1915, every Haitian president had been overthrown, and many of them killed in office; on the eve of the U.S. intervention, there had been mob violence following the murder of President Guillaume Sam. This unrest presumably left Washington with no option but to send U.S. Marines and Navy forces to take over Haiti. Washington argued that invasion was necessary to prevent Haiti's complete collapse and keep this Caribbean country from defaulting on its financial obligations to foreign creditors, a development that could have justified unwanted European intervention (ONR 1969, 37).

In the United States' full-scale nineteen-year occupation of Haiti (1915–1934), the large Haitian standing army was abolished, and a national police constabulary—the Garde d'Haiti—was created in its place (Diederich and Burt 1969, 39). The United States also assumed control over all Haitian government institutions except the Departments of Justice, Education, and Post Office. In order to ensure U.S. control over the new Garde, U.S. Marines held command positions. Thus even though this new security force was supposed to be ultimately under the control of Haiti's president, "In fact . . . the President appeared to have less power than the American commander of the Marine regular forces, who frequently issued orders directly to the Chief of the Gendarmerie" (ONR 1969, 40), that is, the Garde d'Haiti.

Almost immediately, the new Garde d'Haiti, which had jurisdiction throughout the country, became an extension of the U.S. occupation. Indeed, as Goldwert (1962, 48) points out for the Caribbean and Central America as a whole, these constabularies introduced a new distribution and balance of power in the politics of recipient nations such that "power [came to be] centralized in well-equipped constabularies led by [U.S. Marine] officers."

This, in turn, generated conflict and resistance. Haitians were irked that few of the U.S. Marines who commanded the Garde spoke Creole or French. That some American officers "had biased racial attitudes" also provoked disdain, according to the U.S. military itself, which in retrospect thought that it had made "a serious error of judgment" in assigning U.S. Marines from southern U.S. states to the Garde "on the mistaken assumption that Southerners would know how to deal effectively with Haitian Negroes" (ONR 1969, 44). In any case, Haitians were angered that prostitution and out-of-wedlock births had increased substantially with the presence of U.S. Marines.

However, the biggest source of Haitian dissatisfaction with the Garde grew out of the revival by U.S. occupation forces in 1916 of an older Haitian corvée law permitting the use of forced labor in road construction. Under the corvée, local Haitian officials supplied the Garde with lists of peasants who were then delivered "notification cards" to report for work at construction sites. A peasant who did not present himself for work could pay a tax, but because most were extremely poor, forced unremunerated labor was their only real option.

Not surprisingly, enforcement of the corvée law gave U.S. Marines and their Haitian gendarmerie a very bad name because the Garde "virtually shanghaied [peasants] and [forced them to] work . . . in what amounted to chain gangs" (Birr and Curti 1954, 129). The Garde "brutalized the laborers, treating them like criminals" once on the job (ONR 1969, 45). As many Haitians saw it, the Garde had been used by the United States to repress them or extract labor from them (ONR 1969, 47).

The Garde's behavior led to "a dramatic increase in anti-American-ism" and helped generate a guerrilla resistance movement as peasants took to the hills, there to be recruited into *caco* units—irregular peasant-based guerrilla militias. By spring 1919, in Haiti's northern and central districts, Charlemagne Peralte had raised a caco army of five thousand men and mounted a successful attack against the U.S.-backed Garde (ONR 1969, 47). The U.S. forces in Haiti offered a $2,000 bounty to Haitian Jean Conze for the capture or assassination of Peralte. Accompanying Conze on this mission was Herman Heneken, a U.S. Marine captain. In the end, it was Heneken who murdered Peralte and brought the caco leader's "almost naked body . . . to . . . [gendarmerie] general headquarters . . . in Cap Haitien," where it was tied to a door (Diederich and Burt 1969, 40). Heneken was awarded the U.S. Congressional Medal of Honor; Jean Conze received the Haitian Medal of Honor and Merit. There is no record as to who received the U.S. bounty (Diederich and Burt 1969, 40). Yet although the United States had eliminated a troublemaker, it had not neutralized the cacos. Indeed, the United States was embarrassed that the Haitian Garde had been unable to control the cacos and was also concerned that the Garde was so poorly regarded by other Haitians.

The Garde was a visible arm of U.S. intervention, making apparent the connections between the United States and Haiti's dominant economic and political elite. Thus, rather than eliminating turmoil, the new U.S.-officered constabulary had increased internal conflict by centralizing and consolidating national power for leaders loyal to the United States.

The Nicaraguan Constabulary

According to Dana Munro, an early-twentieth-century U.S. career diplomat posted to various Caribbean and Central American countries, there was no national army in Nicaragua before the 1912 U.S. intervention; "Family feuds, sectional hatred, [and] local bigotry" dominated political life (in Goldwert 1962, 22). For example, between 1913 and 1924, there had been ten revolutionary coup attempts in Nicaragua, and the country had been under martial law for virtually the entire period.

According to Munro, Washington reasoned that a nationally based "nonpartisan" constabulary would bring order out of political chaos and eliminate the factional infighting that dominated Nicaraguan politics (Munro 1964). So, in 1923, as U.S. diplomats helped the Nicaraguan government rewrite its election laws for the upcoming presidential elections, the United States proposed establishing a centralized constabulary force for Nicaragua (FRUS 1923), to help the Nicaraguan government keep order and enhance its legitimacy during the elections. Of course, Washington did not want it to appear that the United States was itself hoping to use the constabulary to control Nicaraguan politics.

For international validation, Washington sponsored a Central American conference on arms limitations. Its primary outcome was the Central American Treaty of Peace and Amity (CCAA1 1922–1923), which pledged all the participants to withhold political recognition from any government coming to power through coup or revolution. The treaty recommended Central American countries' establishing constabularies, with training by "suitable instructors" already "experience[d] . . . [in other countries] organizing such corps" (CCAA2 1922–1923; also Millett 1977).

The United States had already had ample experience training police constabularies; by 1923 it had established such national police forces in Puerto Rico, Cuba, Haiti, the Dominican Republic, Panama, the Philippines, and Liberia. In most of these countries, the U.S. War Department had provided the constabulary training. However, Panama (after 1905) and Nicaragua (1923–1927) were special cases: their police assistance was provided extragovernmentally through a State Department–arranged training contract between the host governments and private U.S. police specialists.

In many ways, Washington's involvement with the Nicaraguan constabulary was a prototype for later U.S. police training programs in Latin America, because these too had to have at least the appearance of being legitimized by international law. This was particularly necessary in 1923 in Nicaragua because at that time there was no U.S. law that permitted U.S. armed forces to train foreign government police where there had been no full-scale U.S. occupation, as in Cuba, Haiti, the Dominican Republic, and the Philippines. There was also no mechanism for granting U.S. pay or retirement credits to U.S. specialists brought in by foreign governments to advise them. In fact, Congress did not pass legislation until 1926 permitting the U.S. military to assist "the governments of the Republics of North America, Central America, and South America, [as well as] . . . Cuba, Haiti, and [the Dominican Republic] in military and naval matters," the rubric under which police assistance to "independent governments" was categorized at the time (Sixty-Ninth Congr. 1926, 565).

Yet there was still an informal tradition in the War and State Departments of arranging police training contracts between foreign governments and "private" U.S. citizens. For example, in 1905 the United States government had recommended that the Panamanian government contract with Samuel Davis to train the Panamanian police. When Davis died from yellow fever, Washington suggested George W. Jimenez, a former New York City policeman (McCain 1937, 79).

The U.S. proceedings in Nicaragua demonstrate that when political, administrative, or legal reasons stood in the way of Washington's openly and directly establishing a constabulary, the U.S. government sought unofficial means of accomplishing its objective. For example, in Nicaragua in 1923, the two most viable options for setting up a new constabulary were either to recruit trainer "volunteers" from the United States Legation Guard in Nicaragua, a detachment of 100 U.S. Marines that had been backing the U.S. presence in Nicaragua since 1912, or to arrange a private police training contract between a U.S. citizen and the Nicaraguan government. Either alternative required Nicaraguan approval, and it complicated matters that powerful sectors of Nicaragua's elite strongly resisted U.S. involvement in their country's internal affairs. As Secretary of State Charles Evans Hughes pointed out, the presence of U.S. Marines in Nicaragua might give rise to the hypothesis that the U.S. "Government is maintaining in office a government which would otherwise perhaps not be strong enough to maintain itself against the attacks of its political opponents" (in FRUS 1923, 607).

Nicaragua's foreign minister, General Emiliano Chamorro, warned that Nicaraguans might regard a U.S.-established constabulary as Washington's attempt to influence his country's 1924 presidential elections, cautioning that open U.S. involvement in Nicaragua's electoral process could cost his U.S.-backed Conservative Party thousands of votes (FRUS 1923, 607). Chamorro would, however, support the constabulary project if U.S. military volunteer trainers left Nicaragua before the October 1924 presidential elections. Washington accepted Chamorro's proposal because the United States also leaned toward the more indirect approach to creating a constabulary in Nicaragua.

The constabulary project was taken up again in 1925 when the Nicaraguan congress once more debated the U.S. role in establishing a constabulary there. Washington's proposal brought strong protests and counterproposals from the Nicaraguan congress. This time, the major stumbling block was whether to accept Washington's proposal to constitute U.S. involvement with the police constabulary not just "in . . . a 'Training Branch' . . . [but also in a] 'Constabulary Proper,' with United States [military] officers wielding supreme control over the Training Branch" (Goldwert 1962, 25–26), to be managed by U.S. military volunteers. In the process, the Nicaraguan army would be abolished.

Some Nicaraguan politicians wanted both an army *and* a police constabulary, each separate from and equal to the other. The United States wanted a constabulary and no military at all, with U.S. Marines as the constabulary's trainers and commanding officers. Some Nicaraguan congressmen countered that, at the very least, U.S. instructors should be "under the supreme command of the Nicaraguan government" and not controlled by the United States (Goldwert 1962, 26). There was fairly general agreement in Nicaragua that any U.S. involvement with the Nicaraguan constabulary had to be informal and "voluntary."

Over the objections of the U.S. chargé d'affaires in Managua, U.S. State Department officials and Nicaraguans hammered out an agreement on the constabulary project. The new constabulary was to be headed by Nicaraguans; U.S. volunteers would conduct the training (FRUS 1925, 624); the constabulary was to be a combined "urban, rural, and judicial police force," which would not replace the regular army (Millett 1977, 43). This plan was put into effect through a one-year contract, arranged by the State Department, between the Nicaraguan government and Major Calvin Boone Carter, U.S. Army, retired. Carter, who in 1898 had established the Philippine constabulary, was to be chief of Nicaragua's new constabulary and head of the School of Police Instruction. Carter was paid $600 a month, a very substantial income at the time, and an additional $1,000 for his four U.S. assistants (Millett 1977, 43).

Carter landed on July 25, 1925, at Bluefields on Nicaragua's east coast, and his first official visit was with General Luis Mena, the province's governor, whom Carter described as a "famous old-time rebel." General Mena had been Nicaragua's minister of war under President Adolfo Diaz but had taken up arms against his commander-in-chief because, according to Mena, President Diaz had sold Nicaragua out to the United States (Arévalo 1961, 69). Mena had wanted to become Nicaragua's president—which meant ousting Diaz (Millett 1977). The coup had failed.

For Carter, General Mena symbolized all that was wrong with Nicaragua: he lacked military discipline, was jealously self-interested, and lacked vision beyond what he could gain from controlling local politics. According to Carter, at their first meeting, General Mena lay "in a hammock with a machine gun close beside him, three rifles leaning against the wall, and two bottles of brandy on the floor, all within easy reach." Such a first impression must have reinforced Carter's belief that Nicaraguan politics were like "an old-fashioned family feud" (Carter 1927, 312–13).

Carter later explained that during his twenty months in Nicaragua, there were four "revolutions," a reality of Nicaraguan life that had made the constabulary's work extremely complicated. Indeed, in such a highly charged political environment, Carter's new constabulary was regarded with suspicion from the very beginning. Competing Nicaraguan politicians worried about which side the constabulary would take in any political conflict (Carter 1927, 315). In particular, one nervous Nicaraguan military commander asked Carter what stand the new constabulary would take in the event of a revolution. Carter's response was that his constabulary would "try to suppress uprisings and support the President," to which the officer responded: What "if we had a President we didn't like?" Carter concluded from this exchange that "no President of Nicaragua would dare appoint any but his nearest relatives to [the constabulary's] high command" (Carter 1927, 317), a fact that would surely lead to politicization.

Although apparently troubled by the new constabulary's being inextricably linked to shifting political power and a likely pawn in any political disputes, Major Carter in fact responded to these political pressures in kind. Within months of his arrival in Nicaragua, Carter "actively . . . comfort[ed] . . . and aid[ed]" Emiliano Chamorro, the former Conservative Party foreign minister and President Solórzano's political rival, in a successful revolt against the Solórzano government (Goldwert 1962, 27). Ironically, on his departure from Nicaragua, Carter complained that his constabulary had been a failure because the Solórzano government, which Carter had helped to overthrow, had not given his constabulary sufficient support to get the new constabulary off the ground.

In 1927 the United States again attempted to establish a "nonpartisan" constabulary in Nicaragua. This time, after another U.S. military intervention, the constabulary had a much better chance of living up to Washington's expectations: U.S. Marines disarmed Nicaraguan government forces and set up a constabulary officered by U.S. Marines themselves. Shortly afterward, in order to keep any of Nicaragua's other internal security forces from undermining the U.S.-backed constabulary, Washington rejected Managua's bid to establish a separate police force for the capital city. It was not until 1931, after the United States had established a firm presence in Nicaragua, that the U.S. "finally agreed to the formation of a locally financed municipal police force . . . with the stipulation that such a force be . . . an integral part of the [constabulary, i.e., National] Guard organization" (Goldwert 1962, 36). This arrangement would foster controlled centralization of internal security by subordinating local police to the U.S.-established National Guard, which was in turn linked through national police officials to Washington.

Police Intervention by Other Foreign States

The United States was not the only country in the early twentieth century working to expand its political influence in Latin America by training and directing police. In the early 1900s, French military missions were training police in Uruguay and Peru and for the Brazilian state of São Paulo. The German government reorganized the Argentine, Chilean, and Bolivian police (Fernandes 1974, 165). In 1927 Italy under Mussolini sent a military mission to train the Ecuadorian police, dispatching another mission in 1936 to reorganize the Bolivian constabulary (G-2 Report 1936b). Some Latin American countries were themselves training other regional police forces. For example, in the 1930s, Chile's Carabineiros were brought in to reorganize the Colombian National Police (Dawson 1936).

During this pre–World War II period—when no one country had hegemony over Latin American countries' internal security—various countries vied for such influence. However, such involvement by European and Latin American states was much less invasive of national politics than the U.S. military interventions into Panama, Nicaragua, Haiti, and the Dominican Republic. The case of French trainers in Brazil provides a comparative example.

French Police Training in São Paulo

In 1906 the French were invited to São Paulo state by Governor Jorge Tibiriçá. The French wanted to check German influence in Latin America, gain political and ideological influence in Brazil, and secure favored-nation trading status with South America's largest country (Fernandes 1974, 157). A French military mission arrived in São Paulo at a time when the state's police forces were already being reorganized by Brazilians. In fact, São Paulo had been one of the first Brazilian states to "professionalize" and reorganize its state police; in 1901 the police took a new name, Força Pública, and began to be upgraded. These changes were along the lines of changes at the national level.

In 1889, with the fall of the Empire of Brazil and proclamation of the Federal Republic, a great many formerly centralized government powers were transferred to the Brazilian states—successors to the imperial provinces. Even under the monarchy, maintaining public order had been the responsibility and prerogative of the provinces, although in fact controlled more locally (see Holloway 1993). Under the new republic, many state governors strengthened their power vis-à-vis both local poderosos and the central government by upgrading the state police. In fact, according to Love (1980), during Brazil's First Republic (1889–1930), it was the state governors—rather than the Brazilian central government—who "increasingly restricted the power of the rural seigneurs" (p. 126).

São Paulo's Governor Tibiriçá (1904–1908), following this centralizing lead, wanted French military officers to further professionalize his police, arguing that a well-trained Força Pública would allow him to break the political stranglehold of local oligarchs and regulate labor unrest, as well as protect São Paulo state against federal government incursions. Because Governor Tibiriçá's upgrading of São Paulo's Força Pública occurred at the expense of the coffee planters' personal militias, not surprisingly, his plan had "something less than enthusiastic support from the landowners" (Love 1980, 126).

Labor unrest was also on the governor's mind. Indeed, the governor's request for French training for state police forces had come just one year after workers at the Paulista Railway Company had staged São Paulo's most important strike of the early twentieth century (Dallari 1976, 89). Apparently the poor police performance against strikers had convinced Tibiriçá that his police needed more preparation for labor unrest.

Furthermore, a reorganized state police would improve São Paulo's capacity to resist Brazilian federal government encroachment on the state's power. The most immediate threat had been generated by a feud between São Paulo state officials and Brazilian president Francisco Rodrigues Alves (1902–1908) over the governor's proposed federal "valorization" program.[1] It would require the federal government's cooperation with São Paulo state in subsidizing the state's coffee crops. But this policy angered other regions' agricultural interests (Love 1980, 45–47). Indeed, Tibiriçá's valorization proposal was hotly opposed by President Alves, a northeasterner with a solid base of support among his region's sugar interests. They wanted federal subsidies for their product instead.

By 1906 the dispute between São Paulo planter interests and the federal government had become so heated that the *Jornal do Comércio*, a conservative business-oriented newspaper, urged President Alves to send a warship to block coffee shipments from leaving São Paulo's port of Santos (Fernandes 1974, 161). Probably not at all by chance, the French training mission arrived in São Paulo on March 21 of that same year to reorganize the state police forces: if nothing else, a professionalized state police might be able to protect São Paulo from federal government intervention.

But there was national resistance to the French training mission. Brazilian newspapers complained that French training would create "Imperialism by the States"—turning São Paulo into the "Prussia of Brazil" (in Fernandes 1974, 161). One Brazilian journalist, fearful that French training would undermine Brazilian "national unity," pointed out that if each state contracted with foreign advisors for police training, Paraná state would have to secure the Germans to counterbalance French influence in neighboring São Paulo; Santa Catarina would need to invite the Russians to offset Paraná's German-trained police; and Rio Grande do Sul state would have to counter by hiring Japanese trainers to offset Santa Catarina's Russian-trained police, and so on (Fernandes 1974, 158).

Even members of the Força Pública themselves granted neither the need for, nor the legitimacy of, French training (Fernandes 1974, 160). In fact, some of these state police physically attacked their French trainers. Moreover, French training angered São Paulo City police forces: It seemed blatantly partisan to give one arm of São Paulo's social-control apparatus, the Força, training, modern equipment, and higher pay while virtually neglecting the city's own police forces (Fernandes 1974, 160).

There was also increasing conflict between São Paulo's state police and the Brazilian army. On the one hand, the Força's increasing size posed a potential threat to the federal military's role in protecting the unity of the country. For example, by 1908, the Força had an active strength of 5,000 men, growing by the mid-1920s to 14,000 (Love 1980, 127). The army then had only 5,675 troops in São Paulo state (McCann 1977, 242), outnumbered almost three to one by the Força Pública. Moreover, after 1910, Força officers were paid as well as, or better than, federal army officers, and the Força had its own hospital, social insurance programs, and a primary school for enlisted men— many of them illiterate or foreign-born (Love 1980, 127). By the 1920s, the Força Pública even had an air unit, organized and trained by Orton Hoover—a relative of the U.S. consul in São Paulo, Charles S. Hoover (Brown 1920). Thus there was good reason for federal officials to suspect that São Paulo's modernizing of its police might make these forces more loyal to the state than to federal authorities, a suspicion that grew quickly into a reality.

Yet at the same time the professionalization and upgrading of São Paulo's Força Pública did not fully guarantee their support of the governor's needs and expectations. For example, in São Paulo city's 1917 strike, elements of the Força refused to take action against striking workers. The police rebels "identified with the workers . . . because of [the police force's] . . . own low wages" (Dallari 1976, 92). And in 1924 a group of police from the Força Pública defied the governor by joining a rebel army in its big march across Brazil, led by a group of lieutenants (the Tenentes) who had revolted two years before at Rio's Fort Copacabana against President Artur Bernardes' support for Brazil's planter-dominated federal system.

This "Prestes Column," under its leader Luis Carlos Prestes, one of the original rebel Tenentes, marched across thousands of miles of Brazil in two and a half years (Flynn 1978, 45–47; Levine 1970; Love 1980).

Some regiments of the São Paulo Força Pública defied the governor and joined five thousand other dissidents identified with the Tenentes against a rival federal government force of more than twenty thousand. These rebels kept São Paulo city in their own hands for eighteen days (Flynn 1978, 45).

The governor's response to this disloyalty from elements of his Força Pública was in fact to increase the Força's strength from 8,829 to 14,000, replacing those who had allied with the Tenentes with recruits whose loyalty could be newly shaped. The governor granted pay bonuses to those officers and soldiers who had known "how to defend and uphold the basic institutions of the nation and the state." He instituted military-style training, uniforms, equipment, and sophisticated arms and ammunition for the newly reconstituted Força Pública (Dallari 1976, 94) and awarded fringe benefits comparable to those of other state employees.

Love argues, however, that the Força Pública's "professionalization was probably a direct cause of its officers' participation in the 1924 [Tenente] rebellion—[in other words] modernization had its ideological side effects" (Love 1980, 128). In any case, the state's governor soon took steps to create a police force more predictably loyal to his interests by offering special rewards and further professionalization, often with assistance from the French.

Comparative Internationalizing of Policing

There are many parallels between the French training of São Paulo's Força Pública and U.S. establishment of the Nicaraguan and Haitian constabularies. In the first place, these police projects were initiated at times when the host country or region was in great political turmoil. In São Paulo, French trainers were brought in during rising foreign immigration into Brazil with concomitant labor unrest—all associated with threatened federal intervention in São Paulo. Likewise, U.S. establishment of Nicaragua's and Haiti's constabularies came not only when the United States was expanding into markets and resources abroad but also while local factionalism and conflict threatened these expansionist designs both in and of themselves and because they increased the possibility of European intervention.

Both French training of São Paulo state police forces and U.S. establishment of the Haitian and Nicaraguan constabularies nurtured centralization of internal control and facilitated political manipulation by those controlling police centralization. For example, in São Paulo, French training and the governor's other steps to professionalize the Força helped increase the governor's control over internal security, reduce the power of competing local and regional oligarchs, and enhance the governor's political power. In Nicaragua and Haiti, the U.S.-organized and -controlled police constabularies increased centralization of internal control and introduced a new balance of power into national politics—with the U.S. becoming a central player in this power nexus.

But in both cases, foreign police assistance in fact exacerbated local public and political turmoil. There was conflict over the legitimacy of French training within São Paulo state itself, between São Paulo and other Brazilian states, and between São Paulo and the Brazilian federal government. The training also generated conflict among the forces of social control themselves—between different levels of police within São Paulo and between the state police and the federal military, thus leading to a devolution of control toward more security force violence.

In Nicaragua, the establishment of new constabulary forces generated conflict among the Nicaraguans, even among those who had cooperated initially in setting up a new constabulary, and the U.S.-established constabulary then became involved in a coup against the elected Nicaraguan president. Likewise, the use of Haiti's Garde to enforce a forced-labor law fueled peasant resistance to the Haitian government and its constabulary; a Haitian constabulary officer and a U.S. Marine led an assassination mission against a political foe of the U.S. occupation. The Nicaraguan constabulary and the Haitian Garde in short order had become highly politicized, and an arm of external authoritarian control, conjoined to the beginnings of devolution.

However, as the examples illustrate, foreign police training and centralizing does not necessarily make recipient police more loyal to those controlling their training. In Nicaragua, the constabulary that Carlos Solórzano's government allowed the United States to establish and train led to a coup against his own regime. São Paulo's Força Pública demonstrated at least twice that foreign training and professionalization provided no insurance against police disloyalty to state power. Indeed, Love suggests that the ideological content of French training may have actually helped create Força officers' support for the Tenente antigovernment movement (Love 1980, 128).

Political Policing: Internationalization, Centralization,
and Devolution

Such disloyalties notwithstanding, public officials and politicians in
diverse, including international, cultural settings have recognized that
professional police can help them maintain and consolidate political
power—whether at the neighborhood, municipal, regional, national, or
international levels. Within systems of unequal distribution of political
power, one group, political faction, class, or nation-state can use its
more centralized control over police to enhance its political advantages
over those who do not have control over their police. Yet as the previous examples have suggested, such political manipulation of the police can lead to a partial devolution of the social-control system—
ranging from minor forms of insubordination to police-initiated coups.
This has often been followed by efforts to increase government control
over internal security forces through forms of police professionalization that promote increased centralizing and militarizing of policing,
and thus their nonlocal, authoritarian character, without, however, increasing their resistance to devolution, as we shall see.

3 "Good Neighbor" Policing

By the early 1930s, the U.S.-established constabularies in Central America and the Caribbean had become powerful National Guards that could be used to take over executive power. In the Dominican Republic, for example, president Rafael Leonidas Trujillo Molina had risen from poverty through the ranks of his country's National Guard to build and consolidate his power over political and social life, "armed with . . . [his] nation's first modern army"—the U.S.-established and -supported constabulary that had become the National Guard (Goldwert 1962, 21).

When U.S. Marines withdrew from Nicaragua in 1933, they left Anastasio Somoza as chief of the National Guard. The former minister of foreign affairs, he soon became Nicaragua's strongman president. Somoza had created, as "Chief of the Guard, . . . a third political force . . . [that reduced] the historical [political] parties [to] . . . political midgets" (Goldwert 1962, 47). Through the same process, as Haiti's U.S.-trained Garde grew into a decisive force in national politics, François "Papa Doc" Duvalier used this national gendarmerie to consolidate his position as President-for-Life.

Washington had learned by the 1930s that establishing and training a foreign country's police gave the United States strong influence over that country's local politics. Yet in the 1930s internationalizing U.S. influence through police assistance had to be indirect if the U.S. were to uphold its asserted role as Latin America's "Good Neighbor" and demonstrate an "aversion to use of force as an instrument of national or international foreign policy." As Latin America's "Good Neighbor," the United States had announced that it would respect the "equal sovereignty of states and justice under international law" (Haines 1977, 373–74).

Under such ideological constraints, the process of internationalizing U.S. assistance to foreign police took two relatively indirect and politically invisible forms: through treaties and agreements allowing the exchange of suspects and information, and through a country's request for FBI assistance in establishing new secret service organizations. The success of such U.S. penetration turned in part on the dictatorial climate in some of the Latin American countries receiving U.S. police assistance, and in part on the quality of relations between high U.S. diplomatic officials and the recipient country's national and local police officials, who may not always have represented the interests of their own nation's executive power in requesting U.S. police assistance.

Centralizing Power

As far as the indirect nature of police assistance was concerned, the 1930s was a relatively easy time for the United States to play the role of Latin America's "Good Neighbor": more than half these governments were under strongman rule (Haines 1977, 373–74). Often held in place by a strong military, leaders were interested in quick action to gain further control over regional and local police forces. Latin American leaders eager to consolidate their power often sought foreign assistance in reorganizing their national police forces—as in 1935 when Colombian central government officials contracted with Chile's Cuerpo de Carabineros to make the Colombian National Police into "the largest armed force in the country." At the end of such training, according to a U.S. military attaché's communiqué, Colombian government officials planned to absorb the police of "the various [provinces] . . . into . . . the [new] National Police" organization (Greene 1936), presumably to block any local police force in Colombia from threatening the central government's power.

For this reason, the new strongmen also sought to block foreign governments from assisting regional and local police systems—as in 1933 when Brazilian president Getúlio Vargas prohibited a Minas Gerais state governor from contracting with the French military to train that state's police, as São Paulo state had done in the early twentieth century.

In Argentina a military coup had installed José Uriburu as the new strongman president in 1930. Uriburu followed a pattern of political consolidation like that of Brazil's Getúlio Vargas, but less successfully, given the fragile political coalition on which he depended. Uriburu subordinated all state and local forces to the national military, and then, to further stabilize his regime, he began upgrading the Buenos Aires Capital City's police forces (Rodriguez 1981). Crowd and riot control tactics and technologies for the police were improved. Ford patrol cars were purchased to help the police deal more efficiently "with riots, fugitive gunmen, and any other cases . . . [where police] presence may be considered necessary" (Fleming 1931, 2). Other improvements included a new automobile and motorcycle "flying squad" with a "wireless receiving and transmitting apparatus, portable machine guns, and explosive tear gas bombs." The radio equipment had been purchased from the U.S. Standard Electric Company (Fleming 1931, 2).

Uriburu also upgraded his police system by linking Buenos Aires's 250 kilometers of private telephone wires into a "close-meshed net to assist in the capture of escaping criminals," according to the U.S. military attaché (Fleming 1931, 1). This communications network was connected to more than two hundred street emergency call boxes to facilitate police and military control of crime and civil disturbance. The Union Telefonica, a subsidiary of U.S.-owned International Telephone and Telegraph, had established the police communication system for exclusive use by the army, which, during the 1930 military coup, had been forced "to use the public telephone system [, causing] much confusion" (Fleming 1931, 2).

A series of Argentinian governments throughout the 1930s, including the liberal civilian Agustin P. Justo's administration (1932–1938), built up a systematic intelligence network, in which "political policing was . . . perfected and bureaucratized" (Kalmanowiecki 1994, 12) through the creation of "routine procedures for monitoring, containing, scanning, and eventually breaking up" activities deemed dangerous to the state (p. 6). According to Kalmanowiecki, this surveillance apparatus, which "increased the state's capacity to act at the national level" (1994, 11), embraced the police system. "The repressive practices [that had been] inaugurated under the [military] Uriburu regime endured and were even perfected and further developed during the [civilian] Justo administration [, when] the police [apparatus] underwent further centralization and nationalization" (Kalmanowiecki 1994, 5).

About the same time as Uriburu had come to power in Argentina, Getúlio Vargas—Brazil's civilian strongman—assumed Brazil's presidency through a military coup. Like Uriburu, Vargas recognized the importance of controlling the police. For Vargas, this meant taking swift action against any state governor who might reinforce state police forces and threaten Vargas's own central government's power. Thus, one of Vargas's first moves was to limit the state governments' budgets for police (Love 1980, 259), taking special action against São Paulo's powerful Força Pública by nationalizing its air wing.

Many Brazilian state governors moved quickly to circumvent Vargas's restrictions on their control over state police by increasing budgetary support for local police (Love 1980). Consequently, by 1936 São Paulo's city police were receiving more funding than the state police (Love 1980, 258). According to Love, such budgetary shifts represented not only the governors' longer-term motive to suppress strikes and fight urban crime but also a more immediate "eagerness to evade Vargas' stringent limitations on state [police] expenditures" (Love 1980, 259).

In Minas Gerais state Gústavo Capanema, the acting State Federal Intervenor (a federally appointed governor), in 1933 attempted to bring in a professor at the Lausanne Institute of Police Science in Switzerland to "reform" the state police. When this plan fell through, Capanema approached the French government for a military mission to provide such training (Capanema 1933). Capanema's attempt "to engage foreign specialists for the Minas Gerais state troops" was viewed by the Vargas administration "with . . . utmost distaste" because the federal government thoroughly disapproved of state officials' contracting for foreign upgrading of their states' police forces (G-2 Report 1933, 1). The U.S. military attaché in Rio reported that Minas Gerais governor Capanema was using the threat of bringing in foreign police trainers to gain political leverage against Vargas: if Vargas would name Capanema the state's permanent intervenor, Capanema would abandon his request for French assistance. In the end, Capanema was given the permanent intervenor post, and Vargas detailed army officers to train Minas Gerais police.

The U.S. military attaché favored this political deal because it would make Minas Gerais police into "an auxiliary force of the Federal army, . . . [an] important advance toward direct control [of such police] by the federal military authorities" (G-2 Report 1933, 2). But many Brazilian state officials did not share the U.S. attaché's perspective. A political official in São Paulo—Minas Gerais's neighbor to the southwest—refused to support the Vargas "dictatorship [because it] has dissolved state militias [i.e., state police] . . . toward . . . the partial or total suppression of the autonomy of the states [themselves], . . . especially . . . of São Paulo, Minas Gerais, and Rio Grande do Sul" (Marcondes 1932). Among Brazil's most politically and economically important states at that time, such opposition was a political threat to Vargas's fragile ruling coalition.

One faction of this coalition, the Liberal Alliance, favored a strong centralized government—Vargas's own position. Another faction, the Constitutionalists, wanted to block any new federal encroachment on state autonomy—the position of São Paulo's political leaders, for example. At the very least, the Constitutionalists wanted their own state parties to share power with the federal government. How such power came to be divided and shared depended in part on where power was located to control a state's police forces. Within the ongoing struggle over the shape and scope of state and federal power, many leaders recognized the value of police forces for achieving their own political goals.

The United States had also demonstrated such an awareness in 1931, when a Brazilian official in Rio requested the U.S. ambassador to Brazil, Edwin W. Morgan, to secure "two or three officials of the police of New York City, who are specialists in the modern methods adopted in New York for the organizing of police service, . . . to go to Rio de Janeiro to organize the Brazilian police system" (State Department Memorandum 1931). In forwarding the request to Washington, the American ambassador himself had demurred and maintained that the government of Brazil was "not sufficiently stable nor . . . its financial situation sufficiently secure to assure foreign nationals that the terms of the contract . . . [would] be observed." Washington rejected the unnamed Brazilian official's request, arguing that it was "inexpedient for foreign governments to assist Brazil either by recommending or lending their officials or those of states or municipalities in reorganizing [police] work." Morgan agreed to reconsider Brazil's request for police assistance once Brazil had reestablished constitutional government (Morgan 1931). But in the end, Washington did increase its involvement with Brazilian police: there was much police cooperation during the Vargas dictatorial "Estado Novo" period (1937–1945)—although this aid was usually ad hoc and informal, as the following case demonstrates.

Internationalizing through the Back Door: Brazil

In November 1935, a series of military revolts in Brazil's northeastern cities of Recife and Natal and the federal capital of Rio de Janeiro against the Vargas regime "challenged the established order in the name of popular revolution and the ANL" (National Liberation Alliance) (Levine 1970, 104). The ANL had been broadened earlier in 1935 when the Brazilian Communist Party had joined the Alliance, making it into a National Front organization, with its honorary leader the popular hero Luis Carlos Prestes. By the mid-1930s, the ANL had become a viable political force in Brazil, with its broad-based membership posing a visible challenge to Vargas's power.

The military revolts provided a pretext for Vargas to take federal action against this political threat. In the months immediately following November 1935, as many as 20,000 people were arrested in Brazil; in the immediately following years, largely politically motivated arrests ranged between 2,000 and 5,000 annually (Levine 1970, 130). These were processed after January 1936 by Vargas's autonomous investigative agency, the National Commission for the Repression of Communism, which held star-chamber proceedings (Levine 1970, 126).

In 1937, to further consolidate his power, Vargas created his repressive, highly centralized "Estado Novo"—the "New State." At the capital, Rio de Janeiro, the New State was ushered in with "the solemn public burning . . . of the flags of the twenty states of the federation," symbolizing the country's turn toward centralized, corporatist rule (Flynn 1978, 94). The new 1937 constitution vastly strengthened presidential power—especially under state-of-siege provisions and a new national security law, the "Lei Monstro" (Monstrous Law), so labeled for its harsh provisions (Flynn 1978, 103). The Lei Monstro provided the legal foundation for harassing the political left, arresting liberal journalists, and deporting "undesirable" foreigners (Levine 1970). In Rio de Janeiro alone, there were as many as one hundred arrests monthly in mid-1937, primarily of people alleged to have participated in or supported the 1935 military uprisings (Flynn 1978, 83).

The U.S. government's involvement with Brazilian police was quiet but supportive. The U.S. military attaché in Rio claimed that Vargas's new national security legislation "emphasizes the individual rights of citizens and requires police authorities to proceed within the law" (G-2 Report 1936). U.S. ambassador Hugh Gibson was working closely with the federal capital's political police, the DOPS (Departamento de Ordem Político e Social), as his memoranda to the State Department attest. Particularly revealing are Gibson's details of the arrests in 1935 of "Harry Berger" (in fact, Arthur Ernst Ewert) and his wife, Elise Saborowski ("Machla Lenczyki") (see Cancelli 1993; Morais 1985; Pinheiro 1991). Ewert, a leading member of the Comintern in the 1920s and a former German Communist Party Reichstag deputy, and Saborowski— like Berger, a Third International (Comintern) agent—had arrived in Brazil with U.S. papers in early 1935 and been organizing to promote the Comintern manifesto, that workers should arm and seize government power.

From the moment of Ewert and Saborowski's arrest, Ambassador Gibson and his "special assistant," Theodore Xanthaky, were in contact with the couple, since they had entered Brazil with North American identities. For example, on December 28, 1935, just a few days after the couple's arrest, Gibson had cabled the State Department that Xanthaky had "arranged in full agreement with the police for certain improvements in the treatment of [these] prisoners in the belief that this will encourage them to talk" (Gibson 1935, 5). Even though Brazil's own Justice Department officials had not been allowed to see Ewert and Saborowski, Xanthaky—"through [his] personal connections with the [political] police"—had succeeded "in having long private talks with [the Ewerts]." Indeed, Xanthaky had been given "full authority to see [Ewert and Saborowski] alone when[ever] he like[d]" (Gibson 1936a, 1).

Meanwhile, the U.S. embassy disavowed publicly any knowledge of Ewert and Saborowski's mistreatment by Brazilian police (Levine 1970). Yet after spending almost three months in Rio's House of Detention, the couple appeared before a Brazilian judge, where they charged that they had been deliberately deprived of adequate food and water and systematically tortured. Ewert had been forced to watch while his wife was stripped naked, dragged across the floor by her hair and breasts, and repeatedly raped and beaten by police (Levine 1970, 127). Ambassador Gibson could not have been unaware of their mistreatment, given his assistant's frequent talks with them and in light of the ambassador's close collaboration with important officials of Rio de Janeiro's DOPS, the capital's political police.

These were Felinto Müller, chief of DOPS (Departamento de Ordem Político e Social), and DOPS police captains Henrique de Miranda Correia and Francisco Jullien. Gibson informed the State Department that Jullien and Miranda Correia had "been tremendously friendly and cooperative" with the U.S. embassy in its efforts to track down Communists in Brazil. Among other things, the DOPS had given the U.S. embassy "access to their secret files, while refusing such facilities to everyone else, including their own foreign office" (Gibson 1936c).

Describing Miranda Correia and Jullien as "two extreme[ly] able young men," the American ambassador wanted the U.S. government to reward the two DOPS captains for their service to the embassy (Gibson 1936c). As the ambassador explained, the officers had been

so convinced of the essential importance of their efforts to keep track of communist activities, that when officials [sic] funds have not been forthcoming they have repeatedly hung up their belongings with a pawnbroker in order to carry on. (Gibson 1936c)

As for their particular mission, Jullien and Miranda Correia were part of the police team dispatched to capture Luis Carlos Prestes, the ANL leader. A Brazilian official had promised that if Jullien captured Prestes, the policeman would be given "a six-months' holiday abroad for the purpose of learning how to deal with radicals" (Gibson 1936c).

Ambassador Gibson urged the State Department to give both Jullien and Miranda Correia "as much encouragement as possible" (i.e., arranging for them to visit the United States), because in Gibson's opinion, the officers were "working with genuine devotion to build up an adequate and efficient service for the maintenance of public order" (Gibson 1936b). In Gibson's opinion, "Brazil [would] continue for many years to be an important center of radical activities," and the United States "ought to begin laying plans . . . for making sure of the fullest possible volume of [intelligence] information." Gibson reasoned that if the United States trained a Brazilian police official who had influence, "we shall probably continue to have facilities for knowing what is going on." In Gibson's mind, helping Brazilian police to get police training in the United States was "something like giving the goose a correspondence course in laying golden eggs" (Gibson 1936c, 2). Gibson warned that if these two Brazilian police officials were not successful at securing guidance from the United States, they would turn to the British, who "would jump at the opportunity to bring [them] into [their] camp" (Gibson 1936c, 1).

On March 5, 1936, a police squad led by Captain Jullien arrested Prestes and his wife, Olga Gutman Benário ("Maria Prestes"). Police Chief Felinto Müller turned Olga, a Jew of German parentage and a Comintern agent (Cancelli 1993; Morais 1985; Pinheiro 1991), over to the German Gestapo (Nash 1945), presumably through the international agreement between Brazil and the Gestapo to track down and capture political "undesirables" and to monitor "movements dangerous to the state." The other signatories to this agreement were the British Secret Service and other European and Latin American security organizations (MEMCON 1945, 1).

The U.S. ambassador to Brazil was fully aware of the U.S. government's collaboration in this agreement with the Gestapo, as were Brazil's Enrico Gaspar Dutra, minister of war (and from 1946 to 1951 president of Brazil), Gois Monteiro, chief of staff of the Brazilian army, and of course Felinto Müller himself, as chief of the DOPS political police (MEMCON 1945, 2). In fact, Brazil's foreign minister, Oswaldo

Aranha—without fully admitting that such an agreement had existed—stated in 1945 that in the late 1930s, "the relations between . . . [Brazil] and the Nazi police were better than they should have been for the interests of Brazil" (Berle 1945).

Olga—then pregnant with Prestes's child—was deported by Brazil via Gestapo officials to Nazi Germany. After her daughter, Anita, was born in Berlin's Bernimstrasse Women's Prison, Olga was transferred to Bahrenberg concentration camp, where in 1942 she was reported to have been executed in a gas chamber (Morais 1985, 293). Before the outbreak of World War II, Anita had been allowed to leave Germany for Mexico with her Brazilian grandmother and aunt, but only after international pressure had been placed on the Nazi government to release Prestes's child to her Brazilian relatives (Morais 1985). Prestes remained in a Brazilian prison for nine years (Levine 1970, 122).

Captain Miranda Correia's next placement was on special assignment at the Brazilian embassy in Buenos Aires, where the police official helped Brazil and Argentina hammer out an agreement for "prevent[ing] . . . acts of international terrorism" (Cancelli 1993, 75). After that, Miranda Correia was secretly transferred to Germany, where he spent a year working with the Gestapo. At the end of his stay in Germany, Heinrich Himmler awarded Miranda Correia the highest honor given by the Nazi government to friendly foreign nationals (Cancelli 1993, 79).

U.S. Domestic Policing and Latin American Espionage in the 1930s

As U.S. ambassador Hugh Gibson had promised, once Prestes had been arrested, Miranda Correia and Jullien were rewarded by Washington: Miranda Correia received an invitation from President Roosevelt to visit police departments in Washington, D.C., and New York City (Cancelli 1993, 73). The State Department arranged for Jullien to visit police departments in Chicago and New York City and pay a call at the FBI headquarters in Washington, D.C.

But what professional expertise in particular might Jullien have learned at police departments in Chicago and New York City? In fact, there may have been little that American police could have taught this DOPS political police official, already well schooled in violent methods of extracting information. The "parrot's perch"—on which a bound up prisoner is hung by the knees like a roasting pig and then beaten, with water forced into the mouth and anus—was already a solid fixture of DOPS precincts (see Cancelli 1993; Mingardi 1992; Pinheiro 1991). In fact, in the United States, Jullien would have been exposed to much of what he already knew or seen how to improve existing techniques for extracting information.

The Wickersham Commission—established in 1931 by President Hoover to evaluate urban U.S. law enforcement—had disclosed that U.S. urban police relied extensively on brutality to extract information and to secure compliance. Both the Wickersham Commission and the New York Bar Association had found that in 1930 to 1931, the 1,500 detectives in New York City's police force were "left apparently free to administer whatever kind of persuasion suited . . . [their] experience— fists, feet, rubber hoses, blackjacks, and nightsticks being the predomi- nant weapons"; of the 1,235 suspects who had been arrested by the New York City police and defended in 1930 by the Voluntary Public Defenders Committee, 23 percent had been beaten by police, either on arrest or in "third-degree rooms" (Wickersham 1931, 100).

A 1928 U.S. grand jury report had declared the Chicago police "rotten to the core" (Mosse 1975, 282). A technique popular with Chi- cago's police for obtaining confessions was to heave a city telephone book at a suspect's ear—the phone book would knock a man down but leave no lasting marks (Wickersham 1931, 126). Most Chicago police precincts had a "goldfish room" where suspects were taken and "given the works"; this included liberal use of the rubber hose, grinding sus- pects' molars to the roots (cooperative dentists carried this out), club- bing suspects' throat and abdomen, dragging women around by the hair, and squeezing and twisting men's testicles (Wickersham 1931, 126–36).

But the State Department saw New York City as an especially appro- priate place for Jullien to improve his policing skills because the city was active in "following local communist activities" (Duggan 1936). In fact, by 1936 the New York City police had spent more than eighty years battling labor unrest, and almost six decades squaring off against anarchists and later "Bolsheviks," who soon became the "Communists."

Indeed, by the 1930s, specialized local police intelligence "red squads" across the United States had become key elements in repress- ing labor and left-wing activities. These Red Squads had been estab- lished in the early twentieth century in response to labor strife, usually in close cooperation with industrial and business organizations (Krajick 1981, 8). In fact, in some U.S. cities, the ties between businessmen and the Red Squads were so close that their relationship was "blatant[ly] patron-client" (Donner 1990, 33).

As just one indicator of the extent of police political repression inside the United States in the early 1930s, the American Civil Liberties Union reported that "during the first three months of 1930, [there were] . . . a total of 930 arrests involving free speech cases, exceeding the total for any entire year from 1921 to 1929. . . . [Moreover, in 1930] the number of meetings broken up by police exceeded by far the total for any year during the 1921–29 period" (in Goldstein 1978, 202). As for labor, never before had businesspeople "hired so many private police, strikebreakers, thugs, spies, and agents provocateurs, and never before [had they] laid up such stores of tear gas, machine guns, and firearms." Moreover, "a total of eighteen thousand strikers were arrested [in the United States] from 1934 to 1936" (Goldstein 1978, 218). This was the "professional" climate into which Jullien was introduced in the 1930s.

The FBI as Latin America's "Good Neighbor"

In the mid-1930s—with the rise of Nazism in Europe and growth of pro-Nazi groups in the United States—Roosevelt had "reactivated the FBI as a political spying agency by asking it to undertake an investigation of the Nazi movement in the United States." Then, in 1936, FDR directed the FBI "to broaden . . . political intelligence activity . . . to include communist groups" (Goldstein 1978, 213). J. Edgar Hoover was to coordinate all information about Communists and right-wing extremists with State Department and military intelligence (Goldstein 1978, 215).

Although Washington had not specifically identified cross-national police training as part of its intelligence gathering or its "Good Neighbor" foreign policy, it clearly wanted access to intelligence information gathered by Latin American police. One way of accomplishing this was for the FBI to penetrate existing police organizations abroad and establish new ones there controlled by indigenous government officials linked to the United States. Sometimes such officials themselves initiated a request for FBI assistance, as in 1938 when both the Dominican Republic and Haiti asked for an FBI operative to investigate Nazi activities there. The Brazilian and Colombian governments requested FBI assistance in establishing new national secret service organizations. Whereas the State Department refused Haiti and the Dominican Republic's requests, it recommended a positive U.S. response to Brazil and Colombia.

Brazil's Foreign Office had asked for FBI assistance in October 1938 after Brazilian authorities reportedly turned up a Nazi plot to foment rebellion in Brazil, Uruguay, and Argentina. According to Foreign Minister Oswaldo Aranha, there was "unmistakable evidence of a large and well-planned organization directed by a German General and aimed at the establishment of a Nazist [sic] regime in Brazil" (Aranha 1938, 1). Aranha—claiming that Germany, and perhaps Italy, Poland, and Japan, were planning to divide South America into colonies—wanted Washington to send several FBI men to Brazil to "organize and direct a proper [Brazilian Secret] Service" (Scotten 1938, 1). The new secret service was to be "a special corps of 5 to 16 persons who would serve directly under [the Foreign Ministry], . . . [as] people of [the] highest personal trust, . . . paid through a special fund" (Fontoura [1938?]). These agents were to give intelligence information only to Brazil's foreign affairs minister; the police would get the necessary information from him.

Brazil's new secret service organization seemed founded on the foreign minister's distrust of Felinto Müller's DOPS, or the political police, and indeed seemed primarily intended for keeping track of Brazil's other police organizations, rather than improving Brazil's internal security. As we have seen, just two years earlier, Müller had blocked Brazil's Foreign Office from interrogating the two important Comintern agents, Ewert and Saborowski. Foreign Minister Aranha wanted his country's new secret service to be separate from—and even unknown to—the existing undercover intelligence section (S-2) of Müller's DOPS—even though both would be based in the federal capital, Rio de Janeiro. An obvious benefit for Aranha and others from such a secret service was that it could monitor Müller's S-2, which had routinely been used as a weapon by those who controlled it—putting even cabinet members and Aranha's diplomats under surveillance (Levine 1970, 56).

In 1940 a U.S. military intelligence officer reported from one of his intelligence contacts that there was "an integrated system of secret police [in Brazil] which is headed in Rio by Captain [Felinto] Müller, who reports directly to Getúlio [Vargas]." According to this informant, Müller's S-2 "was not a secret police in the sense . . . [of] the Gestapo, but . . . a gum-shoe agency of plainclothes men . . . constantly snooping around the [Brazilian] army . . . checking up on individual officers and their beliefs" (G-2 Report 1940, 1).

In spite of the turmoil among Brazilian officials as to who could be trusted—or perhaps because of it—the United States granted Aranha's request for an FBI man to assist setting up a Brazilian federal secret service. J. Edgar Hoover wanted to assign Special Agent Edgar K. Thompson to the job. Hoover described this agent as a young bachelor with a thorough knowledge of Spanish—the FBI had no one who spoke Portuguese. The bureau nevertheless considered Thompson ideal for this Brazilian secret service project: Thompson had already worked for a while in Puerto Rico.

But the State Department had a series of problems getting the FBI project off the ground. While U.S. Public Law 63.76 (Cong. HR 3134) permitted civilians and U.S. nonmilitary government employees to be detailed to foreign countries as technical specialists, the FBI itself had no budget to support agents in the field abroad. U.S. PL. 63.76 stipulated that such costs were to be paid by the "host" country. On the eve of Thompson's departure for Brazil, there was still a great deal of confusion about how this FBI special agent was to be paid. The State Department could confirm only a day or two before Thompson's departure that the Brazilian government would be able to pay part of his stipend. So, in a last effort to get supplementary funding for Thompson, the State Department requested from President Roosevelt a "special appropriation" to cover some of Thompson's expenses. FDR gave quick approval, declaring that the Brazilian secret service project was "very important." In the president's mind, "It should be done" (Welles 1938).

In the end, the Brazilian government paid Thompson's $900 travel costs, plus $1,000 toward his monthly salary, and a living allowance of $2,160 (Hull 1939)—the FBI's special agent had a suite in Rio's posh Hotel Glória (Thompson 1939c). In addition, Thompson received his regular FBI salary and a 50 percent bonus for this "hard duty" mission (Welles 1938). Indeed, the FBI agent's total support of around $8,910, including his salary and the housing stipend, was enormous by late-1930s U.S. standards, when the U.S. median annual family income was in the range of $1,784 (Statistical Abs. 1943, 363); less than 1 percent of the U.S. population earned more than $7,500 annually (USDC 1989, 301). But Birr and Curti (1954, 299) point out that it was common for U.S. "technical specialists" to receive very luxurious salaries and living support abroad.

Once the financial arrangements for Thompson's FBI project had been resolved, Thompson left for Brazil, sailing into Rio de Janeiro's Guanabara Bay in early 1939 on the USS *Uruguay*. Thompson's FBI assignment, of course, was to "work in [Brazil's] Foreign Office, rather than with the police," because as Foreign Minister Aranha explained to Thompson, Brazil's "police organizations . . . were very inefficient." Admonishing Thompson not to have any contact with the DOPS political police, Aranha wanted the FBI's special agent to work undercover as a businessman conducting an economic survey of Brazil (Thompson 1939a).

Thompson's active travel schedule suggests that the FBI's special agent may have attempted quite a lot of intelligence gathering. During Thompson's five months in Brazil, the FBI special agent traveled extensively in the South, visiting primarily cities with large concentrations of Italians and Germans (Thompson 1939b). Even though the U.S. State Department had warned Thompson not to gather any intelligence for the FBI, the FBI director in 1940 wrote that Thompson's mission to Brazil (and later to Colombia) had given the FBI an opportunity "to gather a great deal of most interesting information" (IC 1940, 2).

Thompson's final June 1939 report to the FBI on his work in Brazil indicated that a number of problems had hampered his projects there, because he had not been able to incorporate Rio's DOPS into an FBI-controlled intelligence-gathering apparatus. The primary stumbling block had been resistance from Müller, who as chief of the capital district's political police had made it clear that he did not "want any foreigner 'fooling around' in [or outside] his department" (Thompson 1939d). In fact, Thompson thought it had been a mistake for Aranha to secure FBI assistance without consulting with Müller because as Thompson saw it, "the Brazilian government can only operate with the support of the police and armed forces" (Thompson 1939d).

When his Brazil assignment was considered completed, Agent Thompson was scheduled to be transferred to Bogotá to respond to the Colombian government's request for U.S. assistance in setting up their own secret service (Braden 1939c). In fact, some months before Thompson's transfer to Colombia, Colombian foreign minister Lozano y Lozano had requested that the New York City police establish a secret service in Colombia. The U.S. ambassador to Colombia, Spruille Braden, thought that Colombia's goodwill was extremely important at "a time when alien activities of possible enemies to the U.S. may be a threat" (Braden 1939b, 2). The State Department supported its ambassador's wishes, adding that Colombia needed a secret service because of the "special problems resulting from the proximity of Colombia to the defense of the . . . [Panama] Canal Zone" (Welles 1939a). But Braden recommended against allowing New York City police to assist the Colombian government with such a mission. As Braden saw it, because any "American agents [could] be useful in keeping watch [in Colombia] . . . on alien activities which could be inimical to the U.S.," such assistance should come only from a U.S. federal agency (Braden 1939a). In the end, Ambassador Braden prevailed, and Colombia was to get an FBI man to establish its new secret service.

With World War II about to break out in Europe, there was great urgency in addressing Colombia's request for FBI assistance. The State Department therefore wanted Special Agent Thompson transferred directly from Brazil to Colombia. Ambassador Braden wanted Thompson in Colombia immediately, arguing that Thompson's presence would provide an opportunity for the United States to "augment friendship with [that] country" (Braden 1939a). As Ambassador Braden explained in a memorandum to the State Department, a military mission from the Italian Fascist government had been dispatched to reorganize the Bolivian police, and Italian police had also been "employed as instructors [for the police of] Venezuela and Peru," making any "lack of [a] cooperative attitude [by the United States even] more noticeable" (Braden 1939b, 2).

But Thompson's reassignment was held up by a bitter dispute between J. Edgar Hoover, the Colombian government, and the State Department. FBI Director Hoover vehemently refused to dispatch Thompson to Colombia. On the face of it, Hoover's resistance is curious, for the record indicates that the FBI's ambitious director had his sights steadily trained on an FBI monopoly over intelligence gathering in Latin America. But Hoover had a personal feud with Colombia and the State Department. This conflict apparently dated to late May or June 1937, when the Colombian government discovered that "an American negro," then working as a chauffeur at the U.S. embassy in Bogotá, but with an FBI affiliation, had been indicted in the United States—but presumably not tried—for his involvement with "white slavery traffic." The Colombian government was still pressuring the United States to pursue charges against this alleged white slave trafficker; the State Department apparently supported this action. However, Hoover—who always "supported his men"—was refusing to allow the suspect to be taken to trial and, as retaliation against the State Department, was dragging his feet about sending an FBI agent to Colombia. This South American country had become "a fighting word in the FBI" (Berle 1939).

So in late May 1939, Under Secretary of State Sumner Welles asked President Roosevelt to intervene and force Hoover to make "available the services of an agent of the Federal Bureau of Investigation for . . . advising in the organization of an office [in Colombia] similar to the Bureau." FDR's handwritten response on the margin of Welles's memo was, "O.K., tell Justice" (Welles 1939b).

But no sooner had Special Agent Thompson arrived in Bogotá than Hoover began pushing the State Department to release his man from this project. Hoover claimed that he could not spare Thompson in Colombia for more than six weeks. The Colombian government wanted Thompson for about three months; the State Department was set on keeping Thompson in Colombia for six months. In the end, despite Hoover's constant pressure to get his agent out of Colombia, the State Department was able to keep Thompson there as long as the Colombians had wanted him.

As it happens, Ambassador Braden was dissatisfied with Thompson's work. Braden complained that Thompson had done a poor job at ferreting out subversives and had not at least taught Colombia's secret service "Jiujitsu [sic], [the] mechanics of arrest, use of tear gas, [and the] quelling [of] street and strike disturbances" (Braden 1939c). But mostly Braden was angry that the FBI man had done little more than send Washington intelligence reports that Thompson had copied from Braden's own embassy files. According to Braden, the FBI distributed these reports to the State, War, and Navy Departments as the FBI's own intelligence memoranda.

After completing his project in Colombia, Thompson was sent to Ecuador; there is no record of what he actually did there. In his previous Latin American assignments, Thompson had either worked with national police organizations or established secret services. One likely candidate in Ecuador for FBI assistance was that country's national Carabineros. Indeed, Lieutenant Colonel Gilbert Proctor, U.S. military attaché, saw the Carabineros as more important to Ecuadoran security than the national military, arguing that "during the 1940 election, the Carabineros [had been] counted on by the government to put down any uprisings initiated by the Army or revolutionary factions within

Ecuador." As Proctor explained, the loyalty of the Ecuadoran army "is always in question," and the Carabineros could be used to put down a military coup (G-2 Report 1941).

Policing on War's Eve

By the time World War II broke out in Europe, the United States had established solid relations with Latin American and Caribbean police organizations. In fact, the United States had penetrated and shaped many of the region's police institutions, whether through direct military intervention or indirect political contacts. The latter had occurred in the period of state rebuilding in many parts of Latin America by Latin Americans themselves. Recognizing, for the longevity and strength of their regimes, the importance of controlling police, authoritarian Latin American political leaders such as Brazil's Getúlio Vargas and the region's military dictators sought ways of reorganizing and centralizing the police for their countries' internal security. Washington clearly recognized that its own power and security could be enhanced by allying with and supporting the centralizing practices of Latin American national elites, whether they were democratic or not; certainly Vargas was not.

On the eve of World War II, some of these leaders or their political allies (or enemies), sought FBI assistance in establishing new secret service organizations; these could strengthen Latin American regimes' executive power while providing intelligence-gathering opportunities for the United States, if handled carefully. Over time, the new secret services—originally established to root out Nazi agents as well as Communist "subversives"—"became instruments for oppressing [any] local opposition" and, like the national constabularies before them, "helped already repressive [governments] such as Getúlio Vargas's in Brazil and Jorge Ubico's in Guatemala maintain themselves in power" (Haines 1977, 375).

During World War II, the United States would help build police structures. The improved intelligence apparatus that would be created during World War II would be given a single mission at war's end: to monitor and repress insurgency and Communists.

4 From Policing Espionage to Suppressing "Communism": World War II and Its Aftermath

With World War II threatening, the United States strengthened its own domestic security arrangements and monitored more closely Axis activity among its neighbors to the south. One U.S. response in the late 1930s to German, Italian, and Japanese interest in Latin America was to direct the State Department's Latin American Section to "eliminate . . . Nazi espionage activities in the Americas" (quoted in Haines 1977, 375). Toward this goal, the United States had begun training Latin American military officers at U.S. armed service schools and establishing indigenous secret service organizations in selected Latin American countries.

These initiatives were paralleled by similar preparations at home as the war emergency legitimized expansion of domestic counterespionage activity. In May 1938, the House Committee on Un-American Activities, known as the "Dies Committee" for its chairman, Martin Dies (D-Conn.), began investigating domestic activities that might threaten the security of the United States. In November 1938, President Roosevelt gave the FBI permission to expand its domestic surveillance of "subversives" (Goldstein 1978, 247). Police across the country were directed to promptly turn over to the nearest FBI representative any information relating to espionage, counterespionage, sabotage, or violations of the neutrality laws (Donner 1990, 46).

According to Goldstein (1978, 247), it was not long before the FBI had compiled a list of some 2,500 people in the United States allegedly "engaged in activities of Communism, Nazism, and various types of foreign espionage." By 1940, according to his Dies Committee testimony, Chicago Police Lieutenant Make Mills[1] had an index card file "of 5,000 local communists, [and] 75,000 [other] names [from] all over the United States" (Donner 1990, 50). Lieutenant Mills's aggressive intelligence work had been carried out by his own and other cities' police "red squads."

In fact, the FBI could not have accomplished its domestic counterespionage work without local police and their intelligence squads.

These were "a filter for . . . processing . . . privately disseminated data . . . [using] electronic eavesdropping and wiretapping in situations where the [FBI] was reluctant to take constitutional risks" (Donner 1990, 46). Of course, the record now shows that the FBI itself did not shy away from domestic extraconstitutional intelligence gathering. It was revealed as early as 1940 that the bureau (in violation of the 1934 and 1937 Federal Communications Acts and a 1939 Supreme Court decision prohibiting such activity) had been tapping telephones of alleged criminals. In fact, in 1940 President Roosevelt overruled his federal attorney general's ban on the domestic use of FBI wiretaps, declaring that the FBI was "at liberty to secure information by listening devices . . . of persons suspected of subversive activities directed against the Government of the United States" (Goldstein 1978, 249).

By December 8, 1941, as the United States entered World War II, FBI domestic intelligence-monitoring capabilities had been fully mobilized. For example, a 1976 Senate Intelligence Committee report confirmed that by the beginning of 1941, the FBI had even extended its surveillance to the peaceful activities of various citizen groups, to the point where "political belief and association, group membership and nationality affiliation [had become] the criteria for intelligence investigations" (Goldstein 1978, 253). Compared to its domestic purview, the FBI's intelligence work in Latin America was much more limited, perhaps in large part owing to controls on the FBI by some Latin American governments themselves.

Internationalizing the FBI

Nevertheless, as U.S. intelligence capabilities expanded domestically, they were also being internationalized. In 1940 the FBI was given full responsibility for all U.S. intelligence activity in the Western Hemisphere through the bureau's new Special Intelligence Service (SIS), established by Roosevelt's "telephonic directive" of June 24, 1940. Because the only signature on the document is A. A. Berle's (then an assistant secretary of state), FDR could disavow any knowledge of the SIS if it got into political difficulties (Rout and Bratzel 1986, 37). In fact, another two years passed before Roosevelt made public his having established the SIS: it had been operating for some time without formal notification of either Congress or of many of the governments where the SIS was operating.

The FBI's new Special Intelligence Service set about quietly penetrating Latin American police systems. Eager to establish an FBI presence in Latin America rapidly, by June, 1942—just two years after the SIS had begun operating in the region—the FBI had 137 SIS agents in most of the Caribbean and in all of South and Central America, except the European Guiana colonies (FBI 1941). The assumption was that surreptitious police contacts could be used as intelligence sources for keeping track of Nazi activities inside Latin America. Obviously, the friendships created by such cooperation could be used as a foundation for giving the FBI a foothold in the region after World War II.

Although the covert objectives of the SIS did not mention conducting foreign police training, this did constitute some SIS agents' more public activities, as we shall see. However, some high-ranking FBI officials feared training foreign police because, if the recipient country later became an enemy of the United States, it could use its FBI counterespionage training against the United States (MEMCON 1939). Nevertheless, the SIS did share common features with later U.S. police training programs.

In the first place, both SIS and later U.S. police training programs had significant covert components, unknown even to Congress. Second, both SIS and later police programs focused primarily on establishing police links and intelligence gathering, with or without the cooperation of appropriate higher levels of foreign government officials. Finally, some SIS agents and some later U.S. police training officials were implicated in not preventing, or in actually condoning, human rights abuses. Because of such similarities, SIS deserves closer examination, as an early model for internationalizing U.S. security through ties to foreign police institutions.

The Special Intelligence Service (SIS)

In 1940 J. Edgar Hoover's ambitions led him quickly to establish an SIS monopoly over U.S. Western Hemisphere intelligence activities. Nevertheless, most SIS agents were inexperienced at working outside the United States and relatively unsophisticated at intelligence gathering and counterespionage: the FBI provided almost no formal training for SIS intelligence work (Rout and Bratzel 1986, 42). This may be why, just four months after its establishment, Hoover could have SIS undercover agents in Brazil, Argentina, Chile, Colombia, Mexico, and Cuba

(Rout and Bratzel 1986, 37, 45). These agents "maintained [their] . . . extensive program of counter-intelligence, [by] utilizing the services of American business firms." This cover allowed SIS agents to enter a Latin American city without its national government's or the U.S. ambassador and local consul's knowledge and approval (Rout and Bratzel 1986, 40).

U.S. intelligence operations in Latin American countries often exacerbated tensions among U.S. agents and diplomats and increased inter- and intradepartmental infighting. For example, in 1942 the U.S. consul in the city of Natal, in northeastern Brazil, wrote the State Department that there was "every evidence that William Bradley . . . is some type of secret agent, with all indications pointing to the FBI." The consul explained that one of his "most trusted police informants" had told him that Bradley was collecting information on the Axis and keeping "a weather eye trimmed on the American personnel . . . with Pan American Airways." But the consul considered Bradley's efforts on behalf of *American Exporter Magazine* (probably Bradley's SIS cover) "decidedly silly . . . as . . . [is] his export trade knowledge, which is pitifully faltering" (Natal Consul 1942). SIS operations could also raise difficulties among diplomats, as in 1943, when the assistant to the U.S. consul in São Paulo requested that the FBI assign a special agent as "a liaison and instructor to the São Paulo police" but urged that the agent's police work be kept secret "to evade the challenge of the [U.S.] Ambassador in Rio de Janeiro as to the advisability of having an agent as an instructor to the police" (Gannon 1943, 1).

Despite the U.S. ambassador's reservations, SIS agents set up a "secret service" office in Rio itself, "with the help of Brazilians," on downtown Avenida Presidente Wilson—overseen by the U.S. cultural affairs attaché. This gave the United States an opportunity to "know everything that happens at the highest levels in Brazilian politics" (DOPS 1941). But there was an even more problematic side to SIS work. As one part of their secret service activities in Rio de Janeiro, SIS agents collaborated with the federal capital's political police (DOPS) in the interrogation of suspected spies. Rout and Bratzel go on to argue that during World War II, information about police "torture of some prisoners was forwarded [by SIS] to Washington" (1986, 192). Yet SIS agents explained that it was necessary to "look the other way" when DOPS became too heavy-handed with a prisoner because "if [SIS agents] intervened too frequently [to protect] prisoners, [DOPS] might become less cooperative" (Rout and Bratzel 1986, 192). Rout and Bratzel argue that, if J. Edgar Hoover or Undersecretary of State Sumner Welles and Assistant Secretary of State A. A. Berle "were ignorant of what was transpiring in the Brazilian jails, it was essentially because they preferred not to know" (1986, 192–93).

In fact, the U.S. ambassador to Brazil, Jefferson Caffrey, was highly influential in Brazilian police circles: he actually recommended the hiring, promotion, and dismissal of Rio police personnel. For example, in 1942, when Alcides Etchegoyen became D O P S chief after the forced resignation of Felinto Müller as D O P S director, Ambassador Caffrey urged that the new police chief immediately dismiss "ten pro-Nazi" police officials in his Rio police department. Caffrey listed for Etchegoyen "a nucleus of fifteen officials for his political police" whom the ambassador trusted (Caffrey 1942). Etchegoyen followed his advice and then went on to give to the U.S. embassy the power to coordinate all counterespionage work in Brazil until Etchegoyen himself could organize a reliable police force (G. Gordon 1942).

Etchegoyen's next step was to seek F B I assistance in setting up "a National Police patterned after the Bureau [F B I]," which Etchegoyen's second in command, Major Denys, asked the U.S. ambassador to facilitate. According to the F B I's agent in Rio, the new police force "would exist for 'political' ends . . . [with] the principal function . . . [being] the maintenance of the government in power." But this agent explained that "a 'political police' has a much more nasty sound in our ears than it has in South American ears." And besides, as the F B I agent saw it, "The maintenance in power of the current [Vargas] government . . . may be a laudable project" (Police School 1943, 2). Therefore, given no apparent caveats by the State Department, the F B I decided to help Etchegoyen set up a national police while warning Bureau agents not to "lend . . . [the F B I's] name . . . directly or indirectly to the creation, organization or instruction of a Brazilian 'Political Police'" (Police School 1943, 1–2).

The F B I agent who was selected to assist Etchegoyen on this project was Rolf Larson, an S I S operative who had been working in Brazil since 1941. Larson was very much an exception among S I S operatives. He had lived in Latin America before entering S I S service—between 1937 and June 1940, he had been a Mormon missionary in Argentina. Larson consequently spoke Spanish fluently, and he even had "a slight knowledge of Portuguese" (Pieper 1940; see also Foxworth 1941, 1).

Drawing on his missionary work, Larson began assembling a covert network of informants in Brazil, including Mormon missionaries. It was Larson's belief that the Mormons represented "an excellent source of information . . . [when] coordinated properly," because the Latter-Day Saints in Brazil were transferred frequently from place to place—giving them an opportunity to interact with people in many parts of the country (Larson 1941, 1). As Larson saw it, the missionaries would be particularly useful in ferreting out Nazi activity in Brazil because they were already proselytizing among "Teuto-Brazilians," Brazilians of German ancestry, mostly in the South of Brazil (Larson 1941, 1).

Another way of ensuring the success of his FBI work in Brazil was for Larson to assemble a network of police contacts. One of these was Plinio Brasil Milano, chief of the Rio Grande do Sul state's political police (DOPS). Rio Grande do Sul was crucial for counterespionage planning in Brazil because this important southern state had a large European-born or -descended population and bordered on Uruguay and Argentina, both of which were leaning toward the Axis. Besides the importance of Rio Grande do Sul to the FBI's counterespionage work in Brazil, Larson also considered Police Chief "Plinio" a man of great vision because he recognized the need for Brazil to have a nationally linked federal-level political police modeled after the FBI. In other words, Plinio's assessment of Brazil's internal security needs was congruent with the FBI's goal for Brazil.

But Plinio faced stiff Brazilian resistance in pursuing his goal of establishing a new federal-level police force: Plinio wanted the administrative nucleus for the new police organization to come from Rio Grande do Sul, rather than from the federal capital's own DOPS organization. Thus, Plinio's request for an FBI agent to work with his Pôrto Alegre DOPS, as a first step toward organizing Brazil's police on a centralized federal basis, was not well received by the Vargas federal government officials. Naturally, they wanted the nucleus for the proposed federal police organization to come from President Vargas's hand-picked police officials in the federal capital, Rio de Janeiro. So, in order to encourage the FBI to work with his state police organization, Plinio had led the FBI to believe that any FBI special agent working with his DOPS in Rio Grande do Sul "would have access to the police files and would be allowed to question prisoners and have all the rights of an official in the [DOPS] Police Department" (Bird 1943). If Plinio's version of the proposal for a unified federal police was not accepted by Rio de Janeiro officials, he planned to establish direct ties of cooperation with the police of other Brazilian states informally, apparently intending to bypass the federal government. Thus the FBI project was already creating the potential for increased competition and conflict within the host country's police.

In any case, in early 1943, the FBI invited Plinio to visit its training academy in Washington, D.C., hoping that Plinio would "return from his trip [to the United States] with the increased prestige and influence" necessary to convince government officials of "the advantages of [establishing] an organization like [the] FBI" (Braddock 1943). Shortly after returning to Brazil, in late 1943, Plinio and "forty crack men" were detailed to Rio de Janeiro "to assist the Rio police in uncovering Fifth Column activities" (Am. Intellig. Svce. Rept. 1943). The FBI was of course delighted that Plinio had been moved, even if temporarily, to Rio de Janeiro. He would be better able to foster interstate police cooperation, although the FBI regarded this a poor substitute for federal organization of the Brazilian police.

Plinio apparently reasoned that one way to get Rio de Janeiro officials to accept the idea of a new federal police organization was for an FBI agent to offer police training lectures to specially selected groups of Brazilian police officials. Plinio requested an FBI agent to set up a police training school in Rio. The FBI agreed to such a request because as one of its agents pointed out, this kind of cooperation "laid the groundwork for the establishment of relations with the Rio de Janeiro police during the war years" (Davidson 1945, 5).

Plinio's role in the FBI-run police school cannot now be determined. In any case, he was not always in Rio and frequently traveled outside Brazil for covert counterespionage intelligence activity. In fact, Plinio was killed at age thirty-six, reportedly shot to death during a counterespionage operation in Montevideo, Uruguay (PAP 1993).

The FBI's police training school continued at Rio de Janeiro's political police (DOPS), with Rolf Larson delivering lectures. Larson's first lecture was attended by eighty people, the majority of them officials from various regional DOPS organizations. In Larson's course, five of the lecture topics covered espionage, counterespionage, Fifth Column activities, and sabotage; two more were on observation and surveillance; and another four focused on interrogation techniques (Bradley 1943b, 3, 5). Course reference books included *The FBI at War and Peace, Total Espionage, Inside the Gestapo,* and *Secrets of German Espionage* (Bradley 1943a, 1–2).

Intersecting Careers and Interests

SIS agents were crucial for U.S. penetration of Brazil's police establishment during the war years. This usually occurred not through spying or coercion but by building strong personal relationships between FBI agents and Brazilian police officials. As one example of how this occurred, in April 1945, the FBI's legal attaché in Rio de Janeiro, without the knowledge of A. A. Berle, by then the U.S. ambassador, informed the FBI in Washington that Rio federal district chief of police João Alberto Lins de Barros was sending his representative, Joaquim de Oliveira Sampaio (brother of the head of PanAir do Brasil—Pan American Airlines of Brazil), to the United States "to purchase sub-machine guns, ammunition, and technical equipment for the Police Department" (Clegg 1945, 1). The FBI agent attached to the U.S. embassy thought that the FBI should respond positively to João Alberto's request because this "would materially aid in the cultivation of [this] new police chief, [who] will be an outstanding political figure in Brazil" (Carson 1945, 1). Favors such as this built friendships that could pay off in the future.

But the FBI could further increase its influence over such police by bringing them to its new Washington, D.C., FBI Academy, an international symbol of modernity and professionalism in police investigative work. Besides improving a Latin American police official's skills at intelligence gathering and counterespionage, a visit might make a police official more receptive to U.S. initiatives. And having been at the FBI's prestigious academy might give the returning police official greater respect and political influence at home for promoting his and the FBI's intersecting interests.

There is little doubt that Pôrto Alegre's DOPS chief, Plinio Brasil Milano, had been deeply impressed by his experience at the FBI's academy in Washington. Plinio's photograph album from his visit includes snapshots of his learning fingerprinting, reading counterespionage texts, and using modern police weapons. In one snapshot, Plinio is standing with J. Edgar Hoover himself. Another set of photographs are of Plinio at the FBI academy's July 1943 graduation exercises, sharing guest-of-honor status with William Jeffers, of the U.S. government's Rubber Development Program. Plinio was, of course, from a country that had abundant and coveted wartime rubber reserves (PAP 1993).

Today, Plinio Brasil Milano—whose picture hangs in most Rio Grande do Sul Civil Police buildings—is considered the patron saint of that state's Civil Police. Fifty years later, the institutional memory of Plinio's FBI training is still strong at the Civil Police (PAP 1993).

As for SIS agent Rolf Larson, after spending almost five years in Brazil, he was transferred to La Paz, the Bolivian capital. There he was to set up a police intelligence school, establish a civilian secret police, and reorganize the Bolivian national police (Davidson 1945, 2). In the end, Larson's sole achievement in Bolivia was to win "the friendship of the Chief of Police [who had made] available to [Larson] such records as [Larson] desire[d]" (Beck 1943, 1). Larson was unable to establish the police intelligence school because of what the FBI characterized as "the absolute lack of mental responsibility of the Bolivian police" (Holloman 1942, 1). Eventually in mid-1950, Larson was stationed in Phoenix, Arizona, where he headed the bureau's local "Communist squad" (Davidson 1945, 12). Rolf Larson had returned to the Cold War United States fortified by a wealth of counterespionage intelligence-gathering skills further developed and tested abroad.

For its part, the FBI's Special Intelligence Service had been successful at penetrating the Brazilian police system. SIS had laid a foundation for the CIA and State Department to further internationalize U.S. security after World War II.

Postwar Reorientation: Anti-Communism to the Fore

In the decade before World War II, Communists and anarchists had been the principal impetus for quietly penetrating Latin American police systems. As the Axis went down in defeat and World War II came to an end, the U.S. State Department began shifting its security concerns from Nazism back toward Communism. Now that the Axis was defeated, it was Communists and ardent nationalists who provided the justification for preparing Latin American police to uncover and neutralize threats to their countries' (and U.S.) national security.

But, in fact, in the immediate postwar years, the U.S. State Department was relatively unprepared to monitor and repress Communism in Latin America. According to the State Department's Division of American Republics, it had to send "all correspondence re[garding] Communist activities in any foreign country . . . [to the State Department's] Division of Eastern European Affairs" (Duggan 1936, 1). Likewise, the State Department's intelligence-monitoring apparatus had an inadequate information-handling system. For example, it did not catalog under a single file heading each individual involved in revolutionary movements abroad. A staffer with the Division of American Republics called for such a cross-tabulated cataloging system "even at the risk of taking up file space" (DAR 1944, 1; see also Pinheiro 1991). The lack of such a system suggests relative unpreparedness at that time for dealing with nationalist and Communist movements and their leaders.

Nevertheless, the State Department was concerned that many Latin American political leaders themselves were slow to recognize the dangers of Communism. A later case in point was Brazil's Getúlio Vargas in his second term of office. According to a State Department communiqué, he was more concerned about developing an internal security apparatus supportive of his power than in making his security forces effective instruments against Communism. Walter N. Walmsley, minister-counselor at the U.S. embassy in Rio, would point out in 1953 that Vargas was selecting men for the federal capital DOPS political police "primarily . . . for their loyalty [to Vargas], and not solely for their anti-communist orientation" (Walmsley 1953, 1). The embassy official reported that some police officials were charging that Vargas was staffing his political police "with men of unquestioned personal loyalty to himself, to be used for violent suppression of the political opposition, whether communist or non-communist." As the embassy saw it, Vargas's police appointments "had the effect of weakening the most effective anti-communist arm of the government in the Federal District for [carrying out] anticommunist repressive action" (Walmsley 1953, 5). Walmsley argued that Vargas's staffing preferences could even weaken the internal security forces of the various state governments, "most of which look to the Federal [District DOPS] Police for leadership and guidance in anti-communist operations" (Walmsley 1953, 5).

Walmsley was enthusiastic about Vargas's earlier appointment in 1951 of Army Major Hugo Bethlem to head the federal district DOPS political police, because as Walmsley saw it, Bethlem was "a young, aggressive anti-communist army officer" (Walmsley 1953, 1). Bethlem already had a good reputation at the embassy; he had requested U.S. embassy assistance for a bimonthly publication of ten thousand copies of "a periodic anti-Communist bulletin" (Barr 1951, 1). At that time, the embassy's cultural affairs officer had told Bethlem that the embassy had no funds for supporting his project, but that the embassy could "furnish him anticommunist articles and editorials from virtually all of the Latin American countries." Bethlem was "quite pleased" with this offer; the cultural affairs officer "promised to send him the first of such editorials as soon as possible" (Barr 1951, 1).

In the meantime, the U.S. embassy's cultural affairs officer recommended that Bethlem seek funding for his bulletin from São Paulo's Serviço Social da Indústria (SESI), a business benevolence and professional association (Barr 1951, 1). SESI had recently set up an office in São Paulo for producing and distributing anti-Communist propaganda, even sending out a U.S. government anti-Communist pamphlet—"Por uma Paz Duradoura" ("For a Lasting Peace")—under attribution only to SESI (Cerwin 1952). According to the embassy's cultural affairs officer, the embassy's own bulletin—"printed in the USIA's [United States Information Agency's] own shop . . . with no attribution to the [U.S.] Embassy"—was being sent "to many members of the [Brazilian] armed forces" (Cerwin 1952).

With Bethlem heading the federal district's DOPS, the U.S. embassy could preserve its influence over this powerful, repressive police organization. But this was at best an ad hoc stratagem for internationalizing U.S. influence over Brazil's internal security. We shall see later how more systematic police training regularized these influences. However, as in the immediate pre–World War II years, so just after the war much internationalizing of U.S. security, at first, still involved only the quiet strategy of developing personal ties with local police officials and then using these relationships to gain influence in their police organizations. Such penetration gave the United States a broader window of information and influence on the host country's internal security system, and through this on its police and political system as well.

But there was as yet still no specific ideologically guided program for transforming foreign police into guardians of containment. As the next section will demonstrate, some new ideology would be crucial for justifying further internationalizing U.S. security through penetration and training of Latin American police systems during peacetime. Only under changing ideological and bureaucratic auspices could U.S. domestic and international security arrangements developed for wartime be carried into the postwar period.

Restructuring for a Cold War: Justifying and Bureaucratizing a National Security Infrastructure

The administration of Harry S. Truman adds an important chapter to the internationalizing of U.S. security through foreign police training.

Changes in the "non-Western world" during Truman's first term (1945–1949)—the rise of nationalist and socialist movements and regimes, along with decolonization and especially the spread of "Communist" ideas and of Soviet and Chinese influence and the U.S. response—would profoundly influence the development of future U.S. programs for training Latin American police.

At war's end there had been calls to dismantle many of the existing U.S. wartime intelligence agencies. Between September 1945 and January 1946, this led to "one of the fiercest bureaucratic battles Washington has ever known . . . over [the future of the U.S.] intelligence [system]" (Ranelagh 1986, 100). The struggle revolved around what U.S. intelligence activities should be, who should control them, and who should have access to them. The U.S. military, important during the war, "was in no mood to shrink back to its [pre–World War II] posture" within the U.S. international security system (Schurmann 1974, 115). In fact, the Joint Chiefs wanted at least what they defined broadly as "military intelligence" to be an arm of the military itself: they did not want this function taken over by civilian organizations.

The State Department, on the other hand, was pressing for a "demilitarization" of intelligence: it wanted to control the security files of the soon-to-be-dismantled wartime security agencies. Troy (1981, 216) maintains that the State Department's renewed expressions of concern about Communism were primarily motivated by its desire to become a central repository for the wartime intelligence files of the various U.S. intelligence organizations. Furthermore, even though the State Department had helped the FBI gain a foothold in Latin America, it now wanted to get the FBI out (Troy 1981). The head of the wartime Office of Strategic Services, William S. ("Wild Bill") Donovan, called for a separate civilian intelligence agency that he would direct: it would coordinate the intelligence activities of the military and the State Department—leaving the FBI out of international intelligence work altogether.

Although it is tempting to see these conflicts as little more than battles over bureaucratic turf, in fact, according to Schurmann (1974), the arguments were symptomatic of fundamental philosophical differences about U.S. postwar security policy and operations. The so-called "nationalists" in the War Department and their supporters in Congress believed that U.S. postwar security was dependent on the United States' remaining militarily strong, particularly by retaining its atomic monopoly. The nationalists opposed demilitarizing U.S. security, whether at home (for example, dismantling the wartime domestic security and international espionage bureaucracies) or abroad (withdrawal of all U.S. military operations). They believed that postwar U.S. foreign policy should be guided by narrowly defined national self-interest, which the military was in the best position to protect (Schurmann 1974).

By contrast, the "internationalists," as Schurmann (1974) labels them, envisioned a world order based on free trade and free enterprise, in which threats to U.S. economic and political interests would be handled according to utilitarian, nonideological criteria. The internationalists were primarily in the State Department and the East Coast business and financial establishment. For them, diplomatic and political measures offered the best solution to international problems, and the State Department was best equipped to direct such diplomatic efforts.

Schurmann (1974) maintains that the predominantly Democratic leaders in Washington at war's end were philosophically closest to the internationalists, although with several ideological qualifications. The White House saw its own Executive Office, advised by diplomatic experts in the State Department, as best suited to make postwar national security policy. This would guarantee that the executive branch retained its wartime national security prerogatives (Ranelagh 1986). All that was needed to ensure this White House preeminence was an operational ideology that could provide justification for pulling together the divergent security organizations and legitimize international security planning during peacetime.

Containment

In 1946, when George Kennan, a U.S. chargé d'affaires in Moscow, first elaborated the containment doctrine, he argued that the Soviet Union represented an aggressive, long-term threat to the West. For Kennan, the only way to block the inexorable character of Soviet expansionism was to erect "powerful dykes around the Russian flood" (in Schurmann 1974, 102). In this early elaboration of his theory, Kennan recognized that not all parts of the world were equally vulnerable to Communist takeover. The most vital were "strategic" countries with industrial capacity and/or valuable raw materials: their resources should be protected. But the Soviets would attempt to take over these countries through psychological and political, rather than military, means, Kennan argued. Thus containment programs had to be proactive, restoring the self-confidence and self-protection of vulnerable nations to help them resist future Soviet aggression.

Ranelagh (1986) maintains that containment caught on so quickly as an ideology in postwar Washington because it "gave voice to a crucial intellectual [viewpoint] that considered the cold war necessary and . . . something to be managed before it gave way to all-out war." According to containment theory, only a government body with a comprehensive knowledge of global problems and issues could effectively formulate U.S. international security policy (Schurmann 1974, 106). Special interest groups, such as Congress or the War Department, could not sufficiently overcome their own particular concerns to allow them to formulate a holistic foreign policy.

In any case, there seemed a need to bring order to the various intelligence organizations that had proliferated during World War II. Indeed, there was insufficient technical and organizational infrastructure to accomplish Cold War security objectives (Troy 1981). Furthermore, existing intelligence agencies functioned independently of each other, and the intelligence system lacked coordination between these agencies: information was shared only as necessary or ordered. There was interdepartmental infighting because there was little centralized control and definition of the U.S. intelligence mission. Finally, the U.S. international security bureaucracy lacked a unified ideological direction (Troy 1981, 210).

Thus, in the dangerous and complicated postwar international order, many policy makers believed that the only way to succeed against Communism was for U.S. intelligence planning and operations to be streamlined, internationalized, and coordinated centrally. Such thinking justified U.S. international security planning. According to Schurmann (1974, 92), the containment doctrine provided just the vocabulary and rationale for retaining international security planning during peacetime, and for giving this responsibility to a single group of executive branch planners; it served to halt, in a way acceptable to both nationalists and internationalists, and executive agencies, the complete dismantling of the wartime security bureaucracies. Containment ideology accomplished this by reconciling each interest group to the loss of its independent control over particular national security affairs by depriving its rivals of their independence, too. This, in turn, accomplished for postwar U.S. international security affairs what the New Deal had done for U.S. domestic policies: it provided a worldview that reoriented, directed, and justified U.S. government policy (Schurmann 1974).

The Truman Doctrine and Foreign Police Centralization

However, even though an ideology that legitimated the need for a proactive approach to international security was becoming a central component of U.S. foreign policy, foreign police did not automatically become an agent for containment. Indeed, the apparent ease with which some of Truman's international security planners could leave foreign police assistance out of containment is suggested by the first draft of the U.S.-Japan peace treaty. According to George Kennan himself, this draft failed to include provisions for helping the Japanese guard their postwar internal security.

Kennan blames General Douglas MacArthur, supreme commander of occupation forces in Japan, for this oversight, maintaining that Kennan himself had urged rewriting the U.S.-Japan peace treaty to include making Japan's "central police establishment . . . [into an] effective means of combatting . . . Communist penetration" by strengthening the connections between Japanese and U.S. security forces (Kennan 1967, 376).

Such a proposal fit perfectly with the policies of U.S. international planners because the United States was already assisting other former enemy countries' police. For example, as soon as the war in Europe was over, U.S. occupation forces were "denazifying" Germany's police. In Korea, the United States was eliminating "all vestiges of Japanese control . . . [by] cleans[ing] and reorganiz[ing] the . . . police system, which had traditionally been authoritarian, arbitrary, highly central- ized, and . . . repressive" (Lobe 1975, 24). In postwar Japan itself, U.S. occupation authorities attempted to "deconcentrate the powers of po- lice agencies, putting them under popular control, and neutralizing them politically" (Sugai 1957, 5). The man in charge of this phase of reorganizing Japan's municipal police was New York City's former po- lice commissioner Lewis J. Valentine. Oscar Olander, of the Michigan State Police, was reorganizing Japan's rural police forces. In addition, "over five hundred U.S. police and intelligence personnel worked as liaison to the Japanese police" (Lobe 1975, 26).

But with the U.S.-Soviet alliance dissolving and the Cold War heat- ing up, Washington was increasingly apprehensive about leftish move- ments in former enemy countries. There was soon a rethinking of the initial approach of "purifying" former enemy police. More emphasis was placed instead on ridding police systems of possible Communist influences. In Germany, for example, "the [U.S.] denazification program was relaxed . . . to help restore a functioning [anti-Communist] internal security force as quickly as possible" (Lobe 1975, 26). This often amounted to restoring Axis sympathizers to their former positions in the police. In Korea, "85 [percent] of the policemen that had formerly served under Japanese employ were simply rehired by the occupation authorities." Such police, "already infamous for their brutal treatment of leftists in Korea, behaved similarly during this regenerative era" (Lobe 1975, 26).

In Japan—with increasing militancy from the left, spreading labor strikes, and allegations of police corruption—U.S. occupation officials took steps to recentralize the police system (Sugai 1957, 7). During this second phase of postwar reorganization, Japan's 75,000-man National Police was placed under the control of the prime minister, making it "entirely separate from the ordinary police and free from interference by any public safety commission." This police organization was then "equipped with American weapons, including mortars and machine guns [*sic*], clothed in American-type [police] uniforms, and drilled . . . Army-fashion" (Sugai 1957, 7). The U.S. police and intelligence personnel who worked with the Japanese National Police force "shifted their counterintelligence work to . . . [focus on] communist infiltration of the police services and root[ing] leftists out of the Japanese internal security apparatus while developing [U.S.-oriented] agents within the [Japanese] police establishment" (Lobe 1975, 26).

The man who directed this phase of Japanese police reorganization was Byron Engle, a U.S. military intelligence officer and top aide to General Douglas MacArthur. Engle, who had headed the Kansas City, Missouri, Police Department before the war, was associated at the time of his assignment to Japan with the CIA. This affiliation apparently continued throughout the 1950s and 1960s while Engle was heading the Agency for International Development's Office of Public Safety (OPS), in charge of foreign police training programs, as we shall see.

Yet Truman's top national security advisors had not yet recognized the central value of foreign police training for U.S. international security. In fact, as in previous decades, foreign police assistance was supplied only where police institutions had already clearly disintegrated or become "disorganized"—in postwar Germany, Japan, Korea, the Philippines, Greece, and Turkey. In general, as in the early part of the twentieth century, such assistance was only part of a general program of military assistance. The Truman administration's foreign police assistance initiatives had neither their own independent budget, nor specially assigned personnel, nor an articulated ideology establishing the unique value of police assistance to U.S. international security. Truman simply inherited the tradition of previous foreign police assistance and generally adhered to the tendency to attach foreign police assistance to military programs.

However, although not specifically recognizing the independent value to U.S. security from assisting foreign police, Truman's international security advisors had established the infrastructure for internationalizing foreign police assistance. In 1947 the National Security Council (NSC) was established as an executive branch organization for coordinating previously scattered U.S. international security planning and operations. The creation that same year of the Central Intelligence Agency, out of the wartime Office of Strategic Services, established a mechanism for centralizing and coordinating intelligence gathering abroad. In theory, if not always in fact, these changes ensured executive oversight of U.S. national security affairs.

This infrastructure would help transform U.S. foreign police assistance into a permanent mechanism for internationalizing U.S. security, under the ideological auspices of defending the "free world" through economic and technical development. This transformation of police assistance, from an ad hoc to a permanent feature of the U.S. national security bureaucracy, was effected through a fusion of the emerging ideologies around containment of the Soviet Union, international Communism, and "free world" economic development.

*Foreign Aid as Security: Internationalization through
the Marshall Plan and Point Four Program*

The Marshall Plan (European Recovery Program), drafted in 1947 by George Kennan and other members of the State Department Policy Planning Staff, operationalized containment along relatively nonmilitarist lines. The argument was that if European economies were economically viable, Europe would be better able to defend itself against Communism. This emphasis on preventive economic approaches to containment established a precedent for linking U.S. economic aid to international security—including, in time, using preventive foreign police training as an alternative to largely defensive and reactive military intervention for promoting internal security.

The Marshall Plan's aid-for-development formula provided a rationale for spreading U.S. containment resources even into regions initially considered relatively safe from Communist penetration. This globalizing of containment was justified to prevent a possible shift in the international balance of power in favor of the Soviets. Communist Party efforts under Soviet tutelage toward taking over vulnerable nations from within, through psychological and political techniques, added pressure on U.S. agencies to find ways of proactively countering such efforts.

Thus, alongside Kennan's initially more focused economic approach to containment emerged a wider global containment strategy, enunciated as the Truman Doctrine by the president on March 12, 1947: it would be "United States [policy] to support free peoples who are resisting attempted subjugation by armed minorities or by outside pressures." The doctrine allowed for extending U.S. containment resources to regions of the world previously considered peripheral to U.S. interests, and it declared the United States to be in a global struggle—with a mix of military and nonmilitary strategies and programs—against Communism.

But only in Truman's second term (1949–1953) did the organizational building blocks for internationalizing U.S. security come into being as the work of the new NSC, the CIA, and the Point Four Program was legitimized by Cold War ideologies. This was the seedbed for expanding U.S. security abroad in the postwar world order. In particular, the developing theory of containment was increasingly linked to economic development. These intertwined doctrines, in turn, were used to legitimize preventive, proactive security planning during peacetime, which provided a rationale for training foreign police as "preventive medicine" against Communism.

Truman's Point Four Program of foreign economic assistance to less developed nations, which became law in 1951, was born of a marriage between containment and economic development ideologies. Communism could be contained by building up a country's own capacity and resolve to resist penetration. One sure way of increasing internal security against Communism was for a country to become more economically developed through technical assistance from U.S. advisors.

Most Point Four technical assistance went to Asia, the Middle East, and Latin America on the assumption that preventive nonmilitary assistance would help such developing regions "avoid the creation of Greek-type [Communist] insurgencies which would [then] require even more costly military intervention" (Schurmann 1974, 96). In the logic of Point Four, if a country became economically self-sufficient through technical assistance from anti-Communist advisors, it would be better able to protect itself against Communist subversion. To this end, Point Four authorized bilateral technical cooperation—advice, training, and "demonstration" equipment—through in-kind contributions from the United States and through recipient-country financing. In other words, the Cold War "menace" required new measures to protect Latin America and other world regions from Communism.

Point Four assistance to Latin America was awarded according to a country's relative ranking on a "subversive pressure" scale, from zero to one hundred. A high subversive pressure score meant that Point Four assistance was urgently needed (Hoover 1952), as in 1952 when Brazil's subversive pressure ranking was ninety-five and Mexico's, eighty-five. The next most urgent Latin American cases were Argentina and Guatemala, with subversive pressure rankings of seventy-five and sixty-four respectively in that year. Point Four assistance would overcome such countries' vulnerability to Communism through technical support for agricultural, health, and "public administration" reforms; police training assistance was subsumed under public administration (see U.S. Embassy 1953, 1).

The standard mechanism for accomplishing Point Four reforms in Latin American public administration was to establish a *servicio* (*serviço* in Portuguese), consisting of a team of officials from the United States and the foreign government working together in the host country's agencies or ministries to improve administrative practices. In the process, nationals would get the necessary training to operate their country's public administration more effectively. The United States recognized that one danger of its collaborating with foreign nationals in a servicio was that U.S. presence in a Latin American government's bureaucracy might create the impression that North Americans were trying to run the host government. This charge was especially likely where U.S. technical specialists maintained a visible presence inside a foreign country's police system. However, negative publicity could be avoided if "advisors work[ed] individually with[in] separate ministries" (FOA/IIAA 1954), presumably decentralizing the U.S. presence to make it less visible.

In any case, most Point Four assistance to Latin American police did not follow the servicio model, remaining largely ad hoc and limited in scope. For example, in 1951, several Rio de Janeiro police requested U.S. embassy funding to study traffic control in the United States. The embassy supported this request, asking a Rio de Janeiro Rotary Club to match funds with the State Department to cover the policemen's travel and lodging. Being unwilling to supply its own funding for this project, the State Department directed the embassy to secure support from the International Association of Chiefs of Police (IACP) (Rio to State, 10/23/51). In fact, throughout the 1950s, the IACP commonly acted as a State Department go-between for securing funds and planning site visits for foreign police. These IACP-hosted visits helped create a professional and ideological bond between U.S. security specialists and visiting foreign police, in much the same way as FBI assistance had done in the previous decade, but without so obvious a government-to-government link.

However, as the next chapter demonstrates, successfully internationalizing U.S. security through penetrating Latin American police systems required much more than such informal, noninstitutional police exchanges. There would need to be new U.S. programs for penetrating and reshaping developing countries' security systems, and new ideologies for justifying and explaining this intervention.

Crisis and Militarism

But new ideologies for expanding existing nonmilitary approaches to containment did not translate readily in the immediate postwar period into an expansion of assistance to foreign police. Instead, changes in the international balance of power after 1947 were providing powerful support for military approaches to containment. In particular, the "fall of China" in 1949, after Mao Tse-tung's Communist defeat of Chiang Kai-shek's U.S.-backed Nationalists, brought widespread criticism of Truman's "weak" foreign policy. A vocal segment in Congress, the "China Lobby," charged that Truman's reluctance to use all-out military intervention in the Chinese civil war had meant the U.S. "surrender" of China to the Communists. There was also criticism of Truman's defense-spending cuts: these had hit the army and navy hardest and favored the air force as the key to U.S. atomic superiority.

There was growing skepticism about George Kennan's earlier warning that the United States could not commit itself to a program of total global containment without suffering high domestic inflation. In particular, the National Security Council asserted in its NSC Memorandum 68 (April 14, 1950) that the U.S. economy could tolerate as much as a tripling of defense spending without incurring serious threats of inflation. According to NSC 68, such increases in spending were necessary because the Soviet Union, bent on world domination, would neutralize the U.S. atomic advantage by 1954. This would place the Soviets in a position to initiate a war against the United States with a reasonable prospect of winning. The almost immediate outbreak of fighting in Korea, blamed on the Soviet Union's backing of its client state in North Korea, helped ensure presidential approval of NSC 68 and a full militarization of containment.

However, it was not long before increased military spending was producing a new round of questions about Truman's foreign policy. Critics charged that even with a sizable military budget, Truman had not been able to take North Korea from the Communists. And the president's new reliance on military approaches to containment had undermined developmentalist containment strategies.

Nonetheless, during the Truman administration, the ideological legitimation and an "enabling" bureaucracy had been developed for launching global police training as preventive containment. This provided a basis for Eisenhower, pressured to reduce military spending, to launch a worldwide foreign police assistance program as "preventive medicine" against Communism. The internationalizing of U.S. security was ready to begin through programs to assist foreign police.

5 Policing Containment

Dwight D. Eisenhower launched his 1952 presidential campaign promising a "new look" for his foreign policy: he would "let Asians fight Asian wars," placing more of the burden for containing the early stages of Communist expansion on the shoulders of vulnerable countries themselves. The working ideology behind this "new look" was further developed in National Security Council debates about U.S. policy should the French pull out of Indochina (NSC 1954a). Eisenhower himself argued that "one of the outstanding failures of the Western world in Asia was its inability to produce good fighting material in the Asian countries"; Admiral Arthur Radford, Chairman of the Joint Chiefs of Staff, agreed that "the real reason the French were still fighting the war [in Vietnam] after 7 years was their earlier reluctance to train any of the Vietnamese" (NSC 1954a, 14). The United States would address this situation by preparing the indigenous forces of "free Vietnam" to fight for themselves (Herring 1979, 31). Internationalized foreign police training would come into its own, with implications for other countries' centralization, militarization, authoritarianization, and devolution.

Policing Communism: Bureaucratizing the U.S. Programs

Eisenhower's containment formula saw the U.S. military as just one element in a "combined U.S.-indigenous defense system" that also included Third World police (IDA 1959a, 4–5). According to William Steeves, the assumption that developing countries' police could be trained to contain Communism had grown out of the 1952 Japanese riots: U.S.-trained Japanese police successfully controlled rioters through "effective riot control techniques. . . . For the first time tear gas was employed"; their success convinced U.S. officials that "the police were key to internal defense" (Steeves 1976, 11).

In any case, according to Steeves, many of Eisenhower's national security advisors already recognized that "internal [security] problems . . . should not be dealt with by military force" alone (Steeves 1976, 12; see also OCB 1955c, 1). One result of such thinking was a new program to train foreign countries' internal security forces. Based on the assumption that criminality and subversion had to be controlled before internal security had deteriorated to the point of requiring military action (Steeves 1976, 2–3), Eisenhower's national security advisors called into question previous foreign internal security approaches that had dealt with foreign police training "on a piecemeal basis, usually acting after a critical situation had already developed, as in Greece or Indochina" or postwar Japan (OCB 1955c, 7). In contrast, Eisenhower's foreign police assistance initiative would "envisage [police as] 'fire prevention'"—detecting and eliminating Communism before it could get out of control (OCB 1955c, 7).

NSC Action Memorandum 1290, dubbed a "Review of Basic National Security Policy," directed, in subclause "d," that the NSC's Operations Coordinating Board (OCB)[1]

present to the [National Security] Council a report on the status and adequacy of the current program to develop constabulary forces to maintain internal security and to destroy the effectiveness of the Communist apparatus in free world countries vulnerable to communist subversion (NSC 1954b, 2).

The police program that grew out of this directive came to be known throughout U.S. national security bureaucracy as the 1290d Program. From then on, foreign police assistance would be reorganized as part of the U.S. national security bureaucracy.

The 1290d Program was thought necessary because "many countries threatened with communist subversion [had] neither the knowledge, training nor means to defend themselves successfully [against communism]" (OCB 1955c, 1). To correct this, 1290d would train foreign countries' "regular and special police gendarmerie and carabinero, constabulary and investigative types of forces" as a first line of defense against Communist subversion (OCB 1955c, 5). However, recognizing that police training alone would not prepare host countries against Communism, in 1957 OCB broadened its internal security initiative and dubbed it the Overseas Internal Security Program (OISP). This top secret internal security program combined 1290d police assistance with a variety of strategies to coordinate international security planning more carefully by integrating military and police assistance with judicial reform, using USIA propaganda to convince vulnerable countries that they needed OISP internal security assistance.

Selling Protection by Internationalizing Police Assistance

It was not by chance that the NSC's Operations Coordinating Board proposed its 1290d Program in the year of the Viet Minh's defeat of the

French at Dien Bien Phu and just as the CIA was completing plans to overthrow Guatemala's democratically elected president Jacobo Arbenz Guzmán. Eisenhower's national security advisors argued that the United States might have prevented the "loss" of these countries to "Communism" if the United States had earlier brought their police and internal security forces into the U.S. orbit. By incorporating U.S. advisors into recipient countries' police systems and using them to orient recipient police toward proactive intelligence and operations, such "friendly" anti-Communist police would be incorporated into U.S. intelligence and political operations.

NSC Memorandum 5501 (January 6, 1955) formalized such thinking by declaring it was "in the U.S. interest to assist countries vulnerable to communist subversion to develop adequate internal security forces" (see OCB 1955c, 1). Recognizing that this would be impossible without first raising foreign governments' consciousness about the Communist threat, the NSC began pushing for broader internal security assistance to countries it considered vulnerable to Communist penetration.

But convincing Latin American governments that they needed such assistance was the biggest hurdle in spreading U.S. internal security assistance. Even governments that had an anti-Communist orientation were falling short of U.S. expectations in this respect. Indeed, according to the NSC, during much of the 1950s, many foreign governments did not accept Washington's analysis of the dangers of Communism. For example, OCB argued in 1955 that many of the countries it had examined lacked "a strong 'national will' to oppose communist subversion." OCB reasoned that in virtually all such countries, "public information instruments exist which could be used to mobilize public opinion in support of the [1290d] internal security program" (OCB 1955c, 6). At the same time, many foreign governments still "did not feel sufficiently threatened by communism to overcome local political problems inherent in establishing new security organizations" (OCB 1958c, 24).

In fact, according to the NSC, "most Latin American governments and peoples . . . believe that the United States overemphasizes Communism as a threat to the Western hemisphere." As a result, such governments took "insufficient precautions against internal communist subversion" (OCB 1959a, 59). For instance, Brazilian president Jucelino Kubitschek resisted the proposition that Brazil's economic development could be promoted by increasing internal security. Kubitschek thought that economic development itself was the best strategy for advancing Brazil's progress, adding that "police repression is no way of changing a man's opinion" (in Rabe 1988, 97). OCB argued that in Brazil the "lack of high-level government interest in combatting communist infiltration ha[d] retarded the development of the [police] program [there]" (OCB 1958c, 24).

Kubitschek countered such thinking by his own proposed "Marshall Plan" for Latin America—dubbed "Operation Pan America"—arguing that the "way to defeat leftist totalitarianism [is to] combat poverty wherever it may be encountered." According to Kubitschek, "the problem of underdevelopment will have to be solved if Latin American nations are to be able more effectively to resist subversion and serve the Western cause" (in Rabe 1988, 110). Secretary of State John Foster Dulles, who saw the equation differently, was pressuring Brazil to intensify its anti-Communist program. For Dulles, there could be no economic and political development without internal national security.

The newly created United States Information Agency (USIA) was given the task of encouraging vulnerable countries to accept internal security assistance. First, the USIA would raise foreign countries' consciousness about Communism and then get their governments to accept an Overseas Internal Security Program. The OCB stressed that "until the countries concerned [had] the determination to control subversive elements, and enact and enforce the necessary security measures or laws, any U.S. assistance to internal security forces [would] . . . be wasted." As OCB explained, "controlling subversion and maintaining internal security depends largely upon the determination and willingness of the threatened peoples and government to take effective action" (OCB 1955c, 18).

Recognizing that "in virtually all countries, public information instruments exist[ed] which could be better used to mobilize public opinion in support of the [U.S.] internal security program," USIA expanded its program of political persuasion in Latin America, using as its model Edward Landsdale's counterinsurgency information campaign against the Hukbalahap (Huk) insurgency in the Philippines. This campaign had included "produc[ing] . . . anticommunist films emphasizing the destructive nature of [the] Huk movement and the constructive nature of the Philippine armed forces' program." It also involved using "mobile units [to] exhibit . . . and distribute . . . films, publications, and posters exposing the Huk movement. . . ." Anti-Huk "films . . . shown to captured Huk leaders in prison camps" were an effort to neutralize their commitment to the movement (OCB 1954).

During the 1950s, USIA produced anti-Communist posters and pamphlets in Mexico and 90,000 copies of an anti-Communist cartoon book for distribution throughout Central America. USIA placed two ongoing anti-Communist, pro-U.S. cartoon strips in more than three hundred Latin American newspapers (NSCPP 1955a). In both cases, the primary subject was the international threat of the Communist Party of the Soviet Union. In Brazil, "before and during" the November 1954 congressional elections, USIA supported "the production and use of a study of the ties . . . between the Brazilian Communist Party and Soviet Russia" (NSCPP 1955a, 21). This study was distributed through intermediary anti-Communist groups to Brazilian newspapers and sympathetic government officials.

One such USIA-affiliated group, the Rio de Janeiro Cruzada Brazileira Anti-Comunista (CBC), distributed anti-Communist posters, flyers, comic books, postcards, and matchbooks. One CBC flyer shows Brazilian novelist Jorge Amado resting quietly in a hammock attached to the outside wall of Rio's Federal Justice Building; three judges—identified in the flyer as members of Communist organizations—are chipping away at the building's foundation. Amado, who was persona non grata with the United States at the time for having gone in 1951 to Moscow to receive the Stalin Prize, is shown directing the judges where to chisel next. The cartoon's caption reads, "Be careful, Jorge—the building might fall on you!" (USIA [1955?]).

Once a country had been convinced of the urgency of the Communist threat, it was encouraged to develop a "properly integrated relationship between . . . military and police-type forces . . . for effective coordination in an emergency" (OCB 1955c, 6). At the same time, OCB emphasized the distinct and important contributions of the police and the military to internal security. As OCB saw it, indigenous police forces were to have

primary responsibility for the detection, apprehension and confinement of individual subversives and small groups of subversives and subversive apparatuses, and the suppression of minor civil disturbances, including banditry and small-scale guerrilla activities. (OCB 1955c, 4)

Indigenous militaries, on the other hand, were to maintain "internal security by suppressing large-scale riots and demonstrations, by repressing guerrilla activities, and by putting down insurrections" (OCB 1955c, 5).

Closely related to restructuring foreign countries' internal security was helping potentially vulnerable developing countries rewrite their laws to protect against Communist subversion. As the NSC saw it, "many [foreign] countries . . . [did not have] adequate laws, [or] effective juridical procedures . . . to deal with communist elements" (OCB 1955c, 6). One way of promoting such legislative reform was to encourage and assist Latin American governments to develop national security laws (see Echandia 1991). These laws then became the foundation for Latin American authoritarian states, as ideologies of internal war prolonged the normally short periods under which Latin American countries could constitutionally be ruled under state-of-siege limitations on civil and political rights (Echandia 1991, 153).

Within the context of helping countries write new laws, a direct means for restructuring internal security was to help governments revise and restrict existing civil and criminal legislative limitations on police powers. For example, in Venezuela, a 1963 OISP legal assistance project recommended disregarding a national law requiring arrest and imprisonment of a policeman who killed a suspected perpetrator of crime. Such police could spend up to three months in jail awaiting a trial and would thus be unable to continue work for the internal security system. Consequently, "under American tutelage, a policeman who killed a terrorist would be examined in one day by a civilian board of lawyers, and . . . quickly restored to duty" (FAA 1964, 76), presumably easily—and legally—excused to continue extrajudicial assassinations.

Police training, the centerpiece of OISP internal security assistance, grew rapidly. For example, in 1955 when 1290d was launched, the United States had civil police programs in only three foreign countries—two of them in Asia and the other in Guatemala. There were 10 police advisors abroad, and 481 participants were being trained inside the United States; no record exists of how many were trained in their own countries (NSCPP 1955b). By the next year, there were police training programs in twenty countries, with 47 police advisors abroad, and a budget of $25 million. This was to train 680 foreign police inside the United States or by third countries and to support the training of 12,500 police in their own countries (ICA Report 1957, 8). In 1958 the United States had 115 police advisors in twenty-four countries and a budget of $35 million (Arnold 1958, 4). Although the police assistance budget was relatively small compared to the military's budgets for this same period, Klare and Arnson (1981, 17) have pointed out that a great many police arms and other repressive technologies can be purchased on such a budget because police matériel is so much less costly than military arms.

OISP's internal security formula for deciding which countries most needed internal security assistance measured the "internal subversion threat" along a continuum from most to least dangerous—beginning with "critical," moving down to "dangerous," then to "potentially dangerous," and ending with "contained but [in need of] watching" (OCB 1955c, 4). Of the nineteen regions rated by OCB in 1955 for their vulnerability to Communist infiltration, four were in Latin America—Chile, Bolivia, Brazil, and Guatemala—thirteen in Asia, one in the Middle East (Syria), and one in Europe (Greece).

In 1955 OCB assessed Bolivia's internal security situation as "dangerous," its most serious threat "the possibility that a coalition of extreme leftist forces, including Communists, might take control of the Government" (OCB 1955c, 26). In April 1952, in a violent mass uprising, the Movimiento Nacionalista Revolucionario (MNR) had assumed control of the Bolivian government. President Paz Estensoro took quick action "to topple Bolivia's oligarchic socioeconomic structure. . . . purg[ing] the army, establish[ing] its own militia, enfranchis[ing] illiterate Bolivians, nationaliz[ing] tin mines, and redistribut[ing] lands" (Rabe 1988, 78). OCB thought that Bolivia's "governing party, the MNR . . . as a whole lack[s] a true understanding of the subversive nature of Communism." Of particular concern to U.S. national security planners was the "14,000-member" mine workers' militia, regarded by the mid-1950s as "highly vulnerable to Communist subversion" (OCB 1955, 26). Ironically, immediately after the 1952 revolution, the United States had supported this militia "as a counter to [the] regular military" (U.S. Embassy 1964, 1). Now OCB proposed that Bolivian military training be continued "with emphasis on counter-intelligence, riot control and anti-guerrilla operations" to "neutralize or minimize the dangerous features of the [mine] workers' militia" (OCB 1955c, 26). OCB also urged USIS to intensify its anti-Communist information activities in Bolivia.

Chile's internal security situation was also rated "dangerous" by OCB because the country's "political and economic conditions, . . . aggravated by unchecked inflation, . . . [gave] the Communists, [and] their left-wing allies, and irresponsible demagogues of all political colors an opportunity to fish in troubled waters" (OCB 1955c, 30). OCB found "Chilean public opinion . . . largely apathetic towards Communism," and the general public and even government officials "looked . . . askance upon any repression of political liberties" (OCB 1955c, 30). To remedy this situation, OCB wanted to bring the heads of Chilean internal security organizations (e.g., *investigaciones* and Carabineros) to the United States "to acquaint [them] with U.S. internal security procedures"; OCB proposed that the Chilean Directorate General of Investigations be urged to "exchange information with the internal security organizations of other American Republics pursuant to the [1954] Caracas Resolution" (OCB 1955c, 30).

Seen in 1955 as slightly less vulnerable to Communist infiltration but much more susceptible to "leftist" pressures from within, Brazil received an OCB internal security rating of "potentially dangerous" (OCB 1955c, 4). OCB planners thought that "political power might fall to persons who would tolerate expansion of Communist influence [because] many [Brazilian] government officials have an inadequate comprehension of the nature and extent of the Communist menace." Jucelino Kubitschek had won the presidency of Brazil with João Goulart—Getúlio Vargas's progressive labor minister—as his vice president. Because there was "little disposition in . . . [this Brazilian] Government to adopt [anti-Communist] measures," OCB recommended "a vigorous anti-Communist informational campaign [with] . . . discreet and informal encouragements. . . given [to] anti-Communist sentiment in the armed forces" (OCB 1955c, 27; see also OCB 1955b, 6).

According to OCB in 1955, the least threatened by Communist subversion, Guatemala's internal security situation was rated as "contained but in need of watching" (OCB 1955c, 4). Castillo Armas, a strongly anti-Communist army officer, had assumed the presidency after the U.S.-orchestrated overthrow of democratically elected Jacobo Arbenz Guzmán. Armas, through his "Preventive Penal Law Against Communism," had suspended habeas corpus and selected as his chief of secret police a man known for brutal repression (Rabe 1988, 43). One of Armas's first acts was to launch a sweeping witch-hunt against political and labor leaders, with thousands of workers and peasants "jailed, tortured, exiled, or killed. . . . Teachers were fired, books were burned" (Dixon and Jonas 1983, 5). In the midst of Armas's campaign against these "social undesirables," OCB recommended "improving the effectiveness of Guatemalan internal security forces [by] expand[ing] the program for training [Guatemalan] police officers in the United States" (OCB 1955c, 33). At a ceremony attended by a high-ranking State Department representative, the International Association of Chiefs of

Police made General Armas an honorary police chief "for his unselfish labor for the good of democratic law enforcement in . . . Guatemala" (*Police Chief* 1955, 4). When Armas was assassinated in 1957 by a member of his own U.S.-trained palace guard, Eisenhower proclaimed the Guatemalan president's death a "great loss to the entire free world" (LaFeber 1983, 126).

Creating U.S. Foreign Police Training

Throughout the 1950s, foreign police assistance was officially administered by the International Cooperation Administration (ICA), the State Department economic development agency and predecessor of the Agency for International Development (AID) (see appendix 3). Some ICA police training assistance was given inside the United States, usually to police officials; most rank-and-file police were trained in their own countries or in such third-country U.S. allies as Panama (for Latin Americans) and Taiwan (for Asians).

In practice, inside the United States, much ICA police assistance was contracted out to U.S. universities: Michigan State University trained the South Vietnamese police, the University of Southern California assisted Iran's security forces, and Northwestern University's Traffic School hosted police from all over the world. Such foreign police assistance inside the United States was usually coordinated by the International Association of Chiefs of Police (IACP), whose State Department contract for facilitating police training ran from January 1955 to December 31, 1963. The IACP's role was three-fold: to secure supplemental training grants from Rotary Clubs, business groups, or other private organizations in a policeman's own country; to arrange U.S. site visits for participating foreign police; and to organize an initial set of orientation lectures given by International Police Services, Inc. (INPOLSE), a CIA proprietary organization. The IACP claimed to have planned and supervised, just between 1955 and 1961, the training of 1,466 police officials from fifty countries (Snook 1961). The State Department budget for such IACP-arranged police training averaged $300,000 annually (CFA 1963, 242).

As for the effectiveness of such ICA-IACP foreign police assistance, Ernest LeFever (1973, 58) has pointed out in his highly favorable report on later U.S. foreign police training programs that U.S.-based IACP-assisted training was "inadequate because it consisted largely of superficial observation tours to various police facilities." Lobe (1975, 45) confirms that "most of the . . . police officials trained [in the United States by the IACP] between 1955 and 1962 were simply shepherded on tours from one city to another with little coherence or direction. Less police training was accomplished than outright tourism." But as Lobe also notes, traveling and visiting in the United States created and solidified U.S. friendships and bonded participating police more closely to the United States, an important part of internationalizing U.S. security through ties with foreign police organizations.

The CIA and Police Assistance

The politics of 1290d police assistance ensured the CIA's interest in this program. Thus the CIA stood covertly behind the seemingly apolitical U.S. university and IACP police training programs. Michigan State University's police specialists were closely connected, both at the university itself and in Vietnam, with the CIA (Hinckle 1966). The CIA seems also to have been involved behind the scenes in the University of Southern California's police program for Iranian police. In any case, Robert Amory, deputy director of the CIA under John F. Kennedy, has stated that the CIA worked closely with the ICA and later AID in all their assistance to foreign police. According to Amory, referring specifically to AID's Office of Public Safety program (1962–1974), the CIA believed that for police training, "the brains are in the CIA . . . [so] we'll just move those brains over to the Agency for International Development" so that thereafter foreign police training could "move back and forth" between AID and the CIA (Amory 1966, 101).

Charles Maechling Jr., who was State Department director for internal defense and staff director of John F. Kennedy's cabinet-level Special Group for Counter-Insurgency (C-I), confirms the CIA's covert involvement in early foreign police training. However, Maechling believes that "the [later] Kennedy-AID police training program represented a conscious decision [for the CIA] to go from covert to overt" (Maechling 1986), which suggests that the CIA became more conspicuously consultants to civil police trainers, or overtly trainers themselves.

Through the Freedom of Information Act and from published research on the CIA's involvement with foreign police, we can reconstruct some aspects of the CIA's relationship with foreign police assistance programs. We know, for example, that the CIA reached out to foreign police officials brought to the United States through CIA control of the seemingly private police training organization, International

Police Services, Inc. (INPOLSE). On the surface, INPOLSE was a private business of civil police consultants, but in fact it was a CIA proprietary firm, "a [secretly] wholly owned and operated subsidiary of the CIA" (Marks 1976, 1). INPOLSE opened its doors in Maryland in 1952 as a CIA front organization. In 1960 INPOLSE operations were transferred to a stately four-story brownstone near Dupont Circle in Washington, D.C.

The secret function of INPOLSE was to serve as a "CIA-controlled training school for police . . . under AID commercial cover" (Agee 1975, 611), providing a vehicle for recruiting foreign police as CIA affiliates, agents, and informants. Lobe (1975, 47–48), in fact, confirms that an important objective of CIA involvement with foreign police was "the cultivation of police personnel who could furnish intelligence to the CIA. Political police, in particular, were CIA targets, . . . [because] they had direct information on communists, 'troublemakers,' politicians, ambitious military men, labor agitators." With proper attentiveness, as the CIA saw it, such political police could be "called on to perform special duties for the United States."

According to former CIA agent Philip Agee, INPOLSE helped "protect the CIA's clandestine training people, so they wouldn't have to go through [ICA/AID] . . . paperwork" (Spear files [1974?]), an arrangement that also shielded the CIA's police training operations from congressional and foreign government scrutiny. The result was that what was taught at INPOLSE headquarters, or at one of its CIA safe houses, exposed the real political objectives of CIA assistance to foreign police. For example, in 1965, CIA agent Agee recommended sending one of his police contacts, Alejandro Otero, chief of intelligence for the Montevideo, Uruguay, police to the United States for "special training." Otero took a general course in the Washington, D.C., AID-OPS International Police Academy, and "special courses" at INPOLSE. There, Otero received training in how to recruit potential agents, do background checks on suspects, and set up surveillance teams; "in special tutorial sessions, . . . clandestine [INPOLSE] trainers showed [Otero] how to install low- and medium-level bugs and telephone taps" (Agee 1974).

The formal role of INPOLSE was to provide a four-week introductory course to ICA-IACP and later AID-OPS foreign police trainees (Branch and Marks 1975; Hearings 1976, 675). Only in 1976 did congressional hearings disclose that INPOLSE assistance had had "the dual purpose of improving allies' internal security, and evaluating foreign cadets for pro-U.S. orientation, which might later enable CIA to recruit them as intelligence assets" (Hearings 1976). By then, INPOLSE had trained "thousands of foreign policemen from eighty-seven countries" and had exported various police weapons—"guns, ammunition, nightsticks, handcuffs, holsters, uniforms, radios, and relatively unsophisticated . . . bugging and surveillance equipment" to police all over the world (Branch and Marks 1975, 1). As an arms exporter, INPOLSE was registered with the State Department's Office of Munitions Control, although even through the Freedom of Information Act, it has been impossible to document the precise extent of INPOLSE arms sales and transfers.

According to Branch and Marks (1975), during its twenty-two years in operation, INPOLSE had a wide market. Its secret training was carried out among police from eighty-four countries, to whom it also sold or transferred police matériel. Yet the total scope of its operations is not even reflected in INPOLSE official budgets, which between 1955 and 1973 amounted to only $320,889.13 (Branch and Marks 1975, 4; Spear files [1974?]). According to INPOLSE officials, this was "only a small fraction of the company's work [with] AID over the years" (Branch and Marks 1975, 4). Indeed, the 1964 U.S. congressional subcontract allocation for INPOLSE did not have a dollar limit, even though most other foreign assistance contracts in that year had spending caps (FAA 1964, 244), suggesting the possibilities for secretly stretching INPOLSE (read: CIA) support for foreign police. Yet, even so, INPOLSE represented but a small portion of all CIA support for foreign police, most of this hidden inside the CIA's unspecified but large "black budgets."

Thus, although we do not know how much the CIA actually spent on foreign police during the 1950s, we can assume that such funding was generous, given the stated importance of foreign police to CIA intelligence and countersubversion work. Indeed, as Director of Central Intelligence William Colby stated in a letter to Senator J. William Fulbright (D-Ark.), any curtailing of U.S. programs to train foreign police would

restrict activities . . . undertaken by the CIA . . . for the purpose of obtaining foreign intelligence information from cooperative foreign security and intelligence services; if the Agency were restricted in these activities, [its] ability to [carry out its] . . . assigned intelligence mission would be severely curtailed. (Colby 1974, 1–2)

The importance of the new 1290d police program to the CIA is indicated by the program's being placed in the agency's deep-cover Counter Intelligence Office (Spear files [1974?]; Agee 1975). This guaranteed the program's important institutional position within the U.S. international security bureaucracy, and also its budgetary resources, flexibility, and secrecy. It also meant that foreign police training was expanding according to the political priorities of the CIA counterintelligence branch.

Rising Doubts and Their Resolution

The police program's attachment to the CIA did not fully protect it from criticism. In late 1957, OCB planners expressed concern that U.S. "programs to strengthen the internal security forces in [Latin America], which are often used as political instruments, may provide grounds for a belief that the U.S. has abandoned the principle of nonintervention and has committed itself to the preservation of the status quo through repression of the political opposition, including noncommunist groups" (OCB 1957, 3). In fact, OCB had recommended in mid-1955 not establishing civil police programs in Honduras and El Salvador because such programs might "identify the U.S. government with . . . regimes repressive of a non-communist opposition, especially in Honduras" (Crenshaw [1955?]). Yet despite this recommendation, ICA soon launched civil police programs in both countries.

Again in 1959 OCB asserted that "the exercise of police authority is vulnerable to abuse, especially in the less developed and newly sovereign nations" (OCB 1959, 13). However, OCB considered that the possible risks to the United States "through . . . association with foreign police activities, including the equipping of police-type forces, and the risk of abuse of police authority, . . . [could be countered] with the exercise of proper care and controls" (OCB 1959d, 4). In particular, the United States could protect its image abroad by limiting internal security support to training and to providing equipment for demonstration use only.

According to such thinking, it was inappropriate to supply foreign police with the "types [of police equipment] not generally identified as police weapons—i.e., machine guns and mortars" (J. H. Smith 1958). Indeed, OCB argued on March 25, 1959, that "every avenue of free world supply [should] be explored before the U.S. [itself] agree[s] to supply equipment not usually associated with police forces" (OCB 1959c, 14). However, just two days later, OCB recommended that such equipment "be made available, whether [through] foreign or U.S. [sources]," because "police-type forces in the underdeveloped and newly sovereign countries . . . often [have] responsibilities not normally associated with police operations in the U.S." (OCB 1959d, 14). The United States had to be free to help foreign police maintain internal security in a range of conditions, including "situations which require[d] action by armed units" (OCB 1959d, 13).

Other concerns about U.S. assistance to foreign police focused on the possibility that such assistance might exacerbate conflicts between recipient country police and their militaries. OCB pointed out that recipient countries' "legally constituted law enforcement and military bodies, as well as the non-communist opposition, resent and fear the introduction of new security agencies designed to combat communist subversion," fearing that any new internal security organization "would be used . . . as [a] political weapon" (OCB 1958c, 24). In a dispassionate explanation of this potential problem, Secretary of State Dulles stated that "when a political leader finds himself in a tight situation, he will undoubtedly turn any such police organization against his political rivals, if he finds it convenient to do so" (A. Dulles [1958?]). But OCB's major concern with this possibility was to make sure that newly professionalized security forces, "under the control of the existing governments, [and] primarily directed at the political opposition . . . [not function] to the detriment of existing security organs" (OCB 1958c, 24). In his particular take on this potential problem, Dulles urged that the U.S. exercise "care . . . in planning the scope of aid to police forces not to develop organizations which might be used to promote rivalry with the armed forces of the country concerned, . . . or to create power complexes that would use these forces for political purposes" (A. Dulles [1958?]). Yet, in fact, Washington often consciously created or exacerbated factionalism within and between foreign governments' security forces—as when the NSC Overseas Internal Security Program had initially given technical support to the Bolivian mine workers' militia to counterbalance the Bolivian military. OISP then withdrew such assistance and directed it to the military to counterbalance the growing power of the workers' militia (Harrison 1956).

Senator Wayne Morse (D-Ore.), believing that internal security assistance promoted dictatorships and repressed civilian opposition, moved an amendment to the 1958 Mutual Security Act forbidding military internal security assistance to Latin America; but his prohibition did not include police assistance. A much whittled-down proposal was also submitted to Congress, urging withholding of military assistance from Latin American countries that lacked "representative" governments. Neither amendment passed, but congressional debate may have been one factor pressuring Eisenhower to open an investigation of U.S. internal security assistance; the other source of this pressure was the inability of police assistance to reduce U.S. military spending, as OCB had optimistically predicted.

Thus by 1958 OCB had begun to admit that although the U.S. foreign police training program had "probably provided an increased measure of internal security in several countries, it [had] not been responsible for any significant diminution in military . . . costs" (OCB 1958a, 7). Eisenhower's response to growing criticism of his Overseas Internal Security Program was to appoint two investigative commissions. The Draper Commission, comprising three retired generals, a retired admiral, and an assistant secretary of defense, was to assess the strengths and weaknesses of the U.S. Military Assistance Program. A subcommittee of the NSC Operations Coordinating Board—the group that had established 1290d police assistance and OISP in the first place—was to evaluate OISP and its police assistance component.

Given the particular makeup of the two presidential commissions, it is not surprising that neither recommended abolishing internal security assistance to foreign countries. The OCB commission argued that although the OISP civil police program had not resulted in substantial savings in military spending, the program should continue because it met "a separate and distinct counter-subversive need"; "internal security programs may be desirable [and] in the U.S. interest for purposes not related directly to Communist subversive threat or the reduction of existing regular military establishments" (OCB 1959c, 3). The Draper Commission's investigation of the U.S. Military Assistance Program concluded that without internal security and the general feeling of confidence engendered by adequate military forces, there was little hope for economic progress: "Insecurity is incompatible with economic development" (IDA 1959b, 2).

Development and Order

Thus the Draper Commission's enunciation of the security for economic development argument offered solid ideological justification for continuing U.S. overseas internal security programs, although it modified the more traditional economic development formula. As Packenham (1973, 125–26) explains it, one offshoot of this older tradition had seen "economic development lead[ing] not only to political stability, but also to a host of other good political things," such as democracy and widespread social well-being.

However, the Draper Commission's conclusions reversed the causal order of this formula by proposing that security assistance could promote economic and social progress. This was not the first time that U.S. international security planners had put forward as a rationale for granting internal security assistance, that technical assistance could promote internal security and economic development. This, at least, implicitly, had been the philosophy of Nelson Rockefeller's IIAA (Institute for Inter-American Affairs, 1942–1950)—an outgrowth of the Office of the Coordinator of Inter-American Affairs (1940–1946) (CI-AA 1947)—and more explicitly of Harry Truman's Greek and Turkish Aid and Point Four Programs. The newer formula of technical aid for security became even more pervasive in the mid-1950s as U.S. government-linked think tanks and university academics began providing ideological justifications for this approach. The Institute for Defense Analysis (IDA) recognized in 1959 that economic growth had "an indirect effect upon security to the extent that it may help ameliorate . . . conditions which promote Communism, extremism, and social unrest." However, IDA argued that security and order are first and foremost "preconditions of independence," and "outside military assistance should be available . . . when it is needed to maintain the . . . security of a country pending [its] economic growth and ultimate ability to maintain its own defense and security forces" (IDA 1959b, 3).

An important foreign policy outcome of this order-for-stability argument was to make foreign militaries and police into "nation builders." Pointing to foreign militaries' potential role in economic development, the Draper Commission asserted in 1959 that "military assistance actually promoted economic progress by improving the educational and administrative skills of [military] officers and men"; the Draper Commission argued that "in some countries the armed services possess the largest reservoir of technically qualified and experienced personnel" (Draper Commission 1959, 95), a potential source of economic development know-how. Guy Pauker, an academic proponent of this military-as-nation-builder thesis, argued that members of a developing country's national officer corps were "best equipped to become an effective counterbalance to the spread of communism" (Pauker 1959, 339).

Yet there was seldom a claim that Latin American police already had a sufficiently large available pool of professionally qualified personnel. The assumption motivating 1290d police assistance was that "civil police forces [could be trained] . . . to assume their proper role in the nation-building process" (Engle 1972, 25).

Introducing Security

In this period (and later), the United States most commonly introduced its police program through a series of small initiatives. As Lobe (1975, 83) explains:

A [U.S.] police assistance program might begin in a number of ways. Officially, a formal request was first received from the recipient government. But this was rarely the case. Rather, the United States usually initiated discussions concerning possible [police] programs. At times, political pressure was exerted when there was no immediate positive response.

For example, a foreign country might simply request or permit the United States to supply traffic control training and technologies; this would then be used to convince the host country that it needed many other kinds of internal security assistance. As one U.S. police trainer explained, "we try to get a man in-country, whatever the program. Once our foot's in the door, we can pry it open by showing them how much more we can help them in ways they never imagined" (in Lobe 1975, 85).

The U.S. public safety program in Brazil seems to have slid in like this through the back door: São Paulo's governor in late 1957 requested a technical study of his state's internal security forces. The International Cooperation Administration completed the study, recommending that "the Brazilians should be encouraged to create a national agency to develop critically needed coordinating and training of [internal security] services"; according to an Operations Coordinating Board secret memorandum (OCB 1959f), "interest was shown by Brazilians in strengthening internal security." So in early 1958, Army General Amaury Kruel—then commander of the federal capital's police forces in Rio—and "two high-ranking police officials visited the United States to observe the coordinating of police operations" (OCB 1959f, 1). Legislation was subsequently enacted in Brazil "to establish coordinating services between the [various Brazilian] states." It was then "determined [by Washington] in March 1959 that the time was opportune for agreeing to Brazilian requests for a long-range Public Safety Program." According to OCB, the Brazilian Communist Party was "successfully impairing the internal security of Brazil by manipulating extreme nationalist sentiment, and facilitating Communist infiltration into all sectors of the national life." The new U.S. public safety program for Brazil was "designed to counter that threat" (OCB 1959f, 2).

General Kruel was a wise choice to help introduce a public safety program in Brazil. An old friend of the United States, Kruel had spent three months in 1943 in military training at Fort Leavenworth, Kansas. Kruel had been among a group of eleven Brazilian army officers to train there, learning about "replacing French fighting methods with United States methods," which meant reducing a "heavy reliance on trench warfare [and] . . . massive defense, [replacing this with] speedy and audacious movement, . . . highly motorized, . . . and a greatly reduced role for horses." Kruel's relationship with the United States must have become even closer when he became head of the Intelligence Section of the Força Expedicionária Brasileira, one of three Brazilian divisions—each of approximately twenty-five thousand men—that participated with the United States in its World War II Italian campaign (J. W. Dulles 1978, 59–60).

The cordiality and military meeting of minds that had flowered during the war years must have been a solid foundation for Kruel's association with U.S. international security agencies during the Cold War. In the late 1950s, no longer leading his military against an external enemy, Kruel took over and improved Rio de Janeiro's police force's ability to act effectively against common criminals—perceived as an emerging internal enemy. Under heavy pressure from Rio businesspeople to do something about the growing number of thefts and robberies of Rio businesses, Kruel must have been keenly interested in improving police coordination when in early 1958 he visited the United States. Kruel returned from his short U.S. training tour with greater appreciation for the Point Four Program's serviço system—the practice of setting up a specialized bureaucracy of U.S. and host country nationals that operated parallel to an existing one, with the new "multinational" bureaucracy a model for reforming the older one—a mechanism for "teaching Brazilians to train themselves" (FOA/IIAA 1954).

In any event, to improve Rio de Janeiro's police system, Kruel hand-picked a group of special police, dubbed the *homens corajosos* (courageous men) for their willingness to die in pursuit of Rio bandits (Huggins 1997; *Time* 1969). He gave this special motorized squad license to take aggressive, violent action against robbers and bandits. Kruel's bandit hunters were not acting outside the formal police institution: they were members of an officially constituted and bureaucratically parallel Serviço de Diligência Especial—a specialized unit within the Civil Police's Esquadrão Motorizada—a motorized patrol unit popularly dubbed the "E.M." General Kruel charged his E.M. with hunting down and disposing of Rio's bandits by any and all means, a mandate that his group of handpicked police must have taken quite literally because it was not long before bodies with signs of torture and marked with skull and crossbones began appearing in Rio slums, fields, and ditches. Pinned to the victims' bodies were hand-printed notes: "I was a thief," "I sold drugs," signed "E.M." (Langguth 1978, 121).

Kruel's secret "death squad" may mark the beginning of a new devolution of such "informal" groups out of the formal police apparatus. Such syncretism is clearly reflected in Kruel's labeling of his "assassination squad" the "E.M."—referring both to the police section to which Commander Kruel's homens corajosos were attached (the Esquadrão Motorizada) and to the Portuguese word for "death squad" (*Esquadrão de Morte*). Yet whatever the origins of this coordination between the formal police system and the "informal" police-related death squads, once the latter had come into being, they quickly proliferated, each with varying degrees of overlap and ties with the formal police system—a case of devolution engendering further devolution.

One of the more publicized spin-offs from Kruel's assassination team was organized by Milton Le Cocq, one of Kruel's "courageous men." This new death squad was dubbed the Turma de Pesada, or "hard-duty team," for its toughness and violence. This death squad in turn spawned a series of others after Le Cocq was murdered by "Cara de Cavalo" ("Horse Face") during a violent campaign against Rio's "marginals" in 1964. The response of Le Cocq's police friends was to form a "Scuderie Le Cocq" club to avenge their colleague's murder. This Scuderie quickly multiplied into a statewide, and then an interstate, network of police-linked death squads—each vowing to kill ten "gangsters" for every policeman murdered.

Such death squad activity was clearly flourishing in Brazil as the

United States expanded its new police training program there. In fact, some U.S. public safety officers—aware of death squad activity— argued that police professionalization, including better salaries and training, would help eliminate vigilantism of this sort (Langguth 1978). However, the record shows that rather than stamping out death squads, some U.S. public safety advisors actually cooperated with Brazilian government officials and local police involved with death squads. U.S. police assistance was supporting devolution of Brazil's police system, as the case study of Brazil will later demonstrate.

6 Counterinsurgency Policing:
Internationalization and Professionalization

The failure of the 1961 CIA-financed Bay of Pigs incursion into Cuba, which Castro-led guerrillas had taken over in 1959, forced President John F. Kennedy to consider more effective strategies for combating insurgency abroad (Rostow 1964). As Kennedy saw it, Cuba, Vietnam, Laos, and Thailand were threatened by "a new kind of war" that the United States was unprepared to fight (U. A. Johnson 1984, 329). Yet it had hampered the development of counterinsurgency strategy that the U.S. national security establishment still considered such regions peripheral to U.S. international security planning (Gilpatric 1970). Indeed, Maechling argues that,

> from the end of World War II until the closing days of the Eisenhower administration, the primary concerns of U.S. strategic thinking had been the Soviet conventional threat to Europe and the Chinese Communist threat in East Asia. [The less-developed world]—with the possible exception of Cuba, Taiwan, and South Korea—[was viewed] . . . as peripheral to U.S. national security interests. (Maechling 1988, 21)

This was so even though U.S. agents and arms had been used to intervene in and overthrow governments in Iran (1953) and Guatemala (1954), and to stop conflicts over the Suez Canal (1956) and in Lebanon (1958). Now the Bay of Pigs had driven home the fact "that the greatest military power in the world . . . could not keep its own doorstep free of Marxist revolutionaries" (U. A. Johnson 1984, 329).

President Kennedy responded to this challenge by asking his senior advisors "to develop a vigorous, multilevel response to the revolutionary threat" (Maechling 1988, 22), a response that would soon reinvigorate existing foreign police assistance. Implementing this broad mandate required developing an ideology to explain the nature of the international threat, as well as developing new or modified strategies to combat it and explain the relative roles of U.S. security agencies in countering insurgency abroad.

The Counterinsurgency Era: A Revised Ideological Strategy

Kennedy's deputy national security advisor, Walt W. Rostow, and a group of like-minded "defense intellectuals" attached to the White House had been working on a theory of economic development that elaborated and made academically respectable the connection between internal security and economic development in "less-developed" countries. According to Rostow's *Stages of Economic Growth* (1960), a developing country was most susceptible to Communist infiltration, not when the country was "underdeveloped" and its population most disadvantaged, but when industrialization had begun to "take off," in his terminology. During this takeoff period, when foreign capital was helping a country industrialize, the potential for social disruption and penetration by Communists was heightened.

Rostow's "modernization theory" argued that without civil order, there could be no economic development and social progress. But the ubiquitous cycle of societal disruption, Communist penetration, violent insurgency, and more disruption could be short-circuited by attacking the economic and social roots of citizen discontent. "Order" had to be created or imposed to create the conditions for economic development through the "takeoff" stage. David Bell, the director of the Agency for International Development (AID), elaborated one rationale for AID's considering counterinsurgency as part of its economic development mission:

A general theory of economic development assumes a minimum degree of personal security . . . , but recent years have taught us that we must often make special adaptations to achieve this. Where we cannot count on "naturally developing" peaceful political situations, we have to work explicitly and deliberately against guerrilla warfare and terrorism [, which create] obstacles to the peaceful concentration on the problem of economic growth. (Bell 1964, 1, 7)

This theory had been developed in "United States Overseas Internal Defense Policy" (OIDP), elaborated in 1962 and dubbed the "C-I Bible." This codified John Kennedy's belief that "a most pressing U.S. national security problem now, and for the foreseeable future, is the continuing threat presented by communist-inspired, -supported, or -directed insurgency" (in Maechling 1988, 28). The OIDP expressly stipulated that military measures were inadequate by themselves to prevent or combat guerrilla insurgency. What was needed were "internal defense programs . . . to deal with and eliminate the *causes* of dissidence and violence [using] every asset, . . . from better information . . . [e.g., propaganda] abroad, to intensified economic development, to training local police" (U. A. Johnson 1984, 332).

Of course, the doctrine of local security forces as the first line of defense against Communism was not new, having been proposed in the early 1950s by academics, formalized in Eisenhower's second "Hoover Commission" (headed by Herbert C. Hoover, son of the thirty-first president), and operationalized by Eisenhower's 1954 1290d police program and the Overseas Internal Security Program (OISP). Yet at that time, this doctrine of preventive medicine had not been fully embraced by U.S. international security and development planners. In fact, as many of John Kennedy's new national security advisors saw it, Eisenhower's OISP and the 1290d police program had fallen far short of its full potential—a problem that could be corrected by assigning foreign police a more institutionally recognized preemptive role in countering insurgency.

Selling Counterinsurgency at Home: Bureaucratic Reorganization

According to Deputy Director of Central Intelligence Robert Amory, it was Attorney General Robert Kennedy who took it upon himself to make "everyone get gung-ho about [counterinsurgency]" (Amory 1966, 100). In fact, the attorney general was the "prime mover" behind the creation of an executive-level Counter-Insurgency Group (C-I Group) that was charged with devising ways to meet the emerging challenges to U.S. security (Gilpatric 1970, 37). This group, established in 1962 by National Security Action Memorandum 124, was to be "the Presidential vehicle for launching, executing, and monitoring a worldwide counterinsurgency effort" (Maechling 1988, 27).

The C-I Group's first task was to develop a "politico-military strategic program to deal with guerrilla and counterguerrilla warfare . . . [by] spread[ing] . . . the counterinsurgency gospel throughout the [U.S.] government by means of foreign policy pronouncements, indoctrination lectures, and articles for publication" (Maechling 1988, 22, 34). As a first step, the group would "review . . . all the [U.S.] government's resources for the internal defense of nations under attack from communist insurgents and mak[e] . . . recommendations for strengthening such nations" (U. A. Johnson 1984, 330). As former Deputy Secretary of

Defense Roswell Gilpatric later disclosed, Vietnam had been "a proving ground for both ideas, tactics, and equipment" to combat insurgency (Gilpatric 1970, 44).

The next step was to convince specifically the U.S. national security bureaucracy that by countering insurgency, the United States could better foster international security and world peace. But the new president faced a problem getting his counterinsurgency program off the ground. Thus, while establishing the C-1 Group officially marked the beginning of the counterinsurgency era (Maechling 1988), much "consciousness raising" was required to get Kennedy's national security establishment to embrace counterinsurgency doctrine fully. Counterinsurgency techniques were underdeveloped and undervalued. As former State Department Director of Internal Defense for politico-military affairs Charles Maechling Jr. has pointed out (1988), in the early 1960s, the United States was still generally unprepared to engage effectively in counterinsurgency warfare.

Consequently, despite its concerns about counterinsurgency, on the eve of the counterinsurgency era, the "Pentagon . . . had [only] a rudimentary counterguerrilla doctrine (i.e., a doctrine for armed combat against guerrilla forces), . . . not a comprehensive *counterinsurgency* doctrine (i.e., a politico-military strategy for overcoming an ideologically driven revolutionary struggle)." In fact, the Pentagon was initially concerned that an overemphasis on counterinsurgency warfare might "generate images of 'elite' units which could disturb [military] morale and raise unwarranted expectations of rapid promotion" (Maechling 1988, 26). And the State Department was both unprepared and unwilling to militarize international development initiatives, and enthusiastic neither about seeing internal security as a necessary condition for economic development nor with equating order maintenance with counterinsurgency operations. Besides, the State Department suspected that "counterinsurgency" was a national security "fad." The Agency for International Development feared that "inclusion of internal security ingredients" within its foreign aid program might cause a "contamination of its economic development programs, especially the Alliance for Progress" (Maechling 1988, 26).

Thus, JFK's new counterinsurgency establishment faced a sizable challenge in spreading the new word throughout the U.S. government. The Pentagon had to be convinced that "subversive insurgency ('wars of liberation') [was] a major form of politico-military conflict equal in importance to conventional warfare" (U. A. Johnson 1984, 330). The State Department and its Agency for International Development had to be encouraged to set aside fears that a major counterinsurgency initiative might "further militarize . . . the [U.S.] foreign aid program" (Maechling 1988, 26).

It is very likely that the thesis of military and police as nation builders already developed under Eisenhower helped neutralize Pentagon and State Department resistance to counterinsurgency doctrine by justifying both the military and the State Department roles in a way compatible with each entity's traditional views of itself. For example, as General Maxwell Taylor said about the relationship of counterinsurgency military training to Third World development, the objective of such training is to "reorient indigenous military establishments away from their traditional focus on external defense [and] toward internal security and counterinsurgency" (Taylor 1965). In the process, Third World militaries would come to play a constructive role in these more rural societies.

According to such thinking, U.S. military assistance for counterinsurgency would create within nations vulnerable to insurgency "a sympathetic image of the [national] military . . . [allowing it to] win the support of the civilian population." The U.S. military would help accomplish this by "including civil government courses in the training programs for foreign officers at U.S. staff colleges," to professionalize the officer corps of Third World countries and encourage military officers "to participate in the political process" in their countries (Maechling 1988, 30–31).

The U.S. Army responded to this challenge by revamping its War College courses and field manuals to include materials on guerrilla and counterguerrilla operations and psychological warfare. The army chief of staff ordered its military schools to devote 20 percent of their curriculum to counterinsurgency (Amory 1966, 100–101). And the army operations manual increased its coverage of unconventional warfare from 2 to 20 percent of its materials (Maechling 1988, 30).

Getting the State Department and AID enthusiastic about counterinsurgency doctrine meant developing their recognition that the United States was fighting a new kind of enemy that required new approaches to economic development and international security. To raise State Department "counterinsurgency consciousness," the C-1 Group created a special six-week seminar, "Problems of Development and Internal

Defense," for all Foreign Service officers assigned to Third World posts (U. A. Johnson 1984).[1] State and AID were encouraged to see developing countries' militaries and police as peaceful counterinsurgency alternatives to traditional military action. Speaking specifically about the role of police in countering insurgency in their own countries, General Taylor explained in 1965 that Vietnam had demonstrated the "need for a strong police force and a strong police intelligence organization to assist in identifying early the symptoms of an incipient subversive situation" (Taylor 1965). This "preventive medicine" doctrine argued that good police intelligence would avoid military conflicts by allowing the suppression of their earliest manifestations.

Promoting Police Assistance: Centralization

To breathe more life into existing foreign police assistance programs, the C-1 Group established a Police Advisory Committee headed by Undersecretary of State U. Alexis Johnson. It was charged with examining the status of U.S. foreign police assistance and devising ways of improving it. The committee recommended doubling existing police programs within one year, with the rationale that "the cost of equipping and maintaining the average policeman [is] one-fifth that of the average soldier" (U. A. Johnson 1984, 338). Indeed, Undersecretary of State Chester Bowles could point out in 1962 that "the total cost of a 225-man [police] riot control company, fully equipped with Willis personnel carriers, tear gas batons, hand arms, and a tank car for spraying crowds with indelible dye comes to only $58,000" (Bowles 1961, 3).

With such arguments in hand, the only apparent remaining hurdle was to convince the national security establishment that, as Attorney General Robert Kennedy enthusiastically explained, "Local police forces could be transformed into an 'early warning system' for the detection—and subsequent suppression—of left-wing political movements before they erupted into armed rebellion" (quoted in Maechling 1988, 32). Yet, in fact, any mandate to reinvigorate the old police assistance program merely opened up a "monumental bureaucratic struggle" over which agency was best suited to oversee expanded civil police training (U. A. Johnson 1984, 338).

The Department of Defense wanted to continue its control over at least the largest police training efforts—as it had done early in the century in the Philippines, Cuba, Panama, Nicaragua, Haiti, and the

Dominican Republic, and in the years immediately after World War II in Japan, Germany, Greece, Turkey, Iran, and the Philippines. National Security Advisor Robert Komer suspected that "the only way to get [police assistance] the attention" it deserved was to transfer the police programs to Defense (Komer 1962a, 1). But he argued that he did not "want a bunch of colonels running programs in which they had no particular expertise." Komer feared the military would transform police assistance "into over-sized MAAG-type [militarized] operations" and it might soil the U.S. "image abroad to have U.S. soldiers training foreign cops" (Komer 1962a, 2). For Komer, the best alternative was to place the police program "under civilian auspices"—controlled by either the CIA or AID—because police training is "a political instrument, not a military bludgeon" (quoted in Lobe 1975, 46).

Yet although the CIA wanted to continue close contact with foreign police—especially paramilitary operations and intelligence—the agency did not want official responsibility for this program. As the CIA saw it, "police assistance is usually not covert, . . . [so] a more overt U.S. organization would be more suitable for such duties." The CIA apparently "feared that, by conducting overt paramilitary work, its personnel . . . would be easily exposed" (quoted in Lobe 1975, 49).

U. Alexis Johnson's Police Advisory Group saw the Agency for International Development (AID)—newly created out of Eisenhower's International Cooperation Administration (ICA)—as the best place for the reinvigorated civil police program. The Police Advisory Group believed that "the emphasis (and the image abroad) of our police programs . . . [should] be civilian, not military" (U. A. Johnson 1984, 338–39). Because the ICA had been the police program's former home, AID was the most logical place for the new program. Robert Komer agreed that putting an economic development agency in charge of police training would "guard against over-militarizing [the] counterinsurgency effort." Komer argued that the U.S. military had "no greater expertise in [the police training] business than the cops recruited by AID and the CIA, indeed, less" (Komer 1962a, 1).

Yet the ICA's record in administering Eisenhower's 1290d Program led some of the advisors on national security to caution that putting AID in charge of police training might continue to marginalize such assistance. As Komer pointed out, ICA police programs had not had a genuinely global focus—their goals, policy, and budgets had been tied to short-run local and regional priorities and problems. In short, "the police programs [had] suffered from neglect in the past" (Komer 1962b, 1). Indeed, Komer charged that civil police assistance had been limited by AID's regional budgets and local and regional power structures abroad. Komer argued that until the police program had "sufficient status and room to operate, it [would] remain at a severe competitive disadvantage vis-à-vis AID's primary activities [; it needed more] operating autonomy" (Komer 1962a, 1).

U. Alexis Johnson's Police Advisory Committee wanted assurances that AID would exercise tighter and more vigorous management over, and attend more seriously to, foreign police training. As a critic of the earlier program pointed out, pre-AID police assistance had "consisted largely of [foreign police taking] superficial observation tours to various [U.S.] police facilities" (LeFever 1973, 58). For his part, Komer doubted that AID could ever be "prodded into doing the right job [because] the police program [had] never found a congenial home [with] ICA" (Komer 1962a, 1). However, in the end, the Police Advisory Committee formally recommended AID as the best place for the expanded police training program.

But whereas "AID leadership conceded that there might be a broad correlation between economic misery and political violence [, many] AID personnel saw themselves as economists and development planners, not as cop trainers" (R. Johnson 1988, 32). Or, as the first director of AID's Office of Public Safety put it, AID people considered themselves "boy scouts" who did not want to engage in the "dirty work" of training foreign police (Engle 1985). And AID officials saw "no justification for diverting badly needed development funding to 'quick fix' projects tied to counterinsurgency campaigns" (R. Johnson 1988, 32).

The Office of Public Safety: Domestic Centralization and Internationalization

President Kennedy cut through AID resistance with a memorandum to AID director Fowler Hamilton:

Though . . . [police programs] seem marginal in terms of focusing our energies on those key sectors which will contribute most to sustained economic growth . . . I regard them as justified on a different though related basis, i.e., that of contributing to internal security and resisting Communist-supported insurgency. (in Lobe 1975, 53)

The president wanted civil police training administered by a separate branch within AID, with its own internal budget, personnel, and logistical autonomy (Lobe 1975, 53). The mechanism for realizing these objectives was the new Office of Public Safety (OPS), established in November 1962 with "powers greater than any other technical office or division in AID." OPS was to have "all the capabilities for independent action and judgment" of other AID branches, but its police programs were to be accorded priority treatment by the rest of the agency. OPS administrator Byron Engle was to report directly to a presidential special assistant for internal defense. This arrangement would ensure OPS ample "independent action and judgment" from congressional oversight, a status guaranteed by OPS's secret relationship with the CIA (in Lobe 1975, 54).

The CIA and OPS: Creating Clients

According to National Security Advisor Maechling, when the Agency for International Development assumed responsibility for police training, the CIA's relationship with foreign police assistance "went from covert to overt" (Maechling 1986). But CIA police activities necessarily required institutional cover, provided by the CIA's mostly covert relationship with the AID Office of Public Safety. In fact, most of the CIA's work with foreign police in the 1960s and early 1970s remained as undercover as it had been in the 1950s. In AID's Public Safety Division, the Office of Public Safety (OPS) "regularly supplied cover to CIA operators all over the world" (Marchetti and Marks 1974, 124).

OPS director Engle himself had a long, secret history of close ties to the Central Intelligence Agency—thus furthering the CIA's covert relationship with foreign police. Engle's relationship with the CIA dated back to his reorganizing Japan's police in the immediate post–World War II years. After that five-year stint, Engle was transferred to another highly sensitive postwar country, becoming chief of the U.S. Police Advisory Group in Ankara, Turkey. In Washington, D.C., between 1955 and 1958, Engle headed the Public Safety Division of ICA, a program that former national security advisor Maechling (Maechling 1986) describes as "a CIA cover," as we have already seen. In the 1960s, according to former CIA agent Philip Agee (1975; see also Spear 1987), as head of AID's Office of Public Safety, Engle simultaneously directed the top secret CIA Counterintelligence Division's "DTBAIL" operation, responsible for funneling specially chosen foreign police into the OPS police training program.

There were a number of ways that the CIA interpenetrated the OPS police program. The Inter-American Police Academy (IAPA) had been established earlier in 1962 by the CIA's Panama Station at Fort Davis Army Base in the Panama Canal Zone to provide training for middle-level foreign police officials (Agee 1975, 262). By the time IAPA operations had been transferred to the new Washington, D.C., AID International Police Academy, located in the Washington, D.C., Transit Building—the "old car barn" near Georgetown University—the IAPA had already trained more than seven hundred Latin American police, primarily in counterinsurgency intelligence and operations (Lobe 1975, 62).

The new AID International Police Academy (IPA), which was considered by AID to be the West Point for police of the non-Communist world, was established in 1963, according to Attorney General Robert Kennedy, to make foreign police into "the very first line of defense" against Communism (Kennedy 1964). In fact, IPA was a mechanism for the CIA to recruit informants and operatives—a process that began, as one agent explained, "by sending a fairly incompetent but well-connected policeman to the IPA," where the agency could "mold [him] into something . . . while he's still malleable"; if such CIA-IPA training was successful, the police participant would be more likely to "listen later" to the CIA (in Lobe 1975, 66).

In penetrating a foreign police organization,

an officer of a local [police] service [was] called upon to perform tasks not known to anyone else in his service, particularly [to] his superiors. Gradually [the police officer] begins to report on his own service and on politics within his own government. Eventually [the policeman's] first loyalty is to the CIA. (In Lobe 1975, 74)

Through its covert relationship with OPS, the CIA was able to develop "a close professional relationship with over a million police throughout the world" (AID Assistance 1969, 3).

Thus perhaps of greatest importance for CIA penetration of foreign police institutions was that the IPA, as the "CIA-controlled police training school under AID cover," offered training to middle- and upper-level police (in Spear [1974?])—just the ones most likely to be in a position to influence their police systems. By this route, the CIA could focus on recruiting informants and establishing relations with political police. It could eventually create new intelligence units and even train paramilitary and other special police organizations and units.

As for exactly how the CIA's intelligence system used its contacts, once a police official had completed IPA training, the official's IPA dossier was sent to the CIA station in his or her country, where "in the event of a crisis . . . a CIA or OPS official could request [strategic] information [from the former IPA trainee] on an informal, friendly basis" (in Lobe 1975, 73). Pointing to the political loyalty nurtured by such IPA training, Senator Abourezk (D-S. Dak.) explained in 1974 that the IPA's primary purpose was to "develop . . . good person-to-person relationships with men (and women) who play, or are likely to play, important roles in [the] government[s] of their countries" (Abourezk 1974b), especially in their country's social-control institutions.

Indeed, most foreign internal security officials who studied at the IPA—60 percent of them from Latin America (Klare and Schechter 1974)—were selected precisely because they already held important positions within their country's internal control apparatus. Many of these officials were then promoted to higher positions by their own superiors after their IPA training. Among a group of late-1960s IPA trainees, slightly more than a third were promoted immediately after IPA training—thirteen to directing police forces and others elevated to responsible command or staff positions within their police institutions. One such official, who took IPA's "Psychological Operations Course," was Brazilian army colonel Moacir Coelho.[2] Coelho was a founder of Brazil's National Information Service (Serviço Nacional da Informação, the SNI) and went on to head Brazil's Federal Police (Polícia Federal)—a nonmilitary national-level FBI-like police organization (*JB* 1974, 1).

OPS: Professionalizing through Foreign Police Training

Whether at the Washington, D.C., IPA or in a foreign country itself, most OPS police training lasted only a few weeks. Such training covered surveillance techniques and intelligence gathering, interrogation procedures, methods of conducting raids, and riot and crowd control (GAO 1976, 15–17; Langguth 1978, 126–31). AID's formal objective for such training was to help security forces develop

investigative capability for detecting and identifying criminal and/or subversive individuals and organizations and neutralizing their activities, and [instilling] . . . a capability for controlling militant activities ranging from demonstrations, disorders, or riots through small-scale guerrilla operations. (AID Assistance 1969)

These objectives were promoted in a variety of teaching settings, both inside and outside IPA. Some IPA trainees went to the academy's bomb-making school at a U.S. border patrol camp near Los Fresnos, Texas. There, in a "technical investigations" course, students learned about "bombs and explosives," "basic electricity as applied to explosives," and "bomb search and investigation." Their CIA instructors demonstrated the use of incendiary devices, the techniques of bomb search and investigation, the use of assassination weapons, and techniques for carrying hidden or disguised weapons (Abourezk [1974?]a). Presumably the argument for learning to make firebombs and to use assassins' techniques was to understand better how to defuse bombs and prevent murders. In any case, the courses taught techniques useful for the future.

Police who took a twenty-two-hour IPA "psychological operations" course at Fort Bragg learned how "to effectively coordinate . . . civil police matters with military organizations . . . in matters concerning internal security, internal defense, and narcotics control" (Harvey 1974, 1). The course's eleven academic subjects included units on "subversive insurgent methodology," "psychological operations in support of internal defense and internal development," "the role of intelligence in internal defense," and "counterguerrilla tactical operations" (IPA [1974?]; see also Abourezk 1975, 2).

At the IPA itself, in Washington, there was a two-track curriculum: the fourteen-week "senior course" for command-level officers and the seventeen-week "general course" for junior-level police officials. The senior officers' course taught units on "prisons as schools for terrorists" and "subversive manipulation and domestic intelligence." Among the fifty-one topics in the general course were "comparative police systems," "disturbance control," "bombs and bomb matters," "internal security," "nature of the insurgent threat," and "crowd and mob psychology." IPA's instructional films included *The Battle for Algiers, Bombs I, II, III,* and *Building Strategic Hamlets* (AID Assistance 1969).

The IPA also used simulation games as teaching devices, including "Operation San Martin," which taught participants how to protect a fictitious country, San Martin, against "Maoland" insurgents. Essentially conceived of as a military problem, this simulation was performed in

IPA's high-tech operations room, in which a large map of Baltimore and environs on one wall was used to depict San Martin. The room was equipped with two-way radios, telephones, a teletype machine, and other communications equipment (Engle 1972, 27). In one San Martin simulation, foreign police participants were divided into three groups. One joined the instructors in creating a disturbance or other internal security problem—this team was to write "Communist propaganda" and plan the disturbance. The second team devised a strategy for putting down the insurrection, presumably using techniques learned at IPA; a third group oversaw and judged the simulation exercise (Langguth 1978, 128; Engle 1972, 28). One Somalian policeman who had been judging this exercise is said to have remarked that the San Martin simulation had been much more difficult than his own real-life police experiences because at "the IPA he [had been] . . . judged by his peers"— suggesting more the relative lack of police accountability in his country (in Langguth 1978, 128) than close control by his superiors.

Yet as realistic as IPA simulations may have been, the most important lesson was not included in their exercises. OPS stood ready "to deliver to threatened countries, in a matter of days, the capacity to put down any internal security threat." OPS was firmly committed to demonstrating that other "governments do not stand alone when they face the challenge of terrorism and riots fomented by internal communism" (AID Assistance 1969, 4).

OPS Foreign In-Country Training: Centralization

Between 1963 and 1973, slightly more than five thousand foreign police were trained at the IPA. Yet, as we have seen, almost one million— the vast majority—received OPS assistance in their own countries during this same period (Abourezk [1974?]c). The content of such assistance varied according to the locus of the insurgent threat (urban or rural) and its extent (small or large). For example, a late-1962 U.S. Army counterinsurgency plan for rural Colombia (Army Special 1962) urged collaboration between the Colombian military and police to neutralize rural banditry and insurgency. The U.S. Army would train the Colombian military, and OPS would assist the police.

According to this counterinsurgency plan, the Colombian government was to undertake a centralized "intensive civilian registration program . . . in order that every resident of Colombia is eventually registered in government files." Colombian security forces were to develop a "central registry system . . . based on an appropriate IBM system" to facilitate capturing "bandits" (Army Special Warfare 1962, 2–3). The new central registry was to include "all personality data [and] organizational [information] on bandit bands," including insurgents. Polygraph operators were to "be trained by the [Colombian] Army and DAS [Secret Police] [to] habitually interrogate villagers . . . believed to be knowledgeable of guerrilla activities"; such "exhaustive interrogation of bandits [was] to include sodium pentothol and polygraph . . . to elicit every shred of information." To pit bandit bands against one another, government "propaganda . . . [was to] allege [that] certain gangs [had given] evidence against others" and . . . fabricate evidence to include pictures of gang members receiving [a] government award (Army Special Warfare 1962, 2–3).

To raise Colombians' consciousness about the need for increased internal security, the Colombian government was to establish its own propaganda program "hammer[ing] on [the] themes [that] banditry is not glamorous but shameful [and that] people who support bandits [are] cowardly half-animals." The campaign was to warn that "all bandits everywhere eventually meet the same violent end, as may people who protect them." Bandits' pictures were to appear regularly on TV, and every rural Colombian village would be "required to post pictures and names of *bandilleros*." To remove "wanted pictures" was to be considered a criminal act against the nation (Army Special Warfare 1962, 2–4).

Whereas some of these strategies were also effective against urban insurgency, urban settings were thought to require counterinsurgency measures directed at other kinds of problems and threats. Thus, in 1962, when the Venezuelan government, then headed by Romulu Betancourt, was threatened by urban guerrilla activity, President Kennedy urged sending increased internal security resources to the Venezuelan government, including secretly dispatching an AID-OPS public safety advisor to the capital, Caracas, to train Venezuelan police in riot control. Most immediately, police trainers had to deal with the fact that "red terrorists in Caracas were trying . . . to kill a policeman a day . . . [while] very few Caracas policemen were killing terrorists" (FAA 1965, 76). It was apparently feared that this internal security situation would have a negative impact on the Venezuelan presidential elections that were to occur the following year.

To ensure national stability during the upcoming elections, O P S police advisors were helping to reform Venezuela's legal system, including eliminating the required arrest of a policeman who killed a suspect. As we have seen in chapter 5, police who murdered a suspect commonly spent up to three months in jail awaiting trial. U.S. internal security assistance encouraged a relaxation of this rule and urged police to make greater use of more lethal nontraditional techniques and weapons. For example, O P S found Venezuelan police hampered in establishing law and order because they still considered a sawed-off shotgun just another type of "fowling piece." U.S. advisors helped Venezuelan police to see that "a sawed-off shotgun is also deadly against lawbreakers" (F A A 1965, 76). In other words, the outright killing of alleged criminals before trial was condoned and encouraged.

O P S police assistance throughout 1962 and 1963 helped the Venezuelan government to successfully maintain order before and after the presidential elections (F A A 1965, 74). Indeed, by instituting changes in the country's criminal justice system to make it more proactive against internal security threats, the United States helped to ensure the election of U.S.-backed President Raul Leoni, despite a tense political situation in the capital. According to the *Los Angeles Times*, the broader consequence of such O P S internal security assistance was that in Venezuela "the tide of battle turned and . . . the cops were outkilling the Communists; enemy casualties included a number of Red students who hitherto had roamed the city in sports cars and carried on their marauding almost without hindrance" (F A A 1965, 76).

Promoting Violence: The Effects of Professionalization

In the early 1970s, a U.S. Government Accounting Office investigation noted that one of the visual aids in I P A's police training curriculum, Gillo Pontecorvo's *The Battle of Algiers*, a film about the Algerian rebellion (1956–1964) against French colonial rule, portrayed policemen loyal to France going out at night in secret patrols to hunt down and kill Algerian nationalist "terrorists." When pressured about the reasons for having this film in I P A's training curriculum, one official explained that although the film had dealt with "questionable techniques of extracting information" with its graphic scenes of police torture, I P A had shown the film "to bring out how abhorrent inhumane methods of interrogation can be." Nevertheless, in revamping the course for 1975, the IPA decided to exclude *The Battle of Algiers* from class presentation (GAO 1976, 16).

Citing particularly IPA's course "Interviews and Interrogations," IPA administrator David Parker himself admitted that it was "quite possible that at some later date the police trained [at IPA] may participate in repression." However, Parker rejected the proposition "that the contents of the [IPA] academy curriculum bear on the causes of such repression" (in Saenz [1981?], 11). As for whether IPA-trained police in fact gained greater respect for human rights from their training, at the end of the training period, students were asked to write a thesis on some aspect of police work—integrating their past police experiences with what IPA had taught them. In an assessment of these policemen's term papers, an aide to Senator James Abourezk (D-S.Dak.) argued that although some IPA trainees had done "little more" than use their thesis as a "formal 'thank you' . . . for . . . attending IPA," another set of papers gave evidence that IPA had advocated "the use of deception: 'black propaganda' (politically dirty tricks) and . . . exaggeration in instilling fear into [the] person being interrogated"; the topics of still another set suggested the possibility that IPA had actually encouraged the use of physical coercion and torture (Abourezk 1974b).

At the very least, a number of IPA trainees had not been persuaded to abandon the use of such violence. For example, a police inspector from Nepal argued that "with the failure of certain suspects and criminals to understand the implications and significance of their own answers to . . . [the] question of the interrogator, I feel that the judicious use of threat and force to some extent . . . when other techniques have failed . . . is a practical necessity" (Excerpts [1974?]). A South Vietnamese investigator's paper argued that there are "favored" tortures that include "drugging (*la narcoanalyse*): intravenous injection of pentothal or scopolamine [sodium amytal] making the suspect lose his judgment. . . . He is in a state of almost [sic] without consciousness. He will respond docily to a question which normally he would refuse to answer" (Excerpts [1974?]).

The U.S. Senate investigator who had analyzed some IPA trainees' end-of-term theses concluded that many came to their training with "attitudes about the use of physical coercion—its usefulness, desirability—that are contrary to basic principles of human rights," and their IPA training, at the very least, had "little . . . effect on . . . attitudes of police who may [already] rely on systematic violations of human rights" as a normal practice. Beyond that, the Senate investigator had a strong suspicion that IPA had provided legitimacy for—and perhaps even made more efficient—foreign police already unrestrained in the use of force (Abourezk 1974b, 2).

Indeed, Senator Wayne Morse (D-Ore.) had already argued in 1964 that the problem with OPS training was that it was being conducted "in . . . countries where [there was] little . . . control over the purposes to which [such training was being] put." Morse maintained that few of the countries receiving U.S. police assistance had "the institutional framework that would make [our police programs] a wise undertaking" (Morse 1964, 10). At a time when such police assistance was expanding, AID administrator David Bell admitted that AID was "working in a lot of countries where the governments are controlled by people who have shortcomings," but argued that AID had to "work with the situation" it found (FAA 1965, 82–83).

Ten years after these assessments, *Washington Post* journalists Jack Anderson and Joseph Spear carried out a hard-hitting journalistic campaign against the International Police Academy, the Office of Public Safety, and AID, accusing IPA and OPS of teaching foreign police how to torture. In 1974 Senator Abourezk reached essentially the same conclusion when after a thorough investigation into past U.S. police assistance programs, he disclosed that a

large proportion of IPA students [had] come from countries . . . [where repression could] be expected . . . to constitute part of the regime's means of maintaining power. [Such police] are not likely to serve as a "civil" police force [while] their increased efficiency strengthens the hand of those governments over their people. (Abourezk 1974b)

Legitimizing Dictators: Authoritarianization

Ideological support for authoritarian regimes became more explicitly articulated in United States foreign policy in 1964, when in a closed-door speech to high-level U.S. diplomats assigned to Latin America, Thomas Mann (Lyndon Johnson's "czar for Latin America") asserted that "the U.S. would no longer seek to punish military juntas for overthrowing democratic regimes" (Packenham 1973, 95). According to *New York Times* reporter Tad Szulc, Mann had argued that "in situations involving dictatorships, the U.S. should not adopt a dogmatic attitude . . . [but] be guided by pragmatism and diplomatic professionalism, dealing with each case on its own merits" (Szulc 1964, 1). The day after Mann's speech, the State Department announced that the United States would be guided in Latin America by national interest and the circumstances peculiar to each political situation as it arose. This "Mann Doctrine" was said to be in line with "the United States' devotion to the principles of democracy" (Packenham 1973, 96) while accepting pragmatically that Latin American dictatorships had to be judged on a case-by-case basis.

However, this apparently paradoxical foreign policy stance raised questions for some of Johnson's national security advisors. For example, Gordon Chase—LBJ's deputy special assistant for national security affairs—wanted to know if the United States "still opposed . . . dictatorships in Latin America (at least publicly and at least in places where we have leverage)" (Chase 1964). Mann's reported response was that as far back as "the 1930s . . . the U.S. had not succeeded . . . in unseating any dictatorships. . . . [it] should stop trying to distinguish among such regimes" (Szulc 1964, 1–2). This led the U.S. ambassador to Guatemala, John O. Ball, to question whether there were no longer any "good guys or bad guys" among the United States' Latin American political allies. Mann's response was that it was "very hard to classify [Latin American] rulers as dictators or democrats"; rather, the legitimacy of a Latin American government had to be judged by its leader's ability to effectively control the country (Szulc 1964, 2).

Bureaucratic-Authoritarian States

Yet measuring "democracy" by the pragmatic criterion of government stability ignored questions about the long-term impact of dictatorship on political participation and on the building of democratic institutions. As early as 1961, Under Secretary of State Chester Bowles had questioned whether U.S. military aid was creating "trained armed forces capable of seizing power and using it for good or evil" (Bowles 1961b, 1). Maechling, Kennedy's director of internal defense, has pointed out more recently that military training programs led "inevitably . . . to unprecedented military involvement in the political process, especially in South and Central America." In particular,

[t]he philosophy of getting the Army out of the barracks and into the life of the people broke down the flimsy partition separating civilian and military author-

ity. Instead of periodic military coups by overweight generals who traditionally left the humdrum aspects of government to civilian bureaucrats, middle- and senior-grade military officers—acting on the premises of the new gospel [of military as nation builder]—began taking over functions of civil administration. (Maechling 1988, 31)

Yet throughout the 1960s there was little recognition of the role of foreign police assistance in promoting this military interventionist mentality. Indeed, even today police training is generally seen more as a peaceful alternative to military assistance. It is this study's thesis that along with military assistance (see Lernoux 1980; Rouquié 1987; Stepan 1973a), such police aid also contributed to the creation of Latin American bureaucratic-authoritarian states, structurally quite different from older-style Latin American military dictatorships, a distinction scholars began making in the 1970s (see Cardoso 1978; Collier 1979; Malloy 1977; O'Donnell 1988; Stepan 1973b).

This differentiation implicitly pointed to an intellectual distinction between state and government: the government includes actors who populate the state's governing institutions, whereas the state organizes domination "by means of a repressive apparatus, an administrative apparatus, and . . . an ideological apparatus" (Cardoso 1978, 9), as an impersonal institution with a monopoly over the legitimate use of force in a given territory.

Applying this distinction to Latin America, scholars argued that the older Latin American strongman governments were being replaced by highly centralized bureaucratic-authoritarian states whose internal security apparatus—including the military and police—had the capacity to penetrate more deeply than ever before into civil society and thereby stifle citizen participation. As Schmitter (1973, 223–24) argued for post-*golpe* Brazil, state centralization had "reached [previously] unprecedented levels through the gradual but systematic subordination of all potential countervailing powers"; in the process, there was "an enormous expansion of the capacity of [the state] for penetrating the peripher[ies] of the polity."

Theorists have described five characteristics of bureaucratic-authoritarian states. First, they emerged in the more industrialized Latin American societies—Brazil after 1964, Argentina after 1966, and Uruguay and Chile after 1973—whereas the older militarism had its roots in social, political, and economic "underdevelopment" and nondifferentiation of functions. Second, bureaucratic-authoritarian states were characterized by institutionalized military rule, their bureaucracies not dependent on the personalistic cronyism of military strongman rulers: "The [bureaucratic-authoritarian] military institution . . . assumes the power in order to restructure society and the state" (Cardoso 1978, 4).

This points to the third characteristic of bureaucratic-authoritarian states: when militaries took control, they became the permanent government, rather than leaving office as soon as they had resolved the political crisis that had brought them to power. In the process, a new brand of state professional—the "transnationalized technocrats"— became directors of the Latin American bureaucratic-authoritarian states. These elites, held accountable to the political and economic requirements of foreign capital, had a low tolerance for political and economic crises. Defining these as threats to their support for and by international capital, such elites expanded the state social-control apparatus to neutralize threats to the state. Such upgrading of repression was legitimized by an ideology linking national security to economic development, which served as the ultimate criterion associated with the value of the bureaucratic-authoritarian states. The national security ideology nurtured growth and legitimization of bureaucratic-authoritarian rule as a means of fostering economic development (Collier 1979; Dassen 1986; O'Donnell 1988).

The transformation of Latin American strongman governments into bureaucratic-authoritarian states is important to this analysis because according to this study's third thesis, bureaucratic-authoritarian Latin American states are in part the product of the internationalizing of U.S. security through foreign police assistance, with a particular mode of centralizing internal security, characterized by authoritarianizing the state and social control. These processes, along with their ultimate devolution, are the focus of the following case study, which describes U.S. police assistance to Brazil in the 1960s and 1970s.

7 Policing Brazil's "Cleanup," 1964–1968

On March 31, 1964, a military coup promoted and supported by the United States (Black 1977; Parker 1979) ousted João Goulart, who had become Brazil's president on September 7, 1961, after the resignation of President Jânio Quadros. On April 2, Brazil's congress in special session declared the presidency vacant and installed Chamber of Deputies head Paschoal Ranieri Mazzilli as Brazil's interim president (April 2 to April 15, 1964). The real power behind this figurehead was a military triumvirate—Army General Arthur da Costa e Silva (president of Brazil from 1967 to 1969), Navy Vice Admiral Augusto Rademacker Grunewald, and Air Force Brigadier General Francisco de Assis Correia de Melo. This junta promised to "eliminate the danger of subversion and communism" and to punish government officials who had been enriched by corruption(Alves 1985, 31).

Less than eighteen hours after President Mazzilli's swearing in, Lyndon Johnson cabled his "warmest good wishes" to the Brazilian people for having resolved their country's "difficulties within a framework of constitutional democracy and without civil strife" (in Parker 1979, 85). U.S. ambassador to Brazil Lincoln Gordon declared that Goulart's "de facto ouster" had been "a great victory for the free world," without which there could have been a "total loss to [the] West of all South American Republics" (in Parker 1979, 82–83).

Ambassador Gordon quickly advised Washington that, to ensure the continued stability of Brazil's new government, "the greatest possible consideration [should] be given to any request [by the new Brazilian government] for economic emergency assistance" (in Parker 1979, 82). U.S. assistance could legitimately ensure the immediate stability of Brazil's interim president under the Estrada Doctrine. Enunciated on September 27, 1930, by Mexico's foreign minister Genaro Estrada, the Estrada Doctrine repudiated allowing "foreign governments to pass upon the legitimacy or illegitimacy of the regime . . . in another country," arguing that a foreign government should not judge "the right of [other] . . . nations to accept, maintain, or replace their governments or authorities" through revolution or any other means (Fenwick 1952, 196; see also Neumann 1947, 28). In his application of this doctrine to Latin American military dictatorships, Lyndon Johnson's national security advisor on Latin America argued in 1964, as we have seen, that the ultimate test of a new government's legitimacy was its ability to maintain itself in power effectively. Thus presumably the United States could in good conscience offer diplomatic recognition and economic aid to Brazil's de facto military government without worrying about its constitutional legitimacy. But the United States further bolstered Brazil's military government by further promoting the new government's "effective control" over the population.

Policing Dictatorship: Centralizing and Authoritarianizing the State and Its Police through Militarization

The Brazilian military consolidated its power through a series of draconian Institutional Acts (IAs), the de facto "constitution" of the new military regime. The first Institutional Act (IA-1), promulgated on April 9, 1964—nine days after the military golpe—rescheduled Brazil's November 1965 presidential elections, drastically reduced congressional powers, and transferred legislative responsibilities to the executive. IA-1 set conditions by which individuals' political rights could be canceled, and it abolished a long list of citizens' other civil rights, particularly those blocking the state's newly initiated and sweeping "cleanup" campaign.

The U.S. embassy's reaction to this formal installation of dictatorship in Brazil was generally positive. Although Ambassador Gordon was troubled that AI-1 had been promulgated "as a fait accompli on the exclusive authority of . . . [Brazil's] military ministers," the ambassador recognized that "a substantial purge was clearly in order," so long as officials maintained judicial appearances (Gordon 1964, 4). National security advisor Walt W. Rostow argued later that Brazil's subsequent military president, General Humberto de Alencar Castelo Branco, had "inherited from [pre-coup president] Goulart . . . a sophisticated Congo." As Rostow saw it, the military government had "devoted itself to cleaning up a hideous mess . . . [while] laying the foundation for future stabilization, growth, and reform" (Rostow 1965).

Moral Rehabilitation through Violence

General Castelo Branco, the country's new president and the army's new commander in chief, launched a countrywide purge to eliminate "subversives" from Brazil's political and administrative systems (J. W. Dulles 1978, 389). This "moral rehabilitation"—dubbed Operação Limpeza (Operation Cleanup)—was in fact aimed at removing supporters of ousted President Goulart from elected office and public service. The ultimate scope of the *limpeza* was foretold from the beginning. On April 2, 1964, as the governing junta was still debating the limpeza's course, three pro-Goulart state governors were deposed and arrested: Pernambuco's Miguel Arraes, Sergipe's Seixas Dória, and Rio de Janeiro state's Badger Silveira (J. W. Dulles 1978, 389). Many more arrests and dismissals would follow, as Operation Cleanup moved like a tidal wave across Brazil: nearly 10,000 civil servants were banished from office, 122 military officers forced to retire, and 378 political and intellectual leaders stripped of citizenship rights through *cassação* (abrogation), which prohibited their holding electoral office or voting for ten years (Black 1977, 28; BNM 1986). This punishment was meted out to former presidents Juscelino Kubitschek (1956–1961) and João Goulart, Peasant League leader Francisco Julião, economist Celso Furtado, former Rio state governor Lionel Brizola, and architect Oscar Niemeyer, designer of the new federal capital, Brasília.

The limpeza was carried out throughout the country by police and military street sweeps involving broad searches, seizures, and mass arrests. By the end of the first week after Brazil's military golpe, more than seven thousand people had been arrested (Black 1977, 28). In another three months, as many as fifty thousand Brazilians were taken into custody (Alves 1985, 37). But Ambassador Gordon doubted that "tens of thousands of prisoners [were] being held [in Brazil] without charges or trials" and proclaimed that the number of prisoners was actually "quite modest, substantially less than the two thousand figure" (Gordon 1964e, 2). Yet *Time* magazine (1964, 49–50) had estimated that during a single week in mid-April 1964, at least ten thousand people had been arrested in the Brazilian limpeza—four thousand in Rio de Janeiro alone.

In any case, Ambassador Gordon did not believe these arrests were symptomatic of human rights abuses: Gordon asserted that Operation Cleanup was being carried out with a characteristic "sense of [Brazilian] moderation" (Gordon 1964b). But *Time* magazine (1964, 49) reported that "in some places [in Brazil] the round-up [of suspects] had degenerated into ugly brutality." Gordon, however, assured the U.S. State Department that arrests did not have "terrorist aspects" (Gordon 1964a)—"most prisoners [were being] detained at locations where they [were] permitted to take sunbaths" (Gordon 1964b). Perhaps so, because in Rio, at least, suspects were crowded into open soccer stadiums, as well as a luxury liner and a Navy transport ship (*Time* 1964, 49). In any case, looking back on this period, the International Commission of Jurists pointed to "allegations from informed sources that torture [was] systematically used against political prisoners" (Black 1977, 33).

Over the course of 1964, reports of widespread torture by Brazilian police and military became so pervasive that President Castelo Branco was pressured into setting up a special commission to investigate these charges, headed by his army colleague General Ernesto Geisel (Brazil's president from 1974 to 1979). The commission found insufficient proof of police and military involvement in prisoner torture, although such information would have been difficult to obtain in any event because, as Ambassador Gordon himself explained, according to President Branco, information about Operation Cleanup was sketchy "due to the autonomy of the [Brazilian] police" (Gordon 1964).

Policing Dictatorships: Professionalizing the Police State through Militarization

However, Ambassador Gordon should not in fact have had trouble monitoring the Brazilian police, because they had been working with U.S. advisors connected to the embassy since police training began in Brazil in 1957. This gave U.S. advisors, especially in Brazil's most important cities, a chance to obtain intelligence from police operations. And, in fact, in late April 1964, right after the coup and throughout May, Gordon was receiving reports from OPS police advisors regarding the progress of Operation Cleanup against alleged subversives. In a typical report in late April 1964, an OPS advisor reported that "following the successful constitutional [*sic*] ousting of [President] Goulart," the Brazilian police and military were "continuing to seek and take into custody known Communists, their supporters, and other subversive elements" (TOAID 1964a, 1). The following year OPS police advisors reported without irony that during the first month after the *golpe*, in Rio de Janeiro alone the police had "apprehended 600 persons involved in subversive activities" (TOAID 1964b, 2).

OPS police advisors worked closely with special military and police inquiry committees, the notorious "IPMs of subversion." Established on April 24, 1964, to process Operation Cleanup arrests, the Inquérito Policial Militar (IPM) committees were to investigate people in all agencies and organizations attached to the Brazilian government (Alves 1985, 35). As such, the IPMs were formal components of Brazil's post-coup military state; established generally "to eliminate subversives," their implicit mandate was to neutralize the supporters of deposed president Goulart. In their investigations, the IPMs were unconstrained by formal rules of evidence or standards of proof. Conducting star-chamber-like proceedings "lacking any formal judicial basis, . . . [and] bound by no fixed rules of evidence or standards of proof" (Alves 1985, 35), the IPMs also made liberal use of violence in investigations. Simple "accusation [by] an IPM was sufficient to begin a series of persecutions that sometimes included imprisonment and torture" (Alves 1985, 36).

The OPS police program in Brazil intersected with the IPMs primarily through former Brazilian police trainees appointed to serve on these investigative commissions. According to a U.S. public safety advisor in the state of Minas Gerais, the May 1964 limpeza there had moved more effectively because a former OPS trainee and DOPS official, David Hazen, had been on the state's "three-man [IPM] board entrusted with processing the cases of . . . persons arrested [in the] 'clean-up' campaign." OPS-Brazil considered this an "important assignment" both for the military government's cleanup and for OPS (TOAID 1964b, 6).

But rather than remaining tribunals for extrajudicial processing of alleged subversives and criminals, the military and police IPMs quickly evolved into "the core of a growing hard-line group, [that was] pressuring for the continuation of the [military government's] extraordinary powers . . . and for the postponement or cancellation of the October [1964 Brazilian congressional] elections" (Alves 1985, 57), in other words for greater authoritarianizing of Brazil's military state.

Internationalizing Authoritarian Internal Control

Authoritarian internal control was carried forward by coordinating police and by centralizing collection and dissemination of information through U.S. assistance for three new bureaucratic agencies in Brazil's military state: a new Federal Department of Public Safety (DFSP), its National Institute of Identification (INI), and the National Information Service (SNI).

The Federal Department of Public Safety (DFSP, Departamento Federal de Segurança Pública)

OPS actively participated in the planning for the new Department of Public Safety (DFSP) for the federal district itself (Brasília, the new capital in the interior) and in reorganizing its police, supplying them technical support and matériel, and setting up the new police training academy. O PS considered its role in setting up the D FSP a positive step toward establishing a new nationwide federal police organization modeled after the U S. Federal Bureau of Investigation. If Brazilian federal officials had a modern U.S.-style police organization in Brasília, they might be convinced of the need for a similar organization, but of national scope.

Among O PS personnel sent to work on Brasília's new Department of Public Safety was A ID public safety advisor Phillip Weatherwax—identified by Philip Agee and by Julius Madar's *Who's Who in the CIA* (1968) as a CIA operative. This activity certainly matched the CIA's general interest in planning new police and security organizations abroad as a way to recruit informants and secure foreign operatives. Weatherwax thought that "the most pressing problem facing the D FSP at this time [was] the lack of competent personnel to staff the . . . organization" (T O AID 1965a, 2); this would be corrected by his assisting in selecting and training new D FSP police personnel with a view toward "activating a meaningful Division of Security" (T O AID 1965a, 6), presumably meaning one that the CIA considered professionally competent.

Weatherwax collaborated on the D FSP project with General Riograndinho Kruel, a former O PS trainee, who had been a supporter of the coup against Goulart; Kruel was the brother of Amaury Kruel, who had set up Rio de Janeiro's first police-linked death squads in the late 1950s. Weatherwax also worked with Riograndinho Kruel's chief of cabinet, Lieutenant Colonel Amerino Raposo Filho. Weatherwax told Washington that the two Brazilian officials were "providing [a] cooperative atmosphere for [the O PS] advisor[y] staff in Brasília by freely admit[ting] that they have shortfalls in the filling of key police personnel positions in the [D FSP] and [in] management of the [new Brasília] Police Academy" (T O AID 1965d, 5).

In order to ensure continuing O PS influence with Kruel and Raposo Filho, in mid-1965 O PS brought both of them to the United States to study the organization and operation of U.S. police on the federal and state levels. Their four-week "VIP tour" included orientation lectures by the CIA's International Police Services, Inc. (INPOLSE), and at the FBI, the Treasury Department, and New York City's Metropolitan Police Department (AID-PIOP 1965).

It was expected that Riograndinho Kruel and Raposo Filho would "use the knowledge gained [from their U.S. visit] to effect changes in their Department [the DFSP] in an effort to improve . . . public safety." At the very least, Brazil's upcoming elections "requir[ed] expeditious programming" for public safety (AID-PIOP 1965). In any case, Washington hoped to use this training tour to underscore Brazil's need for a national police organization modeled after the FBI—a message the United States had been promoting in Brazil since before World War II. Kruel and Raposo Filho returned from their U.S. tour enthusiastic about "how the USAID could . . . assist . . . in . . . develop[ing] a Federal Police] organization" in Brazil (TOAID 1965f, 2).

National Institute of Identification (INI, Instituto Nacional de Identificação)

Building on their cordial relations with Kruel and Raposo Filho, OPS advisors urged development in Brasília of a national identification institute for keeping track of criminals and subversives. The newly computerized INI, which was headed by an OPS trainee, housed a new police communications network—also established by OPS—to facilitate "direct radio contact between Brasília [federal district] police headquarters and the eight regional [INI] offices . . . throughout [Brazil]." The communications network was headed by Major Braggio, who had just completed a six-month OPS telecommunications course in the United States (TOAID 1965b). OPS-Brazil was enthusiastic about the communications system: it would "encourage greater cooperation among . . . police throughout Brazil" (TOAID 1965b, 3) and create "internal security safeguards [there]" (TOAID 1965a, 2; see also TOAID 1965d, 5).

The INI communications network was put to the test during the University of Brasília's September 1965 student demonstrations, when the Brasília DOPS—using U.S.-supplied "Handie-Talkie mobile two-way radios and a stationhouse transreceiver"—successfully routed the protesters. According to OPS reports, DOPS agents had been dispersed "throughout the Federal District . . . at the various educational institutions and other locations where students . . . [were] meeting to discuss and plan the next . . . demonstration." The Handie-Talkies kept DOPS police "in constant contact with the . . . control center," and DOPS agents were able quickly to neutralize the student demonstrators (TOAID 1966c, 3). OPS reported that the DOPS communication network had been "a key factor in controlling the [demonstration] and keeping it from developing into something much more serious" (TOAID 1966b). OPS-Brazil was clearly pleased that the DOPS communication facilities had been "effectively utilized during the student problems" (TOAID 1966c, 3).

Yet such localized coordination of police was just a first step: OPS wanted Brazilian officials to link local police communication systems throughout Brazil to the INI national communications center. A first step would be for Brazilian technicians to learn the IBM "Card Punch System . . . [that had been] designed for IBM equipment [recently placed on-line] at the INI." IBM, with AID funding, would provide training for these technicians to ensure more efficient storage and retrieval of information about criminals and subversives, who in this case were students (TOAID 1965g, 2).

But INI's information storage technology was only as good as the amount and quality of the data it received. The CIA and OPS had already helped Brazilian officials establish a national intelligence service—the Serviço Nacional de Informação (SNI) to ensure a constant and accurate flow of information about internal security threats.

National Information Service (SNI, Serviço Nacional de Informação)

SNI was established on June 13, 1964, a little more than two months after Brazil's military golpe, as an advisory and information-collecting agency under the military president's National Security Council. It is argued in Brazil that the SNI was very much a product of the Brazilian military's own internal security ideas. But its first director, General Golbery do Couto e Silva, was given a good deal of assistance from OPS and the CIA. For example, Public Safety Advisor Cashin prepared "a basic organization[al] chart for the . . . National Information Service [SNI] . . . as a point of departure in developing an organizational structure that will meet the needs of the new organization and be acceptable to the higher [Brazilian] authorities." Concerned about staffing the new SNI with "qualified personnel," the OPS gave the SNI's director "a list of all DFSP personnel who had received training at the CIA's IAPA (Inter-American Police Academy in the U.S. Panama Canal Zone) or in the United States—for possible selection and assignment" to the SNI (TOAID 1964a, 2). OPS did not have to point out to the State Department or the CIA that such assistance could make influencing SNI that much easier.

SNI's primary mission was to "collect and analyze information pertinent to [Brazilian] national security, to counter [mis]information, and to [gather] information on internal subversive affairs" (in Alves 1985, 48). Yet the SNI did not remain simply an information-collecting and -processing agency: it was a central building block in developing Brazil's bureaucratic-authoritarian state, with SNI itself evolving into a "de facto political power . . . almost as important as the executive itself" (Alves 1985, 48; see also Stepan 1973b), presumably with U.S. public safety advisors and the CIA close to the SNI's core.

Two of the military period's five appointed military presidents (not counting the initial interim triumvirate) had been SNI directors before assuming the presidency. This certainly suggests SNI's importance in strengthening Brazil's military state. (*Veja*, July 9, 1997, 54). By the late 1970s, the country's information community—with SNI at its core—employed 200,000 people, including agents, administrative personnel, and regular and occasional informants. In 1979 SNI itself had intelligence files on more than 200,000 people (*Folha* 1979) and had amassed such institutional power that

[e]verybody [feared] the SNI: They were everywhere, [in] DOPS, the Civil Police, Federal Police, armed forces intelligence services—all of them were controlled by SNI, by the higher-ups. Even the military was afraid of SNI. (LO 1993)

In other words, SNI was spying on Brazil's other internal security organizations, a step taken to centralize internal security more tightly, but which would contribute ultimately to a devolution of internal control.

The Second Cycle of Protest and Repression: Increasing Centralization and Authoritarianism

Counterinsurgency, with its heavy military emphasis, was an important component of OPS training in Brazil. Within the first year after the military golpe, a public safety advisor in Paraná state gave a course to Civil Police *Delegados* (Chiefs with a law degree) and senior Militarized Police officials on "the development of and operations against . . . insurgency in South Vietnam" (TOAID 1965a, 4). Paraná, a state in which extensive and highly lucrative agricultural estates were worked by exploited, landless rural laborers, presumably needed to prepare its security forces against Vietnam-like rural insurgency. In rural Pernambuco before the golpe, Peasant League labor organizing on large sugar estates threatened to disrupt the semifeudal hierarchical system that enriched landed sugar barons; OPS-Brazil helped establish there a "special task force of 26 especially selected Civil and Military Police," ostensibly "to reduce banditry, murder, gambling, and narcotics operations" (TOAID 1965e, 1).

Such assistance was part of the preface to a second cycle of repression launched against alleged subversives by Brazil's military government between 1966 and 1969. The Second Institutional Act (IA-2), promulgated on October 26, 1965, declared the executive's right to rule without congressional consent. Direct presidential elections were replaced by indirect elections controlled by the military. Under IA-2, state governors were still to be elected directly, although candidates would only be from the two parties that the military had approved and could control, the Aliança de Renovação Nacional (ARENA) and the Movimento Democrático Brasileiro (MDB).

Ambassador Gordon admitted that IA-2 was "a severe setback in our own hopes . . . that Brazil could maintain [an] uninterrupted march on [the] road back to full constitutional normalcy"; yet in the ambassador's opinion, IA-2 fell

well short of outright dictatorship [because] Congress remains although obviously subject [to] even greater executive pressures, [the] press remains free, and opposition political organizations will be recreated. (Gordon 1965, 1)

Gordon in any case argued against U.S. suspension of diplomatic and economic support to Brazil, because this "would . . . undermine further economic and social progress [and] . . . reduce prospects [for] early achievement [of] full constitutional normalcy" (Gordon 1965, 2)—an analysis clearly related to modernization theory's assumption that because economic development leads inevitably to democracy, any process that furthers capitalist development must be supported and encouraged by the United States even if inherently or evidently antidemocratic.

Yet any hopes for democracy were severely challenged just four months later: on February 5, 1966, President Castelo Branco issued the Third Institutional Act (IA-3), replacing the scheduled direct gubernatorial elections in eleven states with indirect ones by the government-controlled state assemblies. In the event that these assemblies did not act as the military president desired, recalcitrant legislators faced *cas-*

sação, the loss of political rights for ten years. The mayors of state capitals were to be appointed by the federal military executive's hand-picked governors; in any other city—as long as it had not been declared a "national security zone," where mayors were appointed by the military—mayors could be elected directly. After 1967, more and more areas of Brazil would be declared "national security zones."

Protests in the Brazilian Congress and in the streets grew out of the military's ever spreading elimination of civil and political freedoms. The military's response was to close Congress, spawning a citizens' movement urging the withholding of votes for the candidates of either of the permitted political parties in the military-controlled election of 1966. Students from the liberal Ação Popular organization spear-headed a "Voto Nulo" campaign urging voters to leave their ballots blank as a protest against the military's handpicked slates (see Alves 1985).

The immediate outcome of this "vote blank" campaign was the electoral "victory" of the government's ARENA party, followed by the military's reconvening Congress to rubber-stamp a new constitution giving the president jurisdiction over "national security affairs" throughout Brazil and the right to rule by executive decree whenever he declared a national emergency. Crimes against "national security" were to be tried in military rather than civilian tribunals.

Army Marshal Arthur da Costa e Silva was "elected" to the presidency on October 3, 1966, by a military-appointed electoral college. Claiming to favor liberalization *(política de alívio)* of Brazil's political system, Costa e Silva in fact simply gave a slightly more liberal interpretation to the Institutional Acts and the executive decrees already promulgated.

Yet continuing government repression was soon met by further protest in the streets and in the Congress: the Institutional Acts and other executive decrees had effectively blocked most channels to legitimate dissent and struggle. Open elections for political office had been replaced by the military's indirect election process. Even workers' traditionally already limited rights had been further reduced by the elimination of the right to collective bargaining, although labor unions were not yet illegal. In effect, government repression had created its own continuing justification, as "students, intellectuals, labor leaders, and others who had felt the effects of repression . . . seized on . . . elections as an opportunity to register protest." Blank ballots had "become . . . an act of protest" (Alves 1985, 57).

Reconfiguring Policing: Further Centralization

To bring the police system under more predictable and centralized control, the Brazilian military's first three Institutional Acts were supplemented in March 1967 by Law 317—known as the "Police Organic Law." Before the military takeover in 1964, each state's highest police official had been chosen by the state governor; cities' police chiefs (*delgados*) had been appointed by the elected mayors, so that local and state priorities took precedence over national ones. But the new law subsumed each state's regional and municipal police forces under that state's secretary of public security, who by then had become a military appointee, although not necessarily from the military. Under Law 317, each state's secretary of public security's responsibility was to delineate the respective duties and jurisdictions of the state's Civil and Militarized Police.

To help meet any potential challenge to central federal executive authority, OPS reported that it had been "working quietly behind the scenes attempting to advise [Brazilian] Police officials" in writing and implementing Law 317 (TOAID 1968f, 10). OPS thought that by eliminating duplication and overlap between police organizations, and by ensuring better coordination of police operations, the Brazilian police could more effectively combat subversion. Brazil's still relatively decentralized police system had to be made less amenable to local and state influences and more controllable by the military. That some state police forces' matériel and organizational power represented a potential challenge to the federal government, especially if allied with other states, was a distinct problem. Ironically, this had been precisely the case of the conspirators on the eve of the 1964 military golpe, when the governors of Guanabara and Minas Gerais states threw their security forces behind groups conspiring against President Goulart. As Alves (1985, 61) has pointed out, this "lesson was not lost on the [Brazilian] military, which did not wish to see the same instrument turned against it" now that it had come to power—apparently an unpalatable possibility for OPS as well.

By placing each state's police under direct control of the national military and under the direct command of an army general, and by giving each military-approved state secretary of public security jurisdiction over state and local police, the military could more successfully monitor possible threats to its hegemony. As Alves (1985, 61) has pointed out, "The coalition in power [in Brazil] was aware that states' security or police forces would have been a significant political trump card in the hands of the opposition."

OPS-Brazil enthusiastically welcomed the changes in policing that had been ushered in by Law 317, as well as by the first three Institutional Acts. OPS already complained that popular elections had very often disrupted the "continuity of [OPS] programmed operations," because when "the incumbent party [is] defeated, changes of [political] officials . . . and changes within the police . . . [naturally] follow" (TOAID 1965d). Having OPS-trained (and U.S.-oriented) internal security officials in a stable bureaucratic position within their country's internal control bureaucracy was critical to accomplishing OPS political objectives. OPS was frustrated when, because of gubernatorial or mayoral elections, U.S.-trained officials in important positions in Brazil's police system were replaced with people not trained by OPS. OPS would have to begin all over again shaping the consciousness, policing skills, and matériel preferences of the new public security official, a process that might only begin to pay off just as the following election rolled around.

Under Law 317, each state's secretary of public security was to clarify and tighten the jurisdictions of the two main state police forces. The Militarized Police were to be responsible for all uniformed "ostensive" (first-response) street policing, their traditional role. The control of the nonuniformed Civil Police over some aspects of street policing was reduced, particularly their radio patrol operations. However, they were to have exclusive responsibility for *post-facto* investigations of crime, one of their traditional jurisdictions, although sometimes in practice performed also by the Militarized Police.

As for how this new division of labor worked in practice, OPS pointed to Goiás state—which encircled the new federal capital of Brasília—as a model for proper police reorganization: all uniformed street "ostensive" policing was performed by the State Militarized Police (the Brigada Militar) and all investigative and laboratory duties were undertaken by the State Civil Police (TOAID 1968c, 3). In addition, the Goiás State Civil Police "central records and [intelligence] coordinating unit" was to be directed by a former OPS trainee who was on the intelligence unit's planning board, which had "a delegated representative from each of the . . . police divisions and [from the] Brigada Militar." The planning board was linked to Brasília's National Institute of Identification (INI) to "escalate . . . interchange [of information] on a national level" (TOAID 1968a, 7). OPS thought that integration of intelligence was "a prime goal to be achieved" (TOAID 1968b, 1).

Police Coordination and Conflict: Devolution of Control

The more strictly delineated division of labor among police units under Law 317 was ostensibly to reduce conflict and eliminate competition between Brazil's two main police forces. Yet in many parts of Brazil, the new allocation of duties exacerbated existing rivalries as well as promoting systemic devolution toward police death squads, as we shall see.

Some of the most vocal critics of the new police organic law were the powerful Civil Police Delegados. Law 317 had reduced the Civil Police control over street policing, including the setting up of motorized Militarized Police patrols, a change that in fact was never fully implemented. However, the stipulated alterations in Civil Police turf were sufficient to make many Delegados feel as if they were under siege. Thus, in Minas Gerais, State Civil Police officials were "attacking the Militar[ized] Police in the newspapers," alleging that by "giving all material and financial help to the [state] Militar[ized] Police and neglecting the Civil Police[,] . . . the Militar[ized] Police are silently encouraging the Civil Police collapse" (TOAID 1968a, 2). OPS-Washington's response to this conflict was a question: Was this favoring of the Militarized Police "a manifestation of a possible reorganization of the . . . police forces in the state?" (TOAID 1968b, 1).

In Paraná state, Civil Police officials were angered by official demands that there be a Militarized Police "liaison officer" in every Civil Police precinct. As the Delegados saw it, this signaled a Militarized Police attempt to take over the Civil Police's remaining role of booking and investigating crimes. Furthermore, Paraná's Militarized Police officials had asked the State Assembly to "dissolve the Guarda Civil" (the police force usually attached to municipal government) so that the Militarized Police could "take over [this police body's] Radio Patrol operations." OPS-Brazil itself did not express discomfort with its recognition that such action might point to a desire by Paraná's Militarized Police "to control . . . all police functions" in the state (TOAID 1968a, 2).

The conflict between Civil and Militarized Police escalated in São Paulo as well; Civil Police Delegados met to protest the state secretary of public security's alleged favoritism toward the Militarized Police, which had been granted higher pay increases and more sophisticated police technology (TOAID 1968f). The Civil Police Delegados also charged that "some officers of the Força Pública [the São Paulo State Militarized Police] want to take over functions of the judicial [Civil] police," reducing them to little more than conducting *post-facto* investigation of criminality (*JT* 1968d). Indeed, one Civil Police official charged that the new motorized Militarized Police shock troops were becoming "a power base" for expanding even further into Civil Police jurisdiction: the Militarized Police were taking captured prisoners directly to jail and booking them, thus bypassing the intake and investigatory functions of the Civil Police (*JT* 1968c). Many São Paulo Delegados, seeing Law 317 as a "monster . . . a revocation of [the] rights of Civil Police," entered into an "open fight with the new Police Organic Law" (TOAID 1968f, 9).

Thus, rather than reducing competition and conflict between Brazil's two main police forces, the police organic law greatly exacerbated long-standing rivalries (*JT* 1968e). In fact, São Paulo's daily newspaper *O Estado de São Paulo* charged in mid-1968 that police infighting in São Paulo had ushered in "one of the worst crises in the history of our police" (*Estado* 1968). The police organic law—which had been "made to resolve . . . police [organizational and turf] problems . . . has served to increase [such problems] . . . and to unleash a crisis out of all proportion" to its usefulness (*Estado* 1968). Even OPS—which had fully supported police reorganization under Law 317—was beginning to express concern about the "serious dissension between the civil and militar[ized] police" (TOAID 1968b).

In fact, just when the Brazilian government most needed cooperation among the various formal police entities to deal with escalating social turmoil, competition was increasing among police agencies, and even between the police and their associated death squads. The volatility of this situation was vividly illustrated in late 1968 when police from the notorious São Paulo Civil Police's Division of Criminal Investigations—the DEIC[1]—entered a bar where three agents from Brazil's Federal Police, an FBI-like police posted throughout the country, were relaxing over a beer. After a few drinks, the two groups began exchanging insults, which ended up with a Federal Police agent shot by one of the Civil Police. The Civil Police claimed during the investigation that they had not known their adversaries were really Federal Police, a plausible claim because neither police force wore uniforms. In any case, the Federal Police demanded punitive action against their Civil Police attackers, charging that DEIC "police [had been] operating on their own," acting like an informal death squad (*JT* 1968f).

Control of Dissent: The Professional Application of Systematic Violence

As conflict between police forces escalated and death squads began proliferating, political strife was increasing in civil society as well. In this atmosphere of escalating conflict among police forces, as well as proliferating police-related death squads and increasing social conflict, OPS was helping Brazilian police develop military-style motorized patrols and "shock troops" to combat internal security threats and improve the "quality" of policing.

For example, OPS helped train, equip, and suggest personnel for special crowd- and riot-control "shock troops" in the states of Rio Grande do Sul, Paraná, São Paulo, Minas Gerais, Goiás, and Pernambuco, and earlier for the federal district. According to OPS-Brazil, its work with these special police units paid off in May 1967 during a student demonstration in Rio Grande do Sul state, where OPS-trained police riot squads showed students "that there [was] . . . sufficient force to overcome gatherings . . . [and that] the authorities . . . will not tolerate violent [civilian] groups," as OPS-Brazil noted approvingly (TOAID 1967), not commenting on the violence used to carry out this policy.

Another new police unit also considered by OPS to be effective operated in Rio de Janeiro's slums, the *favelas;* in 1966 OPS advisor Dan Mitrione had helped organize and select men for a Militarized Police shock unit "of [40] men over 6 feet tall" to be deployed primarily at night in favelas of Rio (TOAID 1966a, 2). Mitrione has been denounced by the Brazil Nunca Mais human rights group for having used beggars snatched off the streets as subjects for teaching police new modes of torture to extract information (BNM 1986, 14). However, one of his friends, political scientist Robert Daland, claims that Mitrione "knew that Brazilian police were using torture [and] this bothered him greatly," but that Mitrione felt there was nothing he could do about such violence except "throw . . . his weight around" (Daland 1971, 2).

Mitrione is best known for his being kidnapped and murdered in August 1970 in Uruguay by the Tupamaro urban guerrillas, commemorated in the 1973 Costa Gavras film *State of Siege*. Although Jack Lang-guth concludes in his impressive study of Mitrione's life that this OPS advisor was not a CIA agent, a former informant for Brazil's National Intelligence Service (SNI) nevertheless asserts firmly that Mitrione was with "the Company" (LO 1993).[2] In the first place, OPS, as a CIA front, sent Mitrione to countries in the 1960s where the United States would have needed someone more than a police trainer—Cuba, Russia, Libya, Israel. Second, Mitrione had an impressive command of several lan-guages and "spoke Portuguese so fluently that you wouldn't say he was an American" (LO 1993), suggesting his possible training in one of the CIA's excellent "total immersion" language programs.

Like other OPS police advisors, Mitrione was "deeply anticommu-nist—he completely detested [it]." And Mitrione did not teach the standard police topics: he focused primarily on espionage, counteres-pionage, "how communist agents were sent into Latin America, how they infiltrated organizations, how their financial resources entered" a country. Moreover, Mitrione was trained in guerrilla and counterguer-rilla militarized warfare and taught "jungle survival . . . how a person has to react to a guerrilla attack, pain-blocking techniques, [and surviving] torture." In particular, he knew and taught how to withstand "torture without talking [by practicing] thought control—how to shut yourself off." Mitrione explained that "a man's motor coordination is through the brain. . . . You have to control your mind to block the pain." Therefore, if you are "subjected to a violent interrogation, you must always turn off your vital organs." Demonstrating how this worked, Mitrione would "grab a live coal [saying]: 'look, it doesn't hurt. Now you're going to see . . . I'm not feeling any pain'" (LO 1993).

The police squad set up by OPS advisor Mitrione behaved very much like those portrayed in Gillo Pontecorvo's *Battle of Algiers*, the film used in the OPS International Police Academy's training curriculum (GAO 1976, 16), showing nighttime police teams capturing and killing Al-gerian "terrorists" (see chapter 6). Interestingly, according to Brazil Nunca Mais researcher and human rights worker Pastor Jaime Wright, the *Battle for Algiers* was banned from movie houses in Brazil during much of the military period for fear that Brazilian victims of security force violence might recognize that the French techniques of search, arrest, and torture depicted in the film were those used by Brazilian security forces (Wright 1987).

Brazilian military officials, however, apparently wanted to give Brazilian officers more international information on counterinsurgency intelligence-gathering and suppression. So in 1967 the Brazilian army sent a delegation from its own CIEx Army Intelligence to the United States to "study American methods of combating communism" (Lago and Lagoa 1979). But they apparently found U.S. intelligence methods "too rigid" and inappropriate for Brazil. They felt that the United States was waging its own anti-Communist war far beyond its own national borders, in Vietnam. To investigate other countries' counterinsurgency models, the CIEx mission went to Great Britain particularly to examine tactics and techniques being used against the Irish Republican Army, which CIEx decided were best suited to its own purposes. CIEx seemed to prefer "indirect" interrogation strategies—replacing beatings and other harsh methods with Pavlovian conditioning, including sensory deprivation, diuretics, laxatives, and interrogation practices that did not leave visible marks (Lago and Lagoa 1979).

Devolution from Specialized Police to Death Squads

Be that as it may, the absolute autonomy of Mitrione's new official police squad, with its "shoot-to-kill" policy and its practice of operating primarily at night, made his squad behave very much like its informal cousin, the death squad. At the very least, a motorized "hard-duty" patrol of men over six feet tall who worked primarily at night would have darkness to hide its activities yet could still instill fear in the population with these activities. Blaming informal death squads for such violence was ensured after 1966, as Rio de Janeiro's southern favelas had already witnessed extensive death squad activity after the rebirth of these police-related murder teams with the 1964 shooting of policeman Le Cocq by "Cara de Cavalo" (see chapter 5).

There are a number of explanations for how Rio de Janeiro's death squads came into being. In the late 1950s, Amaury Kruel—already mentioned as an OPS associate—had created his special squad of sixteen "courageous" on-duty policemen inside his Civil Police DOPS organization, as we have seen (chapter 5). Kruel's motorized squad, the Esquadrão Motorizado—E.M. for short—had complete autonomy to hunt down and kill bandits and marginals. By 1969 *Time* magazine (1969, 61) reported that Kruel's group had killed an average of one person a week since 1963. Kruel denied that his group was a death squad; he had "merely ordered his police not to fail to kill" (*Veja* 1970).

OPS monthly reports from Brazil show that U.S. police advisors collaborated from at least the late 1950s to the end of the 1960s with Army General Luis de França Oliveira, who had initiated Kruel's E.M. and who is on the Brazil Nunca Mais group's list of documented torturers.

As for death squads in São Paulo, some police from the early 1960s described them in interviews as evolving out of Civil Police motorized patrols called RUDI (Rondas Unificadas do Departamento de Investigações, roving investigative patrols), and out of the RONE (Rondas Noturnas Especiais da Polícia Civil) special night patrols. RUDI and RONE, the latter's emblem an owl with a machine gun under its wing perched on a tree trunk, were initially established in 1958 and 1959, respectively, to combat car thefts and house burglaries just as the first foreign car manufacturing plants were opening in greater São Paulo (M 1993).

Considering the OPS relationship to these police organizations, there is evidence that in the early 1960s OPS-Brazil advisors had a good deal of contact with RUDI, which OPS later described as a "Unified Roving Patrol . . . with three new station wagons manned by four investigators each, equipped with revolvers, rifles, sub-machine guns, tear gas, and two-way telecommunications equipment"; RUDI was "charged with apprehension of 'syndicated' gang personnel, robbers, narcotics peddlers, etc." (TOAID 1969d, 25). The first RUDI police agents were not very well trained, although an OPS advisor had been a consultant to this organization throughout most of the mid-to-late 1960s. One former RUDI official, in fact, explained that he had to teach himself how to shoot by going out into the country and firing at tin cans (M 1993).

RONE, RUDI, and the somewhat later ROSA (Civil Police Rondas do Setor de Assaltos) were "famous for [their use of] violence. Their investigators never thought twice about drawing their gun or beating a suspect" (*Estado* 1969). These squads had a great deal of operational autonomy, reinforced in part by their deployment at night and in part by their being headed by their own Delegado, who as a lawyer could "legalize" any action as falling within his squad's legitimate mission. Indeed, pointing specifically to the way these motorized squads operated, one São Paulo newspaper described them explicitly and without criticism or apology as "death squads" (*JT* 1968a, 1968b, 1968c), in pointing to their shoot-to-kill policy and the bodies left in their wake.

Yet one former RONE commander, arguing that the earliest RONE squads did not do enough shooting, underlines one of the initial pressures for this police unit's devolution into an informal death squad. The former Delegado explains that RONE's first commander, patrolling one day in the police van,

pulled up alongside a stolen car and the guys in the stolen car shot at the RONE car. [But the Delegado] didn't let his policemen . . . shoot at [them]. . . . So the policemen were disgusted [and] went to [a higher official] and said "we won't work with that Delegado any more because . . . he wouldn't let us shoot." So [police officials] reached the conclusion that they needed to shoot. (M 1993)

A former RONE Delegado argues that it was a São Paulo state governor and his secretary of public security who decided that São Paulo needed a death squad, to "reestablish public order—do something good for the community [by] kill[ing] . . . criminals," because "society needed cleaning up—the courts were very slow about deciding things and the law was tying their hands" (M 1993). Before long, one of São Paulo's most infamous Civil Police Delegados, Sérgio Paranhos Fleury, who at the time was attached to RONE, and later to the DOPS political police, established a death squad that

really started cleaning up . . . because if you sent [the criminals] to jail, they [would] get out. . . . [So Fleury's men] killed a bunch [of them]. (S 1993)

A complementary explanation for how São Paulo's death squads got started comes from a former Delegado who, early in his career, was attached to the DEIC Criminal Investigations Division and later with the state's political police (DOPS). As director of the Civil Police DEIC in the early 1960s, this official assembled a special team of police "in the directorate"—that is, a special quasi-secret official death squad under his immediate control, consisting of two other Delegados and eight investigators, all "hard-nosed." The Delegado would call on this group when he "had a very big, very important case, one that even specialized [police] were reluctant to deal with," or when a Delegado from another district said to him, "Look, I can't do anything [with this case] because my investigators . . . seem to be a little reluctant—they're not used to dealing with that kind of people." So others' hesitations had led the Delegado to assemble this team of men "who really liked killing outlaws." The special team would "find out where the [criminal] was and set a place for an ambush": They "weren't going to die. [But] even if [the criminal] didn't resist, they were going to kill him" (S 1993). This

official death squad was closely controlled by the Civil Police Delegado, although he, in fact, denied that it was a death squad at all: "[A
death squad's] purpose was to kill. [My] team didn't go out just to kill"
(S 1993).

But other death squads grew out of this "hard-duty" unit. They had a
much more tenuous relationship to official control. For example, a
former RONE commander explained that as

time went along, [and] the squad [in his precinct] got hooked on drugs, they no
longer had the courage to cleanly execute a guy. So they'd do drugs whenever
they'd go to kill someone. In time, they became friends with a gang of drug
traffickers and, in time, became bandits, more crooked than any other bandit in
the world. (M 1993)

This progression—from a death squad as a component of the formal
police establishment to a much less directly controlled death squad—is
typical of the devolution process, as we shall see throughout the next
two chapters.

An important step in this devolutionary process was to structure
public reaction to such police and quasi-official violence so that it was
not unduly criticized by the São Paulo press, recognizing that "if you
shoot, the press is going to complain." This was accomplished in the
mid-1960s, according to the former RONE official, by transferring a
"Delegado [to RONE] who had been a [crime] reporter; he'll keep the
press in line . . . and then you can shoot" (M 1993).

The assignment of this former reporter as Delegado for RONE is
fairly typical of how police were recruited into RONE: more than anything else, trust dictated a person's acceptance. As the former Delegado
explained, "We brought people into RONE by one man inviting another one: working in the street requires a large dose of confidence in
your partners" (M 1993). One RONE agent, nicknamed "Candonga"
because he was a slick talker—a kind of flimflam artist who could convince anyone of anything—had grown up in the 1950s as a houseboy
on the family estate of São Paulo's powerful governor Ademar de
Barros. The governor is said to have recommended Candonga for
RONE because of the man's imposing height and strength—he was six
feet tall—and because of Candonga's unquestioned loyalty to the governor and his family (M 1993).

The qualifications for RONE were the same as those for other parallel
police-related death squads. In all of them, being fearless, strong, and a

police insider was essential, ensuring an easy interface between the official organization and the informal groups' deviant activities. For example, Fleury, as a RONE investigator, at the same time presided over a network of the city's most brutal informal death squads, many of whose members had come from RONE (M 1993).

The bifurcation of São Paulo's RONE into formal and informal death squads occurred when Fleury was encouraged by the state's highest officials themselves to invite some of his RONE colleagues to join him off duty in eliminating people who were not being dealt with effectively by the formal social-control system of the police and courts. There appears to have been an easy interface here and in several other Brazilian states between specialized Civil Police shoot-to-kill squads and informal "off-duty" death squads. In the process, an almost seamless symbiosis was emerging between the formal police squads and the seemingly unofficial ones without formal state connections. This symbiosis was played down or ignored by OPS when it assisted the motorized police squads that came to be linked to off-duty death squads.

Control and Resistance

In any case, by late 1968, both the formally constituted police squads and the informal death squads were proliferating in Brazil, although not necessarily operating in concert with one another. As we have seen, even as Brazil's internal security system was becoming more centrally controlled and authoritarian in structure and function with encouragement and professional assistance and training from OPS, this system was generating tensions and conflicts, along with a form of structural devolution that undermined fully bureaucratizing and centralizing state control over internal security. Besides the spin-off of death squads, citizen resistance to military rule was increasing, local police were resisting closer links to national government, and the military continued to undercut civic society by reducing citizen political participation. Brazilian journalist Antonio Carlos Fon (1986) adds that by late 1968, student demonstrations and militant bombings and bank robberies during this time of infighting within Brazil's internal security apparatus helped to explain the military government's push to further centralize and authoritarianize society and state, as the next chapter illustrates. But, at the same time, the regime—like OPS—was increasingly anxious to both control and dissociate itself from its own more violent spin-offs.

8 Repression and the Brazilian Police, 1968–1969

Between March 28 and April 4, 1968, protests erupted across Brazil after Militarized Police shot Edison Luis, a working-class secondary school student. Edison Luis had been killed during a demonstration near Rio's Candalária Cathedral, where police had fired indiscriminately into a crowd of demonstrators protesting the governor's withdrawing subsidies for student meals at the Calabouço Restaurant.

At the Seventh Day Mass for Edison Luis in Rio de Janeiro, a large demonstration gathered. Up to twenty thousand police and military had been mobilized to control the mourners. In one account of what happened that day, the Militarized Police "Cavalry wait[ed] for the end of the memorial mass . . . [to] attack . . . the unarmed population as it left the church, [using] clubs and even swords . . . against those who attended the mass" (Alves 1985: 84–85). At another memorial mass later the same day, the police beat and arrested so many that clergy and citizen mourners had to form a circle around the cathedral to protect those inside from further attacks. After the mass, clergy escorted mourners away from the cathedral. As they rounded the corner near the offices of the *Jornal do Brasil* newspaper, the Militarized Police cavalry charged the throng. Nearly a thousand people were beaten by police "using swords and tear gas" against the mourners (Alves 1985, 84–85).

An OPS-Brazil report on events that day gave a much-toned-down account of these "public security" events, explaining that "police on horseback and other police troops [had] dispersed the crowd which had begun to demonstrate" at the cathedral. According to OPS-Brazil, "police took unprecedented security measures . . . by only allowing a relatively small number of persons to enter the church" (TOAID 1968d, 3), with no mention of the police violence that had followed.

Shortly after these demonstrations, the Militarized Police, assisted by OPS-Brazil, began offering a course on "updated procedures to be used in any future demonstrations" (TOAID 1968d, 3). OPS-Brazil explained that in the May to June 1968 Rio protests, students dispersed by the police quickly reorganized into "small groups and roamed [Rio's] downtown area staging small lightning-type demonstrations" (TOAID 1968e, 1). Since the military government had prohibited any formal student protest marches, dissidents were likely to stage more of these quickly executed hit-and-run lightning demonstrations, and OPS was ready to help the police be prepared to quash them.

OPS-Brazil pointed out that "lightning demonstrations" rendered ineffective much prior OPS riot training: Brazilian police had been taught strategies for controlling slow-moving, better-organized groups of protesters—particularly where participants' meetings to prepare a demonstration made possible police infiltration for advance information. Because "lightning demonstrations" made infiltration impossible, police had to learn greater flexibility in combating demonstrations. OPS-Brazil urged the Militarized Police to adopt a less-structured approach to riot control in order to neutralize the more spontaneous "lightning strike" eruptions as they spread. This was to be accomplished by placing squad-size police units at key points in the streets and on the roofs of taller buildings: the rooftop squads could then "advise and coordinate the ground effort" and be available to shoot if the situation got out of their control (TOAID 1968, 11). It was not clear how such situations were defined and how the police targets were to be picked, if the police were not to just fire indiscriminately into the crowd.

In any event, this more flexible model had proven effective in May 1968 at a student demonstration at the U.S. embassy in Rio, where rather than all the riot police being concentrated in a fixed cone formation in the street, plainclothes sharpshooters had been deployed on the embassy roof and across the grounds. The snipers had been able to shoot demonstrators from a number of angles and could see beyond the front protesters to predict the larger group's next movements. The CIA political analyst in Rio praised this method for keeping students from massing their strength (TOAID 1968h, 1).

Ironically, this seemed, in fact, merely to guarantee that large, less militant protest actions would turn into the more scattered and difficult-to-control "lightning demonstrations" that the OPS wanted to help Brazilian police handle. Indeed, the violence that in May had been initially concentrated around the U.S. embassy had spread quickly that day through Rio and raged for hours. Student demonstrators threw marbles on sidewalks, causing riot police to fall; the protesters hurled rocks, heaved iron spears, and lobbed tear gas and Molotov cocktails at police (TOAID 1968h, 1–2). The police dispersed crowds with tear gas, high-pressure water hoses, shock batons, and rifle shots. According to Langguth's account of the day, confrontations between police and demonstrators lasted from noon until nine o'clock in the evening. Police vehicles were attacked and damaged, an army vehicle was set on fire, and workers threw lamps, ashtrays, and chairs at security forces from high-rise office buildings (Langguth 1978, 152). When a Militarized Policeman was killed by an object thrown from a building window, the police retaliated by shooting indiscriminately at all windows from which objects were being thrown (Langguth 1978, 152; TOAID 1968c, 2).

It is estimated that thirty-six people were killed that "Bloody Friday." However, the number of deaths may have been much higher—months later, an officer of the Brazilian Air Force's rescue and parachute squad reported that his unit's "death flights" had pitched scores of demonstrators' bodies into the ocean (Langguth 1978, 152).

OPS Response: Internationalizing Continues

As violent as the police response to this demonstration had been, it did not put an end to conflicts between students and internal security forces. In Brazil's biggest cities, the demonstrations continued, and government repression escalated. In the first six months of 1968, thousands of students were rounded up and jailed by internal security forces.

OPS-Brazil's response to such repression was to increase assistance to the Federal Police and commit more energy to "training . . . police to handle any future demonstrations" (TOAID 1968d, 10). In "Bloody June" 1968, so named for the severity of police repression against demonstrators (Cava 1970, 136), OPS-Brazil seemed concerned only that Rio's police had not been able effectively to control student demonstrations.

OPS wanted to expand assistance to the Militarized Police of the states of Guanabara and Rio de Janeiro. At that time, Guanabara state, which was in fact the city of Rio de Janeiro, was surrounded by Rio de Janeiro state, which thus controlled the land routes for bringing food and manufactured goods into and out of the city from and through the other three bordering Brazilian states. Rio, although no longer the federal capital, was still a major business center and port; Rio de Janeiro–Guanabara contained "vital industrial plants," including the Volta Redonda steel complex, described by OPS as "one of the most important industrial centers in Brazil" (TOAID 1968f, 7–8). The huge plant had been fully equipped by the United States as a reward for Brazil's siding with the Allies during World War II (see McCann 1973).

Given Rio's strategic position and importance for Brazil, the OPS model for teaching internal security planning to the Rio de Janeiro and Guanabara state Militarized Police was "Operation San Martin," the national security simulation game used at the Washington, D.C., International Police Academy to teach how to protect a country or region vulnerable to infiltration from its neighbors (see chapter 6). In the military-oriented IPA simulation, San Martin was surrounded by rival countries and threatened by subversive infiltration, just as Rio and Guanabara states could have been rendered vulnerable by a well-organized protest or strike in or beyond the (Rio) region surrounding Rio city (Guanabara state). Not surprisingly, therefore, the OPS San Martin simulation appealed to Guanabara state Militarized Police officers. With OPS assistance, they mounted a "San Martin" operations room in their downtown Rio headquarters (TOAID 1968i, 9).

OPS taught that an effective means for controlling strikes and demonstrations was to identify participants by photographing protesters, arguing that this method "had proven successful in [previous] . . . demonstrations." It had provided information for postdemonstration punishment and could even frighten demonstrators from future street protest participation. Indeed, as time passed, OPS became deeply involved in helping Brazilian police become more effective at monitoring alleged subversives through infiltration, surveillance, and photographing crowds. For example, OPS reported that a 1970 police training exercise in Rio involved a

group of 15 [police] students [who were] to maintain a discreet surveillance of two suspected subversives. Each team was accompanied by an experienced SNI [National Intelligence Service] agent who critiqued their performance at the end of each day. The students also photographed the suspects and the persons they contacted during the period of the surveillance. (TOAID 1970f, 4)

Yet photographing protesters had drawbacks—student protesters retaliated by photographing police beating demonstrators (TOAID 1968f, 3), leading the police to advance "a theory that photographs [were] being made . . . to study . . . police strategy in encounters with student demonstrators" (TOAID 1968f, 3). OPS recommended that police learn to distinguish the legitimate press from student troublemakers. But the police responded instead by arresting student photographers, which inevitably meant professional journalists being caught up as well, which contributed to charges of press censorship. After a number of highly publicized arrests of newspaper photographers, OPS recommended that Brazilian police begin issuing press identification tags so that police could "properly [distinguish] . . . members of the working press" from student demonstrators (TOAID 1968f, 3).

However, OPS thought that the most effective way of controlling student demonstrations was to improve police coordination. For example, OPS-Brazil wanted Rio de Janeiro's secretary of public security, Army General Luis de França Oliveira, to establish a Special Operations Squad (Grupo de Operaçoẽs Especiais), the GOE—an elite squad made up of police from the state's DOPS political police, the army, state Militarized Police, and firefighters. It seems that França also wanted to reorganize Guanabara's police system by giving "subordinate agencies more administrative autonomy . . . [and] increas[ing] . . . the number of precinct police stations and vigilance squads" (TOAID 1969f, 6–7), perhaps using as a model the "fugitive patrol" that OPS advisor Dan Mitrione had helped set up. GOE would go a step beyond this by integrating several security forces and giving the new police unit greater independence of action. Devolution was in the offing.

The primary criterion for recruitment into GOE "was courage already demonstrated during [a policeman's] professional life." The best candidate was "a man intimately linked to moral principles and the national constitution" (F 1993). The ten police who finally came to serve in GOE were, above all, "trustworthy"—that is, their loyalties to Secretary of Public Security França were unquestioned.

The GOE members were given a military commando course by the Brazilian Air Force Paratrooper Brigade; training in urban guerrilla warfare came from the Brazilian Army, assisted by "American, . . . Arab, and . . . Algerian instructors"—GOE recruits also attended courses on explosives and chemical warfare; according to a former Militarized Police GOE officer, this rich range of training "wasn't only for combat— [for] destroying, arresting, [and] seizing; . . . we trained for everything" (F 1993). In preparing for one mid-1969 mission, GOE got help from an OPS-Brazil advisor who "happened to be visiting" the city's Militarized Police Fifth Battalion headquarters while an "unannounced raid . . . [of] a favela" (slum) was being planned. According to the OPS advisor, this raid was to include "the [Militarized Police] Radio Patrol, the 'fugitive patrol' [of Civil Police], and one company of the Militarized Police 5th Battalion"; four former OPS police trainees were coordinating the raid's briefing operations, facilitated by prior publication and circulation of "wanted lists"—a strategy developed by a former Brazilian OPS participant and encouraged by OPS itself (TOAID 1969f, 8). Such lists were apparently a CIA contribution to such campaigns (e.g., as in Indonesia, 1964–1965; the Philippines, 1950; Vietnam, 1950s–1970s).

Consolidating the Authoritarian State

On the heels of widespread student protest and violent government repression, the Brazilian security forces invaded the University of Brasília and closed it for seven months, but security force violence there led to protests in Brazil's Congress. Outspoken congressional opponents denounced the militarization of Brazilian society. Márcio Moreira Alves, a member of the officially sanctioned MDB (Movimento Democrático Brasileiro) opposition party, called for a nationwide boycott of Brazil's September 7 Independence Day military parade and challenged Brazilian women—in what came to be dubbed "Operação Lysistrata"—to refuse to date officers who engaged in repression or failed to speak out against it (Alves 1985, 93–94).

Military ministers in the cabinet, incensed over what they saw as a direct attack on military integrity, demanded presidential censure of all deputies who had spoken against the military. The Chamber of Deputies reminded them that Brazil's 1967 constitution, imposed by the military itself, granted immunity from punishment for speeches on the floor of Congress. By the first week of December 1968, Brazil was in the midst of a full-scale parliamentary crisis. The response of military hard-liners was to demand cassação of dissident deputies, stripping them of their political rights for ten years. On December 13, 1968, President Costa e Silva promulgated the Fifth Institutional Act (IA-5), described as "the most far-reaching and most repressive of [the] government['s internal security] measures" up to that time (Flynn 1978, 420). IA-5 claimed to be a "compromise" between military hard-liners and Congress over the parliamentary crisis. In fact, many Brazilian political analysts see IA-5 as a "coup-within-a-coup." With its promulgation, the officers who had engineered Brazil's earlier 1964 military golpe were themselves overthrown by "a tightly knit group of soldiers and *técnicos*" from within the original golpe leaders own ranks (Flynn 1978, 425). IA-5 clearly

marked a definite break with the attempt to maintain some form of "controlled democracy," emphasizing [instead] . . . the essentially authoritarian nature of the regime and its apparent inability to handle crisis and challenge other than by ever-more-extreme repression. (Flynn 1978, 422)

The military government's Fifth Institutional Act answered its political critics by giving extensive powers to its own executive, including the power to declare a state of siege unilaterally. Press censorship was greatly expanded, Congress was closed, and all constitutional and individual guarantees were suspended—including habeas corpus for political crimes—and arrests were permitted without formal charges or warrants. Political crimes were to be tried in military courts, and electoral rights were canceled for political crimes (cassação); the private property of such "criminals" was to be confiscated.

It must be remembered that IA-5 was promulgated after violent government repression had already forced the student protest movement into hiding and virtually crushed Brazil's labor movement. Four years of political disbarments and government censorship of political debates had crippled Brazil's only two legal (i.e., government-allowed) political parties. Above all, citizen participation in political and even in ordinary social life had been chilled by military and police searches, seizure, torture, and murder. But IA-5 rendered vulnerable many sectors of the Brazilian population previously spared from security force violence (Alves 1985, 103). The military government undertook a countrywide wave of job dismissals, denial of political rights, arrests, and exile.

Washington's Response to IA-5: International Support for Authoritarianizing

A few months after IA-5 became law, Washington suspended economic assistance to Brazil. Yet this " 'cosmetic' protest against . . . tightening of the dictatorial noose" did not include suspending assistance to Brazilian police; indeed, the number of Brazilian policemen brought to the United States for training during the period just after enactment of IA-5 almost tripled over the prior year (Black 1977, 146).

OPS knew that its proposals to further assist Brazilian police came on the heels of reports of continuing torture and murder by Brazilian security forces. OPS acknowledged that IA-5 was having "the effect of substituting martial law for due process of constitutional government" (TOAID 1969a, 1). But OPS justified its support for these police, because, as OPS saw it, the limited dissatisfaction in Brazil over IA-5 was concentrated in "small elements of the informed and concerned [public], particularly those . . . directly affected" by IA-5. And according to OPS, such groups had "only voice[ed] (*sotto voce*) disapproval of the seizure and exercise of governmental power by the military elite." OPS assured Washington that in any case, such dissatisfaction was not likely to threaten Brazil's internal security (TOAID 1969d, 2), OPS's prime consideration. However, OPS did wonder whether the Brazilian government would be able to continue to "contain opposition without further damage to its internal and international image" (TOAID 1969c, 1). This might require some managing. Along these lines, in early March 1969, OPS-Brazil commended Paraiba state governor João Agripino for "put[ting] out [the order] for [his state's] police to stop all *public* beatings" (emphasis added) (TOAID 1969d, 15), presumably in an effort to keep police violence behind closed doors. The governor credited OPS with "contributing to [this] professionalism" of the Paraiba police.

A new Brazilian National Security Law, promulgated on March 31, 1969, even more sharply limited freedom of assembly, of association, and of the press. Newspapers were forbidden to "publish news or fact [that was] slanted in such a way as to dispose the population against the constituted authorities" (Alves 1985, 118). All strikes were forbidden in essential services. None but the two government-approved political parties could operate at all. And even the approved parties were forbidden to "offend persons in a position of authority for political or social reasons" (Alves 1985, 118). As the International Association of Jurists pointed out at the time, the National Security Law was "a formidable weapon of repression" (in Flynn 1978, 424).

OPS-Brazil's response to the National Security Law was to inform OPS-Washington that the law had been merely "designed to facilitate Government action against those involved in anti-Government propaganda and acts of sabotage as well as criminal acts which affect the economy" (TOAID 1969e, 2; see also TOAID 1969h, 2). OPS-Brazil did concede that if Brazil's Federal Congress were to reopen, "much of [its] function as an element of government will have been emasculated, as . . . [is already] the case . . . [with] the federal judiciary, leaving the Federal Executive in [an] . . . unchallenged leadership role" (TOAID 1969e, 1). But OPS-Brazil explained that most Brazilians were "politically uninvolved and uninspired to express . . . dissatisfaction" with the law (failing to mention that such expression had been further suppressed by the law itself). In any case, OPS pointed out that some lower segments of the Brazilian public were actually supportive of the military's restrictions on political freedom—"reduction [in] the [status] of professional politicians [had] . . . general popularity at the *feijão preto* (black beans) level" (i.e., among the poor) (TOAID 1969d, 2).

In any case, this militarized authoritarianism suited the goals of OPS-Brazil, which considered the elimination of oversight by Brazil's Congress an opportunity to push its own centralizing and professionalizing agenda with its military and police contacts. In August 1969, OPS urged that a proposed reorganization of Brazil's Federal Police be pushed "through [by] the [military-appointed] Minister of Justice, . . . preferably before Congress . . . reconvened [in order] to enable [police reorganization] . . . by Presidential Decree rather than [through] the lengthy legislative process" (TOAID 1969e; see also TOAID 1969h).

Further Centralizing Internal Security: Operação Bandeirantes

IA-5 and the National Security Law had been promulgated at a time when Brazil's entire internal security apparatus did not yet constitute an integrated security system. Indeed, in the words of one Brazilian military analyst, in 1969, "when terrorist actions began [in Brazil], the [country's repressive] system did not have the capacity to put out the fires" (in Lago and Lagoa 1979). For example, in 1969 the various states' social and political police (DOPS) were not effectively centralized under the military nor even linked among the states themselves. To one Brazilian military analyst, there was a great range in the different states' DOPS's ability to take on an expanded internal security role. According to his evaluation, the São Paulo DOPS had a "good" intelligence apparatus, whereas the Pôrto Alegre city and the Minas Gerais state DOPS were only "pretty good," and the city of Rio de Janeiro's DOPS were only "so-so." Other state DOPS police were apparently not even good enough to be considered (Lago and Lagoa 1979).

It would therefore be wrong to assume that a well-coordinated internal security system in Brazil or even in any of the separate states was ready to enforce the ever widening national security legislation enacted in 1968 and 1969 (e.g., IA-5 and the National Security Law). In particular, central coordination between the police commands and their elite shock and intelligence squads, as well as among Brazil's various police forces and between police organizations and the military, was seen to be insufficient.

Law 317, designed to coordinate all Brazilian police, was still falling short of expectations, even though under it there had been attempts to weave police into an internal security system by placing police under tighter military control. As a first step toward more coordinated policing, Operação Bandeirantes (OBAN) was secretly established in São Paulo city on July 2, 1969, to be applied nationally in 1970 as a new internal security organization called DOI/CODI (to be examined in chapter 9). OBAN's general purpose was to coordinate the activities of the state's various police and military internal security organizations and facilitate the rapid collection of intelligence information. Its more specific goal was to "identify, locate, and capture subversive groups that operate in the Second Army region, especially in São Paulo, with the objective of destroying or at least neutralizing [them]" (DOPS Record 1974, 3). OPS-Brazil, in its "neutral," professional way, described OBAN as "a combined military-police operation aimed at suppressing terrorist activities and apprehending known and suspected subversives" (TOAID 1970b, 7).

According to a former Delegado from the São Paulo Civil Police's DEIC Criminal Investigations Division, the core police for OBAN came from a specially selected group of hard-nosed police the Delegado had originally assembled in his DEIC division's directorate. These police were already "very bestialized" when he incorporated them into his new official, secret death squad in the directorate, but they became even more so in the course of carrying out their specialized work for him. Being experienced in search, capture, and interrogation, this group of violent police was then invited to enter OBAN (S 1993), becoming the nucleus for this notoriously violent internal security organization.

OBAN is said to have been the brainchild of the general in charge of the Second Army, José Canavarro Pereira, who was in frequent contact with OPS-Brazil. Indeed, there is evidence that the idea for OBAN was born in February 1969 at the First International Security Seminar in Brasília (Fon 1986), where a proposal had been advanced to create an organization for coordinating and centralizing Brazil's fight against subversion. According to OPS, seminar organizers—Generals José Bretas Cupertino, then director general of the Federal Police of Brazil, and Carlos de Meira Mattos, the country's Militarized Police inspector general—gave OPS-Brazil credit for "close assistance [and] . . . impetus toward integration of [Brazil's] internal security forces" (TOAID 1969d, 2). OPS-Brazil had apparently argued at the seminar that integration and centralization of Brazil's security forces was "a vital element in strategic planning for national security" (TOAID 1969d, 2). OBAN was a trial run in São Paulo for such a nationwide internal security system.

OBAN also assumed a consciousness-raising role, dedicating itself to a propaganda campaign for "motivat[ing] the civil population toward its own defense against terrorism." The campaign included encouraging and providing assistance in setting up "telephone chains" and "chain letters." These would promote allegiance to the military government and check the spread of "terrorist" rumors, with the warning that "if you break the chain, you or a loved one could be the victim of a [subversive's] assault or fire bomb." OBAN also set up "rumor clinics," based on psychologist Gordon Allport's World War II research, to block "subversive" rumors by planting informants in labor unions, universities, business and commercial associations, sport and social clubs, and other civic organizations—with the objective of eventually turning "every member of the population into a secret police to prevent terrorism and . . . Communist subversion" (DOPS Record 1969c). That is, the population would become part of a totalitarian infrastructure, based on total involvement in the state repressive apparatus.

Because of the way OBAN was structured and operated, it has been described as a pilot Vietnam-style Phoenix Program for Latin America (Saxe-Fernandez 1972). Phoenix had been established in South Vietnam just two years earlier as a countrywide intelligence network consisting of CIA, Vietnamese, and U.S. Army operatives and was designed to unify Vietnam's fragmented intelligence apparatus and "neutralize" the National Liberation Front's political infrastructure (Saxe-Fernandez 1972, 25). The Phoenix Program carried out its mission through interrogation, intimidation, torture, disappearances, and murder, with estimates that between 1968 and 1972, while Phoenix was under U.S. administration, 26,369 Vietnamese civilians were killed under the program, and another 33,358 imprisoned under brutalizing conditions (Klare and Arnson 1981, 25). Interestingly, Theodore Brown headed the CIA's Phoenix Program in Vietnam immediately after being OPS chief public safety officer for Brazil (actually serving as OPS Latin American branch chief).

One important difference between Phoenix and OBAN was that Phoenix—although highly secretive—was formally constituted and funded by the United States: as a CIA operation, Phoenix also had OPS funds. In contrast, São Paulo's OBAN was extraofficial and privatized, financed through local businessmen and national and multinational corporations, among them Ford and General Motors (Flynn 1978, 435; Langguth 1978; Weschler 1987, 74).

One of OBAN's most energetic fund-raisers was São Paulo industrialist Hennig Albert Boilessen, president of São Paulo's Ùltragás Corporation. Langguth (1978) writes that many who knew Boilessen suspected that the industrialist had links to the CIA. Or, as Langguth (1978, 122) has put it, there was more than one way in which the wealthy Brazilian industrialist—whose house was on São Paulo's opulent United States Street (Rua dos Estados Unidos)—"lived off" the United States.

OPS knew about Boilessen's involvement with OBAN, for he was described in one OPS secret memorandum as "a close associate of high-level [Brazilian] Government officials and active in unofficial anti-terrorist circles" (TOAID 1971a, 1). Boilessen's connections to antiterrorist groups were apparently known to others: on April 15, 1971, the industrialist was gunned down as he left his house by militants of the Aliança Libertação Nacional (ALN) and MR (Movimento Revolucionário) Tiradentes groups. A pamphlet left on Boilessen's body charged that the industrialist "had been singled out for revolutionary justice because he had placed the resources of his organization at the disposal of torturers and assassins of the Brazilian people" (TOAID 1971a). OPS-Brazil sent this information on to Washington. But when Theodore Brown, OPS–Latin America branch chief, was asked in 1971 what he knew about OBAN, he told a Senate hearing that he had "heard [the] expression," but it "slips my mind [as to] what [it] is" (CFR 1971a, 43).

Institutionalized State Violence

In fact, as we have seen, OPS-Brazil advisors had been at the International Security Seminar where the idea for OBAN had been broached as an extraofficial, top secret internal security organization. OPS-Brazil had encouraged Brazilian internal security officials to set up OBAN and had then supported it, even as this organization was carrying out violent raids and engaging in torture and murder. According to a 1973 Amnesty International report, OBAN had been responsible for some of the Brazilian military dictatorship's most brutal torture (Flynn 1978, 435).

OPS-Brazil reported in February 1970 that it had a "favorable relationship" with the São Paulo Delegado who headed OBAN and spoke approvingly of OBAN's "successful actions . . . [and] well-coordinated raids on targets pinpointed through joint intelligence operations" among local, regional, and national intelligence agencies. According to OPS-Brazil, OBAN's raids had resulted in "arrests of suspects and captures of illegal weapons and subversive propaganda" (TOAID 1970b, 7).

One victim of OBAN torture reported in a letter, passed clandestinely among militants in Brazil, that it was "difficult to describe the screams of men being tortured [at OBAN]: The [screams] come involuntarily from the depths of their lungs; they can't be demonstrated. [But] anyone who has heard them will never forget them." Tortured for two hours by OBAN operatives, who all called themselves " 'Guimarães' to avoid anyone knowing their identities," this victim contrasted the anonymity of his torturers with the striking and painful reality of their brutalizing technologies. Field radios were hooked up to his anus, lips, tongue, or nose, with "the shock provoking . . . muscle contractions so strong that if the torturer [didn't] put something in [the victim's] mouth . . . [he] would eat his tongue" (DOPS Record 1969b). This was the hidden reality behind OBAN that OPS-Brazil was supporting through its training.

One of the more publicized cases of torture involved Frei Tito Alencar, a twenty-seven-year-old Dominican friar from the Brazilian northeastern state of Ceará and an activist in the Catholic Church's Young Christian Student group (JEC). After his arrest in São Paulo by OBAN on November 4, 1969, for allegedly being in contact with the ALN guerrilla group led by Carlos Marighella, Tito was held in an OBAN facility. In one OBAN interrogation session, Frei Tito was kicked and beaten with rods and fists, followed by an extended round of electric shocks. One of the friar's accusers forced him to "receive the Eucharist" by putting a live electric wire to Tito's mouth, causing it to become so swollen that the priest could not speak. After hours of such brutality in his tiny OBAN torture chamber (two by two meters in size), without any furniture except for a stand holding the implements of torture (DOPS Record 1969b), Frei Tito had to be carried back to his cell, where he lay all night on the cold cement floor. The following day, OBAN security forces kicked and then beat Tito with "hard little boards" (known as the *palmatória*), alternating beatings with electric shocks and cigarette burns. At one point during this five-hour torture session, Tito was forced to "walk through the 'Polish Corridor' "—a gauntlet of soldiers who beat Tito until he could not walk.

Following this treatment, OBAN interrogators initially decided to attach the Dominican friar to the "parrot's perch"—where Tito was to be suspended upside down with his wrists and ankles tied to the rod while being administered electric shocks. But the OBAN team decided that the friar would be more valuable in the next day's interrogation session after a good night's sleep. Before returning Tito to his cell, an OBAN security officer warned the friar that if he did not talk in the next day's session, the interrogator would "bust [your] insides." It was well known among victims of the parrot's perch that this device transformed the victim's "body . . . into a mass that no longer obeys the brain" (DOPS Record 1969b; see also DOPS Record 1977). That night, Frei Tito resolved that the "only . . . way out [was] to kill myself" (Alencar 1970, 2).

So, after four months of persistent torture by OBAN, the friar had to be rushed to the University of São Paulo Hospital das Clínicas after slashing his wrists. For Frei Tito, even death by suicide—a mortal sin—was preferable to another OBAN torture session. Tito survived and from the hospital was able to write a deeply disturbing letter about his treatment. This was smuggled out and distributed to religious groups in and out of Brazil, which used it as evidence in their campaigns against the Brazilian military regime's practices.

CIA Director Richard Helms, testifying in 1971 on Brazil before a U.S. Senate Subcommittee, acknowledged that the "potentially most damaging criticism of torture by [Brazilian security forces] has come from prelates of the [Catholic] Church." Helms conceded that Brazilian security forces had tortured priests "on at least three occasions." But the CIA director declared that "clergymen [who were] involved in subversion should be treated like any other citizen" of their country (CFR 1971a, 26), presumably even if such treatment meant their being tortured. Helms made it clear that his agency had known all along that Brazilian "security forces [were] not beyond using torture, a practice some [Brazilian] officials privately justif[ied] in certain cases on pragmatic grounds" (CFR 1971a, 23). In other words, Helms offered utilitarian grounds for torturers' effectiveness. Yet OPS-Brazil reports never mentioned the torture that was instrumental in OBAN's (and its own) successes. And as we already know, OPS–Latin America branch chief Brown claimed that he knew only "of newspaper items on the subject" of torture in Brazil (CFR 1971a, 18).

Authoritarianizing the State Still Further: Crisis and Repression

By late 1969, the last building blocks of Brazil's authoritarian state were being set in place. The state had been given an aura of legality by the new 1967 constitution and the series of draconian Institutional Acts, all justified by the claim that they were to protect Brazil's national security. Repressive legislation had severely restricted legal citizen involvement in politics and had suspended civil and human rights—among them habeas corpus and freedom of the press and association. Brazil's military government had gained almost total formal control over social, cultural, economic, and political life.

In June 1969, President Richard M. Nixon sent New York governor Nelson A. Rockefeller to Latin America to develop a policy report on the state of the region. This seemingly routine fact-finding visit to Latin America came at a time when a number of Latin American governments were already headed by military dictatorships. Rockefeller's visit was a flash point for protest: "His family's name had been political shorthand throughout South America for imperialism and repression" (Langguth 1978, 159). OPS reported that in Brazil there were "rumors of student and opposition elements' intent to use the occasion to demonstrate against the Brazilian Government and U.S. 'support of the Government'" (TOAID 1969g).

To stave off such negative political activity, Brazil's military government launched combined police and military dragnets leading to thousands of arrests over the weekend just before Rockefeller's visit to Brazil. As Rockefeller departed from Brazil, in the wake of widespread popular protests, OPS-Brazil reported that "security coverage by the police . . . [had been] well-planned, coordinated, and efficiently managed" (TOAID 1969g, 1).

OPS credited its public safety personnel with having "provided back-up . . . in all three cities visited" by Rockefeller, and it reported that the U.S. embassy's security officer gave a "large share of the credit . . . [for the Rockefeller mission's success] to the [OPS] Public Safety Advisors" (TOAID 1969g, 1–2). Having met similar protests from dissenters across Latin America, Rockefeller made a predictable policy recommendation for the region: "The training program which brings military and police . . . from the other hemispheric nations to the United States and to training camps in Panama [should] be continued and strengthened" (Rockefeller 1969, 63–64). The United States, in other words, should further internationalize (and militarize) Latin American police to protect U.S. national security, not to speak of visiting U.S. officials.

But despite Rockefeller's optimistic assessment of the Brazilian military government, by late 1969 cracks had again begun to widen in this government's authoritarian facade. As President Costa e Silva became increasingly incapacitated in mid-1969 from a series of strokes, Vice President Pedro Aleixo prepared to become president. But the vice president's opposition to the Fifth Institutional Act had turned military hard-liners against him. So, they declared, "The constitutional solution was not viable" (Alves 1985, 105).

The tug-of-war over Costa e Silva's successor seemed resolved by the announcement on September 1, 1969, that a military triumvirate made up of representatives from the army, navy, and air force would head the Brazilian government—an internal coup against the military's own 1967 constitution. OPS-Brazil's only response was to report that the creation of this triumvirate had resulted in "a probable further strengthening of military responsibility for internal security and control of the Federal and State law enforcement bodies" (TOAID 1969i, 2), which OPS-Brazil had been in effect encouraging all along. OPS-Brazil recognized that "restoration of the Congress to a functioning role in government and adoption of a new constitution [is] significantly altered with the . . . 'temporary' replacement of [Costa e Silva] . . . by a military triumvirate." Yet OPS assured Washington that there had been very little "visible public effect [from] the change in the Government situation." In fact, according to OPS-Brazil, "there [is] . . . far more fervent public reaction to . . . the victory of Brazil over Paraguay to qualify for . . . the 1970 World Cup soccer championship" (TOAID 1969i, 1–2).

But just three days after installation of the military triumvirate, the kidnapping of U.S. ambassador C. Burke Elbrick in Rio de Janeiro cast a heavy shadow on the government's ability to maintain internal security. Elbrick's abductors—political militants from the MR-8 (Movimento Revolucionário–8) and ALN (Aliança Libertação Nacional) guerrilla groups—threatened to execute the ambassador if the Brazilian government did not release fifteen selected political prisoners within forty-eight hours, with safe transport to Mexico. The situation created conflict among the military cabinet ministers as well as among the various military intelligence agencies. Taking a firm stance, the navy resisted the ultimatum, arguing that its CENIMAR (Centro de Informaçoẽs de Marinha) intelligence section had spent enormous time and resources locating and capturing the prisoners whose release was demanded. Army colonels went further, to demand the triumvirate announce that unless Elbrick was released immediately, the fifteen prisoners would be publicly hanged. In the colonels' minds, giving in to terrorists encouraged more kidnapping. But Brazil's foreign minister, Costa Pinto, apparently under pressure from the U.S. State Department, urged the triumvirate to let the political prisoners depart for Mexico (Sheldon [1979?]).

In the end, the triumvirate reluctantly agreed to exchange the political prisoners for Elbrick's safe release, although without full support from all elements of the military. On September 6, 1969, the day of the prisoners' scheduled departure from Rio de Janeiro's Santos Dumont International Airport, hard-liners in the navy were still intransigent: two hundred army sailors surrounded the aircraft holding the fifteen political prisoners to keep it from departing. Only after hours of closed-door meetings was the navy persuaded to withdraw its troops. Yet even after the prisoners' airplane had taken off, a group of forty air force paratroopers seized a local radio station to protest the militants' departure for Mexico (Sheldon [1979?], 4). As CIA director Helms pointed out in 1971, "many [Brazilian] authorities [had been] particularly angry about having been ordered to release and fly abroad [these] prisoners—many of them dangerous terrorists who had killed policemen" (CFR 1971a, 23). As Helms hinted, the Brazilian government was losing its grip on its security forces.

According to Helms, the Elbrick kidnapping "had hit the Brazilian government and the security forces even harder" than the earlier murder by Brazilian militants of U.S. Army Colonel Charles Chandler: international coverage implied that the [Brazilian] government could not protect . . . official representative[s] of Brazil's traditional[ly] closest friend; Brazilian security forces "became determined to wipe out the terrorists who had so badly embarrassed them" (CFR 1971a, 13). The day after the militants' safe arrival in Mexico and Ambassador Elbrick's release unharmed, the military triumvirate declared Brazil in a state of "internal revolutionary war," a period later described by one high-ranking Militarized Police official as

bloody—so violent; it was . . . just like World War I or II, except in internal terms, where no one respected anything. There were things that only people who lived through it can talk about. (F 1993)

In this climate of civil war, military and police dragnets were carried out in Brazil's major cities, ostensibly to locate the militants who had kidnapped Ambassador Elbrick; in São Paulo, OBAN led its state's search for Elbrick's captors (DOPS Record 1969a). OPS-Brazil collaborated in the countrywide investigation through its state- and local-level contacts. During the dragnets that followed Elbrick's release, nearly 5,000 people were arrested and imprisoned in Brazil, as many as 2,000 in Rio de Janeiro alone (Cava 1970, 136).

In the wake of these widespread arrests, Brazil's military government issued two additional Institutional Acts, striking down citizens' remaining constitutional guarantees against banishment, life imprisonment, and capital punishment. OPS-Brazil's reaction to the "extreme penalties" associated with the new Institutional Acts was to declare them a "step toward more effective terrorist suppression" because the new laws were "applicable to an elastic variety of 'subversive' acts against the Government" (TOAID 1969j, 3).

As for the actual fit between these laws and the terrorist threat, Brazilian political scientist Helena Alves argues that by 1969 only about six thousand people were organized for guerrilla armed struggle in Brazil. Indeed, the CIA chief Richard Helms reported in 1971 that "the number of people engag[ed] in terrorism at any one time [in Brazil had] . . . never exceeded one thousand—a tiny fraction of the [country's] 93 million Brazilians." Helms, in fact, doubted that Brazil was in the throes of a civil war (CFR 1971a, 7), an assessment compatible with Alves's argument that by 1969 Brazil's militant revolutionary organizations had become "ideologically fragmented and unable to unite for coherent armed actions" (Alves 1985, 119), thus clearly unable to mount a civil war.

Yet the military government's position that it was fighting an internal revolutionary war was reinforced by intersecting elements. The rise in politically motivated bank robberies, bombings, and kidnappings had come at a time when the government was already internally divided by the turmoil within the military elite over presidential succession, generating the feeling that the whole society was spinning out of control. Furthermore, the ideology of national security offered a vocabulary for understanding and promoting the belief that Brazil was fighting a special kind of war against internal subversion—"a war without uniforms, situated in the streets, where the enemy was mixed within the general population, [where] the police cannot distinguish by sight the terrorists from good citizens," as Army General Carlos Brilhante Ustra put it. Most significantly, Ustra went on to explain that in such situations, police could easily pull away from central control and begin to "fight each other, thinking that they are taking action against terrorists" (Ustra 1987, 71).

Implanting a "Carceral State"

Brazil's national security legislation was also laying the basis for future devolution. As Brazil's military state became more and more disconnected from civilian influence and control, one by one, institutions that might have mediated between citizens and the government—such as political parties, interest associations, labor unions, religious groups, student organizations, and grassroots movements—were systematically driven underground. Along the way, torture, disappearances, and murder—weapons in the military government's arsenal against internal subversion—had become the military's strategy for closing the "legitimacy gap": as more and more of the politically efficacious population was excluded from political and civic participation, repression was increasingly used to ensure short-term government stability, even if in the long run such tactics undermined the government's legitimacy and threatened its breakup.

In other words, whereas the manifest function of security force violence had been to extract information and confessions and to mete out punishments for crime and subversion more "efficiently" and expeditiously, the latent function of such violence was to institutionalize Brazil's bureaucratic-authoritarian state, at least for the time being. In his application of Michel Foucault to torture in Iran, Darius Rejali (1994, 166–68) argues that within modernized "carceral systems"—where society comes to be organized like a prison—torture transforms the identity of the captive into a "carceral," bringing the victim under the larger systems' control. By forcing its captives "to inform, condemn, recant, or confess to false crimes, the victim is made more easily governable." Through torture, therefore, the victim is socialized into assuming "a hypervigilant conduct that regulate[s] actions in the interests of anonymity," irrespective of the truth or falsity of any confession (Rejali 1994, 154).

One ironic consequence of this social construction of anonymity is that it becomes less and less necessary for the state to govern the population through torture. "It governs by means of the rationality characteristic of carceral institutions," in which a person's behavior is guided by "not a general fear or terror, [but] rather a particular kind of fear and terror"; individuals come to censor their own conduct because "they have a stake in their [own] insularity" (Rejali 1994, 152, 154). In other words, a "carceral rationality" spread throughout Brazilian society to include even sectors of the population not directly affected by torture. And this became a structural support for the developing bureaucratic-authoritarian state. But in the process, for its own purposes, the state was undermining its own centralized, authoritarian powers without being able to recognize, or at least arrest, their disintegration.

9 Fortifying Security and Privatizing Repression: Torture and Death Squads in Authoritarian Devolution, 1969–1970

In October 1969, the selection by a military triumvirate of Army General Emílio Garrastazu Médici as Brazil's third post-1964 military president had given a clear signal that military hard-liners controlled the government. Médici, who had himself headed Brazil's National Intelligence Service (SNI) and commanded the important Third Army Region, would stick to tough policies and use the state's system of social control to ensure their implementation.

The Médici appointment ultimately received the imprimatur of the U.S. Senate in its working consensus on how Médici's government should be viewed: in 1971, during top secret Senate debate over U.S. policies and programs in Brazil (CFR 1971a, 62), New York's liberal Republican Senator Jacob Javits asked CIA Director Richard Helms, "Is it your judgment or the judgment of your agency, if a national election were held and [General] Médici was the candidate, that he would be elected?" Helms answered, "Probably yes." Javits then described Brazil as "a rather strained monolithic dictatorship by consent" (CFR 1971a, 62). "Completely befoggled [sic]," Senator J. William Fulbright (D-Ark.) asked his colleague to clarify "the semantics [of] 'dictatorship [by consent]'" (CFR 1971a, 72). Helms interjected that "if one had free elections in Brazil tomorrow, you would . . . [get] the same fellow [Médici] as President" (CFR 1971a, 73). Fulbright could still not quite swallow the oxymoron, "dictatorship by consent," but he was "perfectly willing to accept . . . that this is the [political] system that suits [Brazilians'] particular temperament and degree of political maturity." Indeed, even Fulbright "doubt[ed] if [Brazilians] could do any better" than Médici (CFR 1971a, 74).

As for OPS-Brazil, its only concern about Médici as president was the possible impact on OPS goals for Brazil: OPS feared that Médici might make extensive changes in top-level internal security positions. If he did, OPS would "once again [face] the task of in-depth project orientation of incoming command and staff-level personnel" (TOAID 1969k, 2).

However, OPS-Brazil presented a positive expectation that Médici would not seriously disrupt, and in fact would promote, OPS internal security work in Brazil: Médici had already named Alfredo Buzaid—"a staunch supporter of strict law enforcement, particularly in dealing with subversive and criminal elements"—to head Brazil's justice ministry (TOAID 1969l, 4).

Authoritarian Centralization: The Formation of DOI/CODI

Helms, as head of the CIA, told a U.S. Senate committee in 1971 that the desirable outcome of police centralization—at least indirectly helped by OPS through its assisting state and federal police units—had come closer to realization by July 1969: The general commanding the Second Army—a region containing São Paulo state—had "claimed that the lack of coordination among the security forces was such that only ad hoc management by the army had kept things from total collapse." The general had made an urgent recommendation, apparently suggested by the CIA itself,[1] "that the commanders of each of the four [Brazilian] armies assume full responsibility for and control of all security elements—and that all-out war be declared on the terrorists immediately" (CFR 1971a, 13–14).

OPS-Brazil supported Médici's creating a special executive-level "commission . . . of top militar[ized] police, and security officials to coordinate all security matters . . . [against] subversion and . . . dealing with internal security problems in [Brazil]" (TOAID 1969l, 4). Because Brazil's national security ideology proposed that, rather than external military force, internal subversion was the greatest threat to national security, this required a Manichaean division of the population into "true citizens" on the one side and "subversives," "terrorists," and "marginals" on the other. This, in turn, provided ideological legitimation for treating the "deviant" and "subversive" part of the population—even if middle or upper class—as enemies to be vanquished by any means necessary.

The timing and composition of the recommendation for a military-police "commission" clearly suggests its possible relationship to the subsequent formation of DOI/CODI—an interconnected national network of both police and military security forces, all under direct military control. From the OPS Cold War point of view, the Brazilian police were getting down to their proper business: fighting subversion through coordinated centralization under military control, not just fighting ordinary crime through a still very decentralized police system.

In late 1969, the first of the new agencies had been established in São Paulo as Operação Bandeirantes (OBAN), the statewide internal defense operations command (described in chapter 8). This model was extended as DOI/CODI[2] throughout Brazil a year later, its mission to secure intelligence and neutralize terrorists.

CIA director Helms saw the DOI/CODI internal security organization as "committees . . . composed of various members of the [Brazilian] armed forces and the police, [in each of which] the ultimate man in command is the army commander in the . . . [corresponding] military districts" (CFR 1971a, 66). The structure of DOI/CODI was designed to help Brazil's security forces overcome "jurisdictional disputes and lack of coordination among the numerous military and civilian intelligence and security agencies," as Helms himself explained (CFR 1971a, 13–14). Although it is difficult to get exact figures on the number of agents in DOI/CODI, it is clear that there were far fewer than in Brazil's other police and military forces. Yet although DOI/CODI was only a small subset of Brazil's internal security apparatus, this organization—because of its direct subordination to the federal military executive—was superimposed on, and accorded higher status than, the other internal security elements. At the organization's creation in 1970, DOI/CODI's privileged status was reinforced by reorganizing Brazil's four traditional army regions into ten DOI/CODI "internal defense zones."

Each of the DOI/CODI internal defense zones had a single CODI, an Internal Defense Operations Command Center. Each CODI identified its region's internal security priorities, analyzed intelligence information, planned "combat" missions (in its military-style terminology), and coordinated DOI squads. These DOI Information and Operations Detachments made up a "combat-ready force [to] combat subversive organizations directly, . . . dismantle their personnel and material structure, and block their re-establishment." According to General Carlos Brilhante Ustra, commander of the São Paulo State DOI, the DOI squads were "eminently adapted to the necessities of countersubversion" (Ustra 1987, 126).

Whereas each CODI region had at least one operational DOI, some of the larger and more strategically important CODI regions, such as those containing the cities of Rio de Janeiro and São Paulo, had as many as four DOI squads. São Paulo's DOI were relatively representative of other state's DOI, each squad containing in all about forty agents from the army and the rest from the "brave and competent members of the . . . Civil and Militar[ized] Police" (Ustra 1987, 126; see also *Isto É* 1978).

According to one military officer, having Civil Police, especially the DOPS political police, in this internal security organization was essential—as earlier in São Paulo's OBAN—because with heightened terrorist activity in Brazil, the military themselves were at first unprepared to collect civilian intelligence, to interrogate prisoners, and to conduct internal security operations generally (Fon 1986). Even as late as 1968, most internal security monitoring in Brazil had still been primarily the responsibility of the various states' secretaries of public security and their DOPS. In São Paulo, the Civil Police Division for Criminal Investigations (DEIC) and the motorized RONE also had experience with capture and arrest. In fact, according to a former Civil Police Delegado who at different points in his career had headed the São Paulo DEIC and RONE, the first group of OBAN operatives had come from DEIC and RONE via the informal death squads that had developed out of these formal police units (see chapter 7). Many of these OBAN operatives were transferred to the São Paulo DOI/CODI once it had replaced OBAN. The Delegado characterized the type of men who went into OBAN and DOI/CODI as "all very bestialized. No one intellectualized. . . . They just killed a bunch—Boom! Boom!" (S 1993).

During the military period, DOI/CODI and its operations remained shrouded in secrecy, and a great deal about it remains secret even today. Yet some information about DOI/CODI has become public through journalists' written accounts; more remains oral—passed by word of mouth from DOI/CODI victims and their families. But of course most police and military who were DOI/CODI agents have been unwilling even to talk about their service in this now publicly much-condemned internal security organization. But some information has been obtained about DOI/CODI from oral history interviews with former DOI operatives, or from police whose work intersected with DOI/CODI.

Specialization and Compartmentalization: DOI/CODI Operations

The biggest states' DOI were divided into three squads: one hunted and arrested suspects (*busca e captura*), another collected intelligence and interrogated prisoners (*informação e interrogação*), and another analyzed information gained from infiltration of associations and interrogation of informants (*informação*) (*Isto É* 1978, 32). A former Rio de Janeiro D O I operative maintains that his D O I also had an assault team (*grupo de assalto*), a backup team (*grupo de apoio*), and a murder team (*grupo de quebra*). This informant, who claimed to have been a member of the murder team, explained that the assault team "goes up front. It's the people who are going to enter the house . . . check out things, search . . . and bring out [the captives]." The support team "isn't seen, but is there to protect" the assault team. As for the murder team, whenever it encounters any captives, it "is going to eliminate them all" (G 1993).

D O I operatives were highly specialized: Those most "identified with [torture were] very cold, . . . very aggressive; [they] had to be." Police who demonstrated these characteristics were "classified for [i.e., funneled into] . . . torture work," to be molded into finely tuned instruments of terror (S 1993). As one former operative explained, "People who had the quality for working in a certain [i.e., aggressive] fashion [were] really exploited by their bosses—by those who want to get the job over with quickly" (J 1993). In the process, police who were chosen for such work were further transformed:

Certain types of police work bestializes men horribly. They get brutal, do things they wouldn't ever have done after ten years' [experience with] . . . routine [police] violence. (S 1993)

Specialization of internal security—what Émile Durkheim would have labeled an "extreme division of labor"—resulted in having some operatives who observed, others who interrogated, some who tortured, and still others who murdered. For example, as a former D O I / C O D I operative described one of his group's missions to the Amazon region, torture began immediately after the D O I / C O D I team's aircraft had taken off with captured "subversives." This murderer began feeling "badly" because captives "were being subjected to all kinds of torture— women . . . were raped and . . . thrown from the [aircraft]." Overcome by one woman's screams, the murderer told the torturers: "Instead of torturing [her], just kill her outright; to keep torturing her isn't for me" (G 1993).

In theory, if not always in fact, there was indeed a strict division of labor within and among the D O I squads and between them and the C O D I center. D O I interrogators were to secure confessions and then turn their information over to C O D I's intelligence and planning analysts. Sometimes a C O D I intelligence agent was on hand during a D O I team's interrogations—to make sure that all relevant information was obtained and that such information was passed on to CODI (Ustra 1987, 20). CODI then handed relevant intelligence information and analysis back to DOI search-and-capture teams to act on.

Rationalizing Repression: Consequences of Efficiency

Human rights advocate Jaime Wright has pointed out that the success of Brazil's internal security apparatus turned on getting information as quickly as possible from a captive so that security forces could hunt down potential "criminal terrorists" before they changed location (Wright 1987). The pressure on interrogators to maintain rapid information turnover is manifested in São Paulo DOI/CODI commander general Ustra's observation that "we all lived in a race against time and against the unknown. Speed was vital . . . to discover and neutralize [terrorist] actions that could cause deaths and great material damage" among the public, the state, and the security forces themselves (Ustra 1987, 71).

Brazil's human rights workers agree that some of the military period's worst torture was carried out by DOI/CODI (BNM 1986, 65). Appropriately, *doi* in Portuguese means "to feel pain." Fred Morris, a Protestant minister who had been a missionary in Brazil and was tortured by security forces, described DOI/CODI's *geladeira* (refrigerator) holding cell in which he was kept: This was a five-foot-square, windowless cubicle "equipped with loudspeakers, strobe lights, and heating and cooling units." DOI/CODI commonly used the geladeira to manipulate a victim's sense of time, essential for quick extraction of information. Captives were isolated from any outside stimuli and administered high-technology attacks on their senses (Colligan 1976, 58).

The geladeira was the ultimate Brazilian rationalized positivistic panopticon or observation room: One victim's account of DOI/CODI geladeira interrogation described the holding room as enclosed within another concrete room, both of them totally closed and without windows. Oxygen was introduced only through tiny holes in the walls. For the first five days of incarceration, the prisoner was nude and hooded, his or her arms tied behind the back. Food was withheld and no sleeping was allowed. The captive had to defecate and urinate on the floor of the cell; every movement was monitored through closed-circuit television (DOPS Record 1977).

During the day, the victim faced beatings—especially the "telephone" torture, in which objects were smashed with great force against the ears. The captors administered electric shocks—"in the fingers, hands, feet, genitals, stomach, chest, and arms." "During the night, bone-chilling sounds were played with the objective of 'destructuring' the captive's personality: Diabolical sounds . . . seemed to penetrate the head like a corkscrew" (DOPS Record 1977).

The torturers subjected their prisoners in the geladeira to cycles of heat and cold, noise and silence, first "lowering the temperature inside the box and playing loud recordings of aircraft noise over the speakers and starting the strobe lights blinking." Then the cycle went on to "heat up [the refrigerator] to about 115 degrees, all lights turned off . . . [to create] dead silence." Once this cold:loud/hot:silence relationship had been established, the combinations were reversed until in some cases "weeks of constant exposure to a changing constellation of sense patterns . . . causes . . . a total nervous breakdown" (Saenz [1981?], 63).

Working in DOI/CODI: Stress and Identity

DOI agents theoretically worked for twenty-four hours at a time and then had forty-eight hours off. But according to the former head of the São Paulo state DOI/CODI, his men "sometimes spent night and day in the stake-out van" (Ustra 1987). A DOI operative explained that it was common for him to be called in to work late at night. When he told his wife, "I'm going out to buy some medicine," she knew he meant, "I'm going to work." He would take his weapons with him, get into his car, "and go . . . away for days; even up to a week" (G 1993).

One intelligence operative who worked closely with DOI/CODI explained that he sometimes had

missions where I would spend ten days on duty—twenty-four hours a day, for ten days. We'd sleep in the police station itself. We were called any time during the night. I would work the whole day; at night we'd take turns sleeping. [Sometimes] we'd stay permanently on duty for thirty days. (J 1993)

A former DEIC agent whose intelligence work intersected with DOI/CODI explained that he quit his organization because the work was

intense and permanent. You couldn't delegate it. The final decision belonged to me only. You ceased to think; you couldn't sleep. The work didn't leave any time for friends—it victimized you. (S 1993)

Clearly, such pressure meant that intelligence work came to domi- nate an operative's life: "I worked all the time, with no real life outside or apart from my work. Even on those rare days off, I still lived, breathed, ate, and slept (when I could sleep) information collection" (S 1993). A DOI operative described his life in intelligence as "a horror" (Veja 1992, 30).

In fact, many agents kept their affiliation with DOI/CODI entirely secret from family and friends. And, in some cases, this identity was even kept hidden from their DOI/CODI colleagues: as a former intel- ligence operative explained, "we worked anonymously." Only the im- mediate head of your sector knew who you were; "you didn't even really know the [other] agent who [carried out] a mission" with you (J 1993). Although local authorities sometimes knew that an intelligence squad was on a mission in their area, just as often his squad "had mission[s] where we couldn't even identify ourselves to the [local] authorities" (J 1993). This imperative for secrecy made one former DOI operative feel "trapped, . . . without friends [and unable] to even unburden myself to [my] wife"; this operative spent "many nights without sleep," feeling completely controlled by his job (*Veja* 1992, 30).

The adult daughter of a former Militarized Police sergeant who be- came a DOI agent described the changes in her father: he joined his state's Militarized Police in 1963; during the twelve years of his regular police work, she remembers him returning home enthusiastic about his work—the police rounds and patrols, his own "heroic deeds." But all this changed dramatically after 1975 when her father joined DOI/CODI— he had to assume a false name and identity, and he switched cars almost daily. His domination by his work in the service of repression had wide consequences for both his professional behavior and his personal iden- tity. His daughter noticed that her father experienced a "profound per- sonal[ity] change." He was obsessed with capturing left-wingers, warn- ing the family "not to speak against the [Brazilian] Government [for fear of] becoming a communist." He took frequent trips out of Brazil, particularly to Paraguay, Argentina, and Chile—Brazil's Southern Cone politically repressive, military-run allies (*JB,* 1985, 17). In the end, what stands out most is both the man's transformation into a "true believer" and his anonymity in work and life. This DOI operative's personal identity was so dominated by what became his secret master status that it came to eclipse and obliterate all other former and parallel identities.

DOI agents' incorporation of their role as repressers was fostered by the use of disguises. The DOI hunt, assault, and murder squads often wore face hoods during an operation. Many DOI/CODI agents also took to wearing hairpieces and fake or even real beards: a former intelligence operative reported that when he began working in intelligence, he let his beard and hair grow to ensure that on missions he "was seldom identified or perceived as being a policeman" (J 1993).

DOI agents also disguised themselves by their clothing. A former DOI agent said that when he reported in his Militarized Police uniform for his first day of DOI/CODI duty, his superiors "looked [me] over, from top to bottom and said, 'Look, you don't need that [uniform] here. Leave, spend three days at home and come back without having shaved, don't get any more haircuts and forget that you've ever put a uniform on. From now on no uniform, . . . just civilian clothes'" (G 1993). On the other hand, to avert public suspicion that it was DOI/CODI that was arresting someone, the operative might sometimes wear an army or Militarized Police uniform so that people would think that the agent was from one of these other security or police units, not from DOI/CODI. Such tactics could further confuse the relationships among these agencies, at least in the public's mind.

DOI/CODI teams almost always hooded their captives. A former DOI operative explained that

the operation lasted [only] a minute. They invaded the house with lightning speed and came out with the people already wearing hoods. They'd put the hood on, handcuff them. The people wouldn't even know where they were being taken. (G 1993)

One former intelligence operative described this DOI technique as "hooding [suspects] with a blanket and throwing them in a car" (*JB* 1985, 17).

For high-profile arrests during the day, where a hood might call undue attention to the action and identities of the security forces, a DOI team might place what appeared to be regular sunglasses on captives—except that the captives' vision would be totally blocked so that they could not see at all. Yet anyone seeing the captive driven away in an unmarked car presumably would not suspect that the victim was in DOI custody (G 1973).

To confuse captives and observers, and to protect their own identities during a murder raid, the members of at least one Rio DOI squad referred to each other by a single code name: "On a raid, we're [all] just

'Pompeu,'" an ambiguous first name after the Roman city buried by Vesuvius, the volcano: "No one could identify us." This meant that "everybody's life—each one's personality—[was tightly] identified [with the group]," explained the DOI/CODI agent. This ensured that the group not only was anonymous but acted in concert. According to him, individuality "can represent a risk to your life: if I'm not comfortable around you, you're not comfortable around me, and we become targets" for dissension, and for getting shot by suspects in the raids, and even, it was feared, for leftist subversion (G 1993).

Thus, to ensure that the organization's secrets were well guarded, DOI/CODI enforced secrecy, fostered invisibility, and encouraged anonymity in its operatives. One intelligence agent explained that disguises made it seem "safer to act. I felt more security, because the moment that I showed myself openly, . . . I would . . . run . . . the risk [of being discovered]" (J 1993). The team members' use of the same given name during missions certainly encouraged their sense of depending solely on each other and their blending of personal identities. DOI work had fostered role engulfment.

Institutional Repression

By the end of the 1960s, torture and murder by Brazilian security forces not only had increased but also had been institutionalized as national central government policy (Cava 1970). By the early 1970s, torture and assassination had become regular instruments used by state officers. According to conservative estimates, between 1969 and 1974 alone, at least 1,558 Brazilians were tortured by police and military during interrogation (BNM 1986, 79), and this number includes only the known political prisoners and no common criminals. According to Alves (1985, 125), political torture was so prevalent in Brazil between 1969 and 1974—and stories of institutional violence were so much a part of everyday life—that "it was difficult to meet a Brazilian who had not come into direct or indirect contact with a torture victim or [witnessed] . . . a [violent] search-and-arrest operation," particularly in the more wealthy adjacent center-south states of Rio, São Paulo, and Minas Gerais. As for Brazilians summarily eliminated, it was estimated that between the 1964 military golpe and 1971 at least 3,000 Brazilians had been murdered or "disappeared" (*Veja* 1983, 47).

The regular use of torture and the threat of murder for extracting information and securing confessions and compliance involved institutionalizing this violence for transforming citizens' relationships with an exclusionist authoritarian state. Given the importance of institutionalizing torture and murder for strengthening Brazil's authoritarian state, let us look at how this regularization evolved. One sign that torture had become a bureaucratized, rationalized instrument of national policy, according to Cava (1970), was that torture was increasingly used not merely to seek information about "subversives" but to quash opposition to the government by any outspoken citizens.

In modernizing repression, torturers and their victims had become increasingly separated from one another. For example, the geladeira holding box kept victims and torturers from face-to-face contact—both had become depersonalized, mere instruments in the state's deindividualizing, impersonal system of social control. And torture techniques were "no longer limited to beatings, pistol whippings, clubbings and the spontaneous violences of individual police anger and sadism"; rather, the newer techniques had become "increasingly . . . sophisticated and complicated and . . . required . . . considerable personnel and organization for . . . implementation" (Cava 1970, 139), in other words, requiring professionalized training and management.

A further sign that torture had become institutionalized was the diffusion of torture techniques and technologies throughout a network of internal security agencies, so that by the end of the 1960s, identical torture techniques were being "employed in different parts of the country, [with] . . . the greatest similarity . . . in the . . . Southern triangle of Guanabara [Rio City], São Paulo, and Minas Gerais" (Cava 1970, 139). The elaborate geladeira, the *mesa de operação*—a diabolical body-stretching "operating table"—and associated technologies had spread throughout Brazil, even though particularly the geladeira was costly and difficult to install, suggesting linkages between local torture centers and Brazilian national and international sources of financial support and institutional involvement (Alves 1985).

Clearly one sign that such institutionalizing of torture was occurring was the creation of the nationally interconnected DOI/CODI internal security zones, with squads that crossed local jurisdictional boundaries and with their specialized torture centers linked to one another nationally. Because a national security region's DOI could be assigned to search-and-capture missions outside its particular DOI/CODI region, security agents from different regions, who previously would not have interacted with one another, increasingly met each other traveling widely in pursuit of terrorists and subversives. In the process, they spread information about torture techniques and technologies and developed interconnecting regional, national, and international ties with one another.

Institutionalizing Torture: The U.S. Role

That these developments normalizing and nationalizing extreme state violence in Brazil served more than just Brazil's national interests is indicated by significant U.S. training, technology, and moral and political support for a police and government involved in torture, disappearances, and murder. The United States not only did not denounce such violence but actively collaborated with police and military known by Washington to be engaging in these abuses of power. In addition to Washington's long-standing relationship with Brazil's DOPS political police, both before and after OPS was established, OPS-Brazil itself had close working relations with Rio de Janeiro's Grupo de Operações Especiais (GOE) and with São Paulo's RUDI, RONE, DEIC, and OBAN—each of which in turn spun off informal death squads of their own. And we have seen that OPS in fact encouraged the establishment of DOI/CODI, whose interrogation facilities were sites of unspeakable brutality.

Among torture technologies, electric shock was commonly used by Brazilian security forces, sometimes by means of USAID field radios, supplied supposedly to keep economic development teams in touch. Langguth (1978, 125) argues that when Brazilian intelligence officers began using field telephones to administer electric shocks, it was U.S. agents who informed them of the levels the human body could withstand. Some of the most gruesome tortures involved a joining of Brazilian ingenuity and U.S.-supplied technology, as with the "Bom Brill"— a Brazilian brand name for a "Brillo"-like metallic scouring pad. This torture involved inserting a Bom Brill into a woman's vagina, hooking a field radio wire to the metal pad, and turning on the electric current. In the victim's sensitive vagina, the mixture of electricity and human moisture produced excruciating pain.

Yet although such atrocities were being spread by the institutionalizing of state violence, OPS-Brazil continued to encourage the military government to pass repressive legislation and enthusiastically sup-

ported "no-nonsense" leaders and other forms of authoritarian government. OPS-Brazil did not urge cutting off or limiting assistance to a
government that was regimenting organized politics, suppressing citizen protest, and subjecting its citizens to systematic violence, torture,
and murder.

OPS Instrumentalism

Brazilian OPS public safety advisors approached their work with a kind
of religious mission, as "true believers" who equated social turmoil with
Communism and saw force as a legitimate method for eliminating Brazilian disorder. Their ultimate expressed goal was the security of the
United States and its democratic freedoms. Their commitment and
methodology in seeking this larger goal resembled the *wertrational* outlook described by Max Weber (1978): they saw their professional
methods and behavior—in this case, the use of whatever force necessary to control Brazilian internal resistance—as guided by moral goals,
and they overlooked any disparity their methods might display with
the wider objectives of democracy and freedom. OPS-Brazil felt that
the most appropriate and rational way to stabilize Brazil's social order
was for police—not the military—to prevent turmoil by all available
means before such conflicts could get beyond the control of the Brazilian state.

   But in fact when such arguments appeared in OPS memoranda in the
late 1960s, its discourse had already turned toward a kind of *zweckrational* instrumentalism (Weber 1978, 24), in which the strategies for
securing Brazil's social order had become ends in themselves. That is,
in the course of providing and legitimizing tools of repression, OPS
had come to see implementing its social-control methods as a goal in itself. Accordingly, all that counted for OPS was instrumental progress:
modernized police organization, improved intelligence gathering, upgraded investigative and control technologies, and more efficient interrogation practices. Using these instruments had assumed the status of
an absolute value, Weber's *zwekrationalität.*

   Pointing to the consequences of such instrumentalism, Weber argued
that "the more unconditionally the actor devotes himself to . . . [a] value
for its own sake, . . . the less is he influenced by considerations of the
consequences of his action" (Weber 1978, 26). OPS, therefore, was
quick to brush aside the undemocratic nature of the Brazilian govern-

ment's Fifth Institutional Act (IA-5) of 1969 (see chapter 8): OPS argued that there was "no evidence . . . that police officials [had] participated at the policy level [in] promulgation of the Institutional Act" (TOAID 1969a, 1). Maintaining that Brazilian police were merely carrying out correctly issued orders from bureaucratic superiors, OPS argued that Brazilian police in enforcing IA-5 were "restricted to carrying out government orders for the apprehension, arrest, and investigation of designated persons" (TOAID 1969a, 1). Apparently from the OPS point of view, this was a technically appropriate role for such police, even though after IA-5, as OPS-Brazil was fully aware, the police were even less constrained by U.S. standards of habeas corpus and other citizen protections.

OPS-Brazil's instrumentalist, zweckrational single-mindedness was a fragmented worldview that justified any undemocratic means to accomplish its narrow goals and kept potentially damaging information on their effects from seeping into its causal scheme. Accordingly, success for internal security came to be measured by the elimination of internal security "problems," especially those that could be measured numerically. To assess the status of Brazil's internal security, OPS used a social conflict "barometer" to judge the amount of force required to neutralize a given level of conflict. Toward the low-level end of this measure of conflict were the spread of crime and the eruption of protests, demonstrations, and strikes; the conflicts considered middle range were the outbreak of riots, guerrilla warfare, and terrorism; the most serious manifestation of conflict was full-scale revolution. Each level of conflict called for a different mix of security force action according to these OPS guidelines. At the conflict barometer's low end, police should be the sole security actors because according to the Office of Public Safety's second director, Loren ("Jack") Goin, "It is politically costly to have soldiers do this kind of law enforcement." For controlling middle-range conflict, OPS called for an interface between police and military, such that "police pass the baton to the military" to stabilize a situation, and "the police take over again when conditions are secure." On the other hand, Goin argued that the military should be the preeminent force in suppressing revolutions, the most extreme form of political turmoil (Goin 1985).

Accordingly, OPS reports in the late 1960s began to list the number of protests, strikes, bank and arms robberies, political kidnappings, and a range of other internal security "problems." The effectiveness of OPS-

Brazil's control strategies thus became measurable by proportional reductions in internal security threats, a methodology that linked social-control problems to their immediate suppression, by whatever means, blinding OPS-Brazil to the long-term and overarching consequences of its zweckrational instrumentalism. Indeed, during one of the periods of heightened state repression in Brazil, in early 1970, OPS-Brazil expressed concern only over the possible impact on Brazilian Federal Police morale of having to carry out the "onerous duty of censoring books and periodicals: The newly imposed requirement of review [i.e., censorship] . . . imposed a tremendous workload on the [Federal] Police, in a role for which they recognized their lack of qualification" (TOAID 1970c, 2). That such censorship hardly accorded with a democratic state evidently had no bearing on OPS-Brazil's concerns for what was going on in Brazil.

From Information Gathering to News Suppression

In fact, institutionalized torture could not have continued in Brazil—particularly when faced with mounting international condemnation—without enforced silence. This was promoted through a well-articulated network of relationships that included the torturers themselves; the medical doctors and psychiatrists who certified that a victim had not been tortured, or who even assisted in torture; the notaries and clerks who failed to record, or openly falsified, a victim's condition (OPS-Brazil had encouraged police to set up a "ticketing" system for certifying the conditions of those arrested); the government's higher officials who fostered, or shut their eyes to, torture; and U.S. and other foreign diplomats and technical specialists who, in order not to have their governments' image soiled through association with a torture complex, either acted as though torture did not exist, or explained it away, or helped to cover it up.

As OPS-Brazil was pooh-poohing the idea that death squad torture and murder were widespread in Brazil, OPS-Brazil reported in January 1970 that Justice Minister Buzaid's Commission on Human Rights had been ordered by military president Médici to drop any investigation or even any further mention of torture (TOAID 1970a, 5). The United States failed to decry this order or Brazilian press censorship, which helped to guarantee the relative invisibility of Brazil's torture complex and the anonymity of its perpetrators and victims. When OPS-Brazil reported that a group of Brazilian military officers had ordered all of Brazil's major news media to cease printing stories about police mistreatment of prisoners (TOAID 1970a, 5), the United States did nothing. Yet such suppression of news contributed directly to the strength and longevity of Brazil's state torture and murder complex.

On one of the rare occasions when OPS-Brazil gave some credence to the possibility that Brazilian security forces were engaged in widespread torture, OPS did so only to justify such activities as one of the by-products of "war." In one of its monthly reports from Brazil, OPS quoted approvingly a 1970 *London Financial Times* editorial that explained that "in a 'dirty war' like that between security forces and terrorists," accusations of mistreatment of prisoners are inevitable. The British newspaper had argued that the Brazilian government was "overwhelmingly supported in this war by the Brazilian people, who want to live in peace and safety" (TOAID 1970d, 2).

Admitting in 1971 that the Brazilian government's violence against terrorists "amounts to a 'holy war,'" the CIA director explained that such violence was "nothing new in Brazil," because, as he (Helms 1971, 22) saw it:

In some regions, particularly [in Brazil's] Northeast, violence is viewed as a traditional—and often quite respectable—means of punishment. In many rural areas, beatings and, in extreme cases, shootings by police and even local landowners have long been a favorite method for keeping the lower classes in line. . . . As long as such treatment does not result in any deaths, the rural populace remains indifferent.

But of course the military's new DOI/CODI was not a private militia under arbitrary and personalistic rural oligarchs: it represented a much more bureaucratic, "rational," and indeed "professional" approach to internal security management as an arm of the military—just what OPS-Brazil had argued for.

Sources of Bureaucratic Devolution: Specialization and Competition

DOI/CODI operatives were highly specialized tools in an internal security system kept humming by the constant and rapid flow of information; their victims were grist for the repressive system's ever more elaborate torture mill. Quite aside from murders to eliminate "malefaction" and frighten everyone else into submission, operatives above all displaced DOI/CODI official goals to favor repression for its own sake. At the same time, the combination of specialization, compartmentalization, and pressure on all security forces to make arrests, get confessions, collect intelligence, and eliminate "dangerous elements"—all carried out in a climate of total war against crime and internal subversion—exacerbated competition among security forces over who would get the credit for capturing and getting information out of the high-profile "subversives." Conflict arose directly from the transfer of some police responsibilities from Civil to Militarized Police, and vice versa, and from these police organizations to OBAN and then to DOI/CODI. Given the ubiquitous likelihood of overlapping services and functions, there was inherent potential for conflict and competition among regular police agencies and between them and DOI/CODI.

Thus extreme specialization and the instrumentalist pressure for results in DOI/CODI led to murderous interagency competition: each specialized internal security unit and organization had to justify its existence and protect its achievements vis-à-vis the others, as we have seen. The stakes were high, time was precious, and the system's rewards went to the units that most successfully and quickly sought, captured, and extracted information from, and eliminated, political subversives. This process led to devolution, as different parts of the internal security system were able to—and in fact had to—turn against each other. This was an important source for the gradual devolution of the security forces from official centralized control toward ever more autonomous torture and murder by informal death squads operating on their own.

Part of this devolution into independent terror squads' competition and conflict was generated simply by the overlapping of their jurisdictions. For example, as we have seen, DOI/CODI overlay existing state, municipal, and other locally controlled police systems, each with various police divisions and squads, thus exacerbating existing security force conflicts. In effect, despite a structure that so finely delineated the functions of different security forces, yet even this could not avoid causing conflict among them: the different security forces' jurisdictions were so narrowly defined that it was impossible for them not to violate one another's turf. And the extreme specialization and compartmentalization among police functions made it possible for each worker to instrumentalize his task as an end in itself, failing to see the wider consequences of his action while on the job.

A particularly dramatic example of such conflict occurred on March 1, 1970, in São Paulo, when a DOI/CODI team raided Delegado Sérgio Paranhos Fleury's São Paulo DOPS facility to "rescue" a DOPS prisoner, Shizuo Ozawa ("Mário Japa"), a Japanese Brazilian militant of the Vanguarda Popular Revolucionária (VPR) guerrilla group. DOI/CODI wanted to interrogate Ozawa in one of its own torture facilities, but Fleury had no intention of letting the high-profile militant whom his group had captured be questioned first by a DOI/CODI squad. In the tumult, knowing that Ozawa might be able to supply information that would help his own DOPS capture other important militants, Fleury ordered Ozawa to lie on the floor and jumped on Ozawa's chest, breaking several of his ribs. Fleury wanted Ozawa to be too injured for DOI/CODI to torture him for information if they snatched him away from DOPS (Fon 1986, 52).

In other words, the ever more widespread violence was not rooted merely in a psychology of "out-of-control" police personalities—although there were such people in all of these agencies, according to their own former members' interviews. Nor was the conflict between internal security organizations merely part of the long-standing interagency police competition for scarce resources, although this certainly was a basis for friction. For example, a former intelligence operative remembers that the military planted in the Brasília police training academy their own agents who had

joined the police without regard for the competitive examinations, or already knew the [answers to the] questions on the test. They would become part of our academy classes and, when the professor left the room, these military plants would work on your head and influence your opinion about the way things were and weren't. (K 1993)

This was a reference to the military's promoting the "national security" ideology. Clearly, the military wanted to be sure that its interpretation of events predominated among the police, which meant overriding civil rights and restraints.

More broadly, a former intelligence operative for SNI intelligence service revealed that "the regular police, even the civil police, were targets of the [military] revolution." This man reported that "there must have been thirty [spies] just like me in my city [Pôrto Alegre] who watched me also. Nobody knew [i.e., trusted] anybody else" (LO 1993). In fact, threats on his life came from other Brazilian security forces.

One former police intelligence agent in São Paulo explained that in the mid-1960s, while investigating "high-level smuggling, including guns and drugs, I got close to the aorta"—even the governor of the state and the state secretary of public security were suspected of being involved in this corruption. It was not long before the agent's life was threatened: "They even threatened to kill my daughter. And I found out that a 'friend' of mine was investigating me. You began not trusting your friends" (S 1993).

Brazil's bureaucratic-authoritarian internal security system, divided by specialized instrumentalism, encouraged by secrecy and subterfuge, and lured into competitive illegality and violence, succumbed over time to the politically negative effects of the dialectic between authoritarianizing centralization and the autonomizing, separating effect of specialization and secrecy.

Sources of Further Devolution: Commodification and Privatization

But beyond this deadly fractioning of the security forces, Brazilian journalist Hélio Gaspari (quoted in Weschler 1987, 86) argues that the violence and illegalities of the military's internal security system "poison[ed] the [whole social] system. A sort of gangrene set . . . in. [There was] an accumulation of peripheral debts contracted in clandestin[e work] which [could] only be rewarded illegally." As Weschler notes (1987, 86), Brazil's internal security "agencies working extralegally inevitably start behaving illegally as well. The torturers become smugglers and blackmailers and extortionists, and no one dares to stop them." As one former Civil Police official has said about the men in one of his police divisions who operated in his police district as a death squad, they

got hooked on drugs [and] no longer had the courage to cleanly execute a guy, so they'd do drugs whenever they'd go to kill someone. In time, they became friends with a gang of drug traffickers and [before long] they became bandits— more crooked than any other bandit in the world. (M 1993)

They were spinning out of control.

Yet this self-consuming police violence and illegality engendered in Brazil's bureaucratic-authoritarian state was not a deviant exception to an otherwise rational-legal internal control system—it was part of the system's operating logic. Devolution toward widespread competitive, uncoordinated, and mutually destructive violence and terror was clearly in part rooted in the military's spreading an unrestrained national security doctrine throughout Brazil's internal security system. So, in the end, the internal security system that had been restructured to coordinate and eliminate competition and conflict among security forces—through centralization, professionalization, elaboration of tasks, and specialization and compartmentalization of functions—in fact exacerbated old conflicts and created new ones and, in the process, led to the disintegration of centralized control over violence.

The Authoritarianizing-Devolution Dialectic: Informal Death Squads and the Military Government: A Case Study

As we have seen, two seemingly contradictory processes operated simultaneously in Brazil and became even more apparent after the Fifth International Act (IA-5), the period of heightened repression that began in 1969. That is, even as Brazil's internal security system was supposed to become more centrally controlled, formally interconnected, specialized, and compartmentalized, aspects of this system were becoming more decentralized—devolving toward debureaucratized and unofficial operation and control. A dramatic and measurable example of these complementary processes is the continued increase in death squads within and parallel to Brazil's official internal security system.

Most interesting was the response of the Brazilian military on discovering that Espirito Santo state's death squads were linked to the police. The military apparently felt they had to move against such death squads because they were answerable only to state Civil Police and the highest state officials. Such devolution could potentially dilute recently passed Law 667, under which all police forces were now directly subordinated to military officers. Police-linked death squads that were under the command of civilian officials of Espirito Santo state would undermine military authority. The military was particularly concerned that death squads might not report arms captured from criminals, diverting them—for profit—to "subversives," defined as anyone who did not cooperate with the military government (*Estado* 1977; Guimarães 1978).

The military began investigating Espirito Santo state's police system's devolution into death squads after three men in the Espirito Santo Civil Police disclosed that gangs of off-duty Espirito Santo Civil Police were not only selling arms, including those they stole, to nongovernment purchasers, but were also involved in car theft and falsification of identity documents. The Civil Police were also accused of engaging in torture and summary execution of captives they had seized, often burying their victims alive (*Estado* 1977; Guimarães 1978). The three police whistle-blowers charged that the state's death squad network included police chiefs and police rank and file from across the state, commanded by the military-appointed civilian governor, Cristiano Dias Lopes Filho, and his brother, State Secretary of Public Security José Dias Lopes. The latter was well known for being tough and mean—able to bring out the "dementia" of cruelty in his police subordinates (Guimarães 1978, 4).

Concerns of the military that this death squad network was getting out of hand must have risen still further when the military investigation ran into roadblocks because the state's highest officials were themselves involved. The governor appointed his own investigative commission— headed by the very man charged with directing the death squads—his brother José Dias Lopes. As secretary of public security and head of the State Civil Police, José Dias Lopes continued to deny any Civil Police involvement in death squads or any associated disappearances and murders. He quickly denounced the three police whistle-blowers, whose boss he was, accusing them of criminal activities and ordering their arrest.

In the meantime, the three policemen's depositions to the military investigative commission had located a cemetery they claimed contained bodies of death squad victims: of 240 people buried there between June and August 1969, the identity of 130 could not be determined from the cemetery records, suggesting that these bodies had been dumped into the hastily prepared graves. In previous three-month periods, the number of unidentified indigents interred in this cemetery had never exceeded fifty—little more than a third of those buried in the summer of 1969 (Guimarães 1978, 4). But the three accusing policemen, forced by death threats and by their own arrest to withdraw their original allegations, exchanged their retraction of all charges against José Dias Lopes for reduced prison time for themselves—having been indicted for involvement in a range of illegalities, including death squad murders.

Nevertheless, in the wake of the governor's severely compromised investigation, another state investigation was opened by an official not linked to the Dias Lopes family. This official found compelling evidence that Espirito Santo death squads were linked to the governor and the secretary of public security; the latter was eventually brought to trial in 1970. The three policemen who had denounced him for involvement in death squads again came forward. This time, with a reexamination of their prior evidence and protection against reprisals, they helped confirm that the statewide death squad network was indeed commanded by José Dias Lopes and supported by the governor. Nevertheless, despite the evidence against him, José Dias Lopes remained in his military-appointed office until the end of 1970; the military no longer supported his and the governor's removal, perhaps because the independent state investigation was also disclosing the military's own relationship to death squads.

Internationalizing Devolution: OPS and Death Squads in Espirito Santo

OPS advisors were already working closely with Espirito Santo state officials when OPS-Brazil stated in a carefully worded report in September 1969 that it had learned "on a confidential basis . . . [about] an on-going state and federal investigation into activities of another so-called 'death squad' operating in the [Espirito Santo] state . . . allegedly composed of police personnel and operating under orders of high police officials." The OPS Espirito Santo advisor expressed great relief that advance warning about the investigation of police involvement in the death squad network had enabled him to "avoid becoming involved in relationships that could have proven extremely embarrassing" (TOAID 1969i, 8).

Nevertheless, because the Espirito Santo death squad network was tied to the state's police establishment, this meant that the state's Civil Police—to which OPS was providing direct program assistance—was in fact at least indirectly linked to the death squads. In 1968 and 1969, OPS had provided Secretary of Public Security José Dias Lopes with police matériel and training support, which continued even after the Brazilian military's investigation of his Civil Police death squads had gotten under way. Indeed, OPS-Brazil reported as late as August 1969 that Dias Lopes "had been able to obtain the necessary [OPS] financial resources to substantially equip the [Espirito Santo] police with some modern transportation and VHF communications [facilities]." To ensure additional ongoing financial support for the state's Civil Police establishment, OPS-Brazil noted approvingly that the governor had had a law passed "imposing a police tax on commercial and industrial establishments, banks and public entertainment, to be earmarked for use by the police in obtaining needed equipment and facilities" (TOAID 1969i, 8). The Brazilian military government could certainly have seen this as state officials' attempting to create a source of police funding independent of central military oversight and control. If so, OPS-Brazil was not only assisting and encouraging businesses to support repressive police closely linked to death squads but also stimulating competition and conflict within the internal security system that it had helped set up, thus advancing the whole process of devolution.

Whether, in fact, OPS funding or matériel was diverted to death squads cannot be determined from the record. If they were, OPS was in interesting company for a "crime-fighting" program: In Espirito Santo's capital, Vitória, a number of illegal businesses—among them gambling and houses of prostitution—had funneled money into police coffers (Guimarães 1978, 4). Because in other states death squads were routinely supported directly but secretly by "legitimate" business and industry and their commercial associations (see chapter 8; for more details see Huggins and Mesquita, 1996a and 1996b; Huggins 1997), that may well have been the case in Espirito Santo, as well.

In any event, in mid-1969, just as ongoing official links to police death squads in Espirito Santo state were about to be reported to Washington, OPS-Washington had José Dias Lopes brought to the United States "for training." At the very least, a trip outside Brazil would have helped take the heat off this U.S.-linked police official, but more than that, it may have lent respectability to a police official who was under investigation by both a Brazilian military and a civilian state commission. In the United States, Dias Lopes first visited AID's International Police Academy, in June 1969. Then in July he spent time with the Michigan State Police (R. Johnson 1988).[3] Only in October 1970 did OPS-Brazil report the resignation of José Dias Lopes as secretary of public security, "in the wake of an exposé of alleged death squad activity in [Espirito Santo state]." According to the OPS-Brazil report, José Dias Lopes "steadfastly denied" any such involvement. But OPS-Brazil finally circumspectly admitted that Dias Lopes was "at least vulnerable to charges of being insufficiently aware of conditions allegedly involving police personnel" (TOAID 1970c, 12). However, OPS-Brazil claimed that no formal charges had been brought against José Dias Lopes—although in fact, they had—but admitted in any case that such

charges would follow installation of a new state governor after the elections among candidates controlled by the military. Just a month before
the November 1970 gubernatorial elections, the two Dias Lopeses, still
in office, were again denounced for involvement with death squad
murders—this time, the newly murdered bodies of eleven "marginals"
had been found (Guimarães 1978).

Yet it was neither these allegations nor the eventual trial of José Dias
Lopes that ultimately caused OPS-Brazil its greatest concern, that the
gubernatorial "elections" might "have a particular effect on the State
public safety organization" (TOAID 1970c, 12). That is, OPS might
have to reorient new public security officials toward its goals and priorities. A single-minded OPS focus on securing Brazil's "internal security" against "terrorists," "subversives," and crime had led OPS-Brazil
into support for the underbelly of the national security state it had
helped to create.

Goals of Internationalizing Police: OPS and CIA Response to Death Squads

In fact, that there was a symbiosis between the formal social-control
system and informal police-linked death squads was well known to
OPS-Brazil, as we have established (see chapters 7 and 8). Only in 1968
did OPS-Brazil in its monthly reports to Washington regularly began to
mention "death squads" explicitly. But then OPS-Brazil alternated between denying their existence and trying to justify them. At first,
throughout 1969 and the early 1970s, OPS-Brazil monthly reports still
evinced skepticism about a "death squad problem" in Brazil; to the
extent that these might exist, OPS continued to claim that few police
were involved in them. For example, in January 1969, OPS-Brazil cau-
tiously reported to Washington that a death squad in São Paulo was
"said to be composed of police personnel with the motive of eliminating known criminals without recourse to law" (TOAID 1969a, 6).

OPS-Brazil did acknowledge that São Paulo newspapers had been
reporting that just during January 1969, death squads had committed
more than thirty murders in São Paulo city, with victims' bodies showing signs of torture; in fact, OPS-Brazil reported that a number of São
Paulo police chiefs (Delegados) had asserted openly that their police
were involved in death squad murders (TOAID 1969c, 6). Assessing the
roots of São Paulo's death squads, one São Paulo state OPS advisor even

claimed that the death squads in his training region had been "inspired by the 'success' of the Rio squad" (TOAID 1969a, 6). By early 1970, an OPS advisor in Rio reported that the state's secretary of public security had told him that several of the city's police precincts had death squads with police from Guanabara (Rio City) and Rio de Janeiro state (TOAID 1970a, 6).

The most common OPS reaction to irrefutable information confirming the existence of death squads continued to be that these murder teams had a generally positive impact on Brazil's crime rate. For example, in late February 1968, OPS reported that São Paulo's secretary of public security had argued that in the wake of death squad assassinations, "a number of criminals have left . . . [São Paulo] City, and there has been a decrease in the crime rate" (TOAID 1969c, 6). In that same report, OPS quoted São Paulo state's top public security official as arguing that a gang of São Paulo bank robbers, "after hearing that they were on a death squad [hit] list," had transferred their operations to Paraná state farther south, apparently preferring "the risk of arrest in Paraná to that of murder [by death squads] in São Paulo" (TOAID 1969c, 5).

The CIA was another U.S. agency that knew Brazil's internal security system was penetrated by death squads: CIA director Helms explained in 1971 to a U.S. Senate subcommittee that Brazilian newspapers had reported that "since 1958, these squads, operating mainly in Rio de Janeiro and São Paulo, . . . [had] killed over one thousand persons allegedly involved in dope peddling, bookmaking, and other types of petty racketeering" (CFR 1971a, 27). Yet Helms did not think death squads had carried out "anti-terrorist killings"—apparently the CIA director's test for whether these murder teams were linked to political assassinations as part of the state's social-control system (CFR 1971a, 27). In any case, in mid-1970, the displeasure of OPS-Washington with OPS-Brazil's even occasionally mentioning newspaper reports of death squads surfaced when OPS-Brazil notified Washington that the "respected" *Jornal do Brasil* newspaper had charged police-related death squads over an eight-month period "with 150 executions . . . in São Paulo, and more than 100 in Rio de Janeiro": An unidentified Washington OPS official penciled in the report's margin, "Why does this [word] 'respected' keep cropping up[?]" (TOAID 1970d, 2), suggesting irritation at OPS-Brazil's lending any credence to newspaper accounts of police-linked death squads.

Nonetheless, Helms himself relied on a *Jornal do Brasil* public opinion poll showing that a majority of Brazilians surveyed considered death squads necessary. Helms (1971, 27–28) explained that "considering the very high petty crime rate [in Brazil,] many citizens may consider them [death squads] a public service." Besides, according to Helms, no Brazilian police official had yet been convicted of death squad crimes. Of course, if charges were ever brought against police officials, they were to be tried in military courts. Indeed, the military protected its subordinate police, except when they strayed too far from military control, as with the Espirito Santo death squad network.

Reprivatizing Social Control

As the conclusion's Afterword will argue, rather than the presence of police-linked death squads in Espirito Santo and elsewhere representing a temporary lapse in military control over the police system, they seemed to signal a controlled "reprivatization" (Shearing 1996) of policing. That is, the "machinery of policing and its control . . . [was shifting back] to political sub-centers" (Shearing 1996, 296) as the state began to act more invisibly through privatized, although police-linked, death squads. In the process, of course, the Brazilian military had to delegate some of its authority and control over internal security to decentralized extraofficial murder squads headed by local and state police and government officials. This they were willing and even eager to do, so long as such informal "vigilantes" promoted the national security state's "internal security" agenda and shielded it from domestic and international criticism of human rights violations.

Yet, as Tilly (1985, 173) pointed out for seventeenth- and eighteenth-century Europe, even "when demobilized, [such outlaws] commonly continue . . . the same [violent social-control] practices." And as Brazil has consistently demonstrated, once "reprivatization," that is, devolution, of social control gets under way, it inevitably assumes a life of its own as each locus of newly reprivatized social control and authority moves farther from the formal social-control system. This devolutionary spiral eventually undermined the whole U.S. Office of Public Safety foreign police training program, as chapter 10 will demonstrate.

10 Closing the Circle:
Devolution Abroad and at Home

By the early 1970s, pressure on Brazil's military government from international public opinion was mounting: reports were widely circulating that Brazil was detaining thousands of political prisoners, and the military, police, and their death squads were torturing and killing suspects. In 1969 the International Commission of Jurists, an organization of some fifty thousand jurists worldwide, had charged that up to twelve thousand people were being held for political reasons in Brazilian prisons and makeshift jails (BIB 1971). After 1969 the Office of Public Safety program in Brazil came under increasing U.S. public scrutiny. Condemnation of OPS came primarily from international nongovernmental human rights organizations, from churches, academics, and their professional organizations, and from political prisoners released from Brazil in exchange for kidnapped foreign ambassadors.

The U.S. media began to follow this rising criticism closely. A February 1970 *Washington Post* editorial (1970, A-14) asserted that there were "too many reports by too many reliable witnesses . . . about the torturing of 'subversives' for anyone to doubt that it goes on" in Brazil. *Look* magazine (Gross 1970, 70–71) published Frei Tito's chilling account of torture by Brazilian security forces. Jack Anderson and Joseph Spear began a series in their syndicated "Washington Merry-Go-Round" column disclosing CIA ties to OPS and denouncing the violence of OPS-supported foreign security forces generally. Anderson called for outright abolition of the OPS program.

In early 1970, Senator Frank Church (D-Id.) opened an investigation into United States policies and programs in Brazil by a subcommittee of the U.S. Senate Committee on Foreign Relations (CFR 1971a). With letters smuggled out of Brazilian jails, statements by political prisoners allowed to leave Brazil, and reports by courageous Brazilian journalists and religious workers, the committee accumulated a full dossier of grim affidavits about Brazilian security force and death squad violence, and about U.S. involvement with the unsavory practices of police and other internal security forces in Brazil.

CIA chief Helms apparently thought it helpful to testify at these hearings that estimates of the number of political prisoners in Brazil depended on the definition of "political prisoner." If this was defined only as someone who broadly criticizes "ideological components of the [Brazilian] government," then there were not "any significant numbers" of political prisoners in custody; but if "political prisoner" meant those who "advocate the violent overthrow of the [Brazilian] government and have engaged in subversive activity such as terrorism, or . . . assisted others who [have done] so," the Brazilian government says "approximately 500 are in jails" (CFR 1971a, 28).

There was considerable official U.S. reluctance even to discuss reports of torture in Brazil. CIA director Helms claimed at Senator Church's hearings that U.S. government inquiries into torture had been stalled because the Brazilian government's human rights commission—already referred to in OPS memoranda (see chapter 9)—had been ordered by the military in early 1970 to drop all investigation into torture. Helms, in any case, admitted that Brazil's "security forces are not beyond using torture, a practice some officials have privately justified in certain cases on [the] pragmatic grounds . . . that it has enabled [security forces] to get valuable information more quickly than any other method" (CFR 1971a, 23–24).

In this same hearing, Theodore Brown, the chief AID OPS police advisor for Brazil, told the committee that he did not believe torture was a big problem. Pressured by Senator Church for his reaction to reports of torture by Brazilian police, Brown excused himself on the grounds that he did not have the "right . . . to judge the Brazilian people or the police" (CFR 1971a, 18).

Brown did, however, have "some concern that the top management of both Federal and State levels of police organization . . . [were] Brazilian Army rather than career police." But this was only because such military commands suffered high turnover rates as officers made their career moves. However, Brown thought that his police advisors could continue collaborating with Brazil's public security officials, "barring development of a political disorientation of the Government . . . from a pro-West, pro-U.S. stance" (TOAID 1971b, 2). Clearly, all that mattered to OPS-Brazil chief Brown was an anti-Communist government, not the government's internal security practices nor its treatment of citizens. The application of pure realpolitik, leading to an explicit technical pragmatism such as Brown advanced, had in fact been admitted six years earlier by AID administrator David Bell, reporting to a U.S. Senate Appropriations Committee that OPS advisors had to work "in a lot of countries where the governments are controlled by people who have shortcomings." Bell had also conceded that "the popularity of the heads of state [varies] in all the countries [where AID is] working," but AID had to work with the situation at hand (FAA 1965, 82).

Closing Down OPS

But the end of AID's Office of Public Safety was approaching. There was mounting testimony in the U.S. media regarding torture and murder by foreign police recipients of OPS assistance. The Brazilian government's exiling of political prisoners to Mexico or Chile in exchange for kidnapped foreign ambassadors brought to light Brazilian security forces' brutal treatment of political prisoners. For example, the *New York Times* reported on January 16, 1971, that "many of the released prisoners, who arrived [in Chile] yesterday, showed recently healed scars, burns, and bruises on their bodies to support their charges of torture of political prisoners" by Brazilian security forces (Oniz 1971).

Growing negative publicity inside the United States was paralleled in Brazil and elsewhere in Latin America by religious and other human rights groups' disclosures of torture and murder by U.S.-assisted security forces. At the end of 1971, a well-known Brazilian figure, ZuZu Angel, fashion designer to the authoritarian state's political elite— among them Iolanda Costa e Silva, wife of Brazil's second military president—called attention to her government's pervasive human rights abuses through her own very public fashion shows. Although she was an unlikely candidate for such a political statement, her son, Stuart Angel Jones, had been "disappeared," and the government would provide no information about his whereabouts. It was generally believed in Brazil that he had been tortured and murdered by Brazilian security forces. His Canadian-born father was a naturalized U.S. citizen, and this drew attention to ZuZu Angel's protests inside the U.S. Her international reputation as a fashion designer (among her clients were actresses Joan Crawford and Kim Novak) added to her visibility (Valli 1986, 24).

For her spring 1972 fashion line, Senora Angel replaced her signature butterfly, flower, and bird prints, all in tropical colors, with a new darker line that included prints of military tanks, cannons firing at angels, imprisoned birds, and black doves flying over undernourished children. The line was presented at U.S. fashion shows, the most publicized at the New York Trade Bureau attended by the cream of New York society; the Mayor's daughter, Katty Lindsey, was one of Angel's models (Koifman 1986, 30).

Persistent reports in the U.S. press of torture and murder by U.S.-trained and -supervised South Vietnamese police added fuel to condemnations of OPS police assistance. Then, in the spring of 1973, the Costa Gavras film *State of Siege* was released in the United States. The film was a docudrama about police repression in military-ruled Uruguay, which had the largest concentration per capita of political prisoners in the world—an average of 1 for every 450 of its 2.5 million inhabitants (*Christian Century* 1976, 454). In dramatizing the Tupamaro guerrilla group's kidnapping, interrogation, and eventual murder of OPS advisor Mitrione, the film depicted U.S. involvement with the police of this militarized country. *State of Siege* provoked heated debate in the U.S. Congress over the nature of AID police training programs. According to Taylor Branch and John Marks (1975, 4), *State of Siege* had been banned in 1973 at the Washington, D.C., Joseph and Rose Kennedy Institute for the Study of Reproduction and Bio-Ethics "because of [the film's] political overtones": at the time, the Kennedy Institute was housed in the same D.C. Transit Building—the "old car barn"—as the OPS International Police Academy (IPA). *State of Siege* helped spread criticism of the International Police Academy and its parent organization, OPS.

Congress began to look into OPS operations. A 1970 report by the Senate's Subcommittee on Western Hemisphere Affairs argued that police aid to Guatemala and the Dominican Republic had pulled "the United States . . . into the bear trap by intervening to frustrate a process of social change (indirectly in Guatemala in 1954, openly in the Dominican Republic in 1965), and the trap has been becoming more painful ever since" (CFR 1971b, 1). In short, OPS assistance had contributed to fortifying repressive governments. In the case of Brazil, the two biggest annual OPS allocations were in 1963 to 1964 (just before and after the original military overthrow of the elected government) and again in 1969 to 1970, just after promulgation of IA-5 and the internal military coup that installed a military triumvirate as Brazil's presidency (Black 1977).

By 1971 questions about OPS foreign police assistance had moved well beyond the Brazil program, which had been a central focus of the 1970 Church hearings. Congressional critics had begun to ask if it was politically appropriate to train any foreign police and security forces at all. A U.S. Senate investigative team was dispatched in 1971 to Guatemala and the Dominican Republic. The team's conclusions regarding Guatemala were that after fourteen years of OPS assistance to Guatemalan police, "the teaching hasn't been absorbed [and] the U.S. is politically identified with police terrorism." The report went on to say that "the Guatemalan police operate without any effective political or judicial restraints. . . . How they use the equipment and techniques which are given them through the public safety program is quite beyond U.S. control." The Senate investigators were also concerned that although OPS advisors were not supposed to participate in operations with Guatemalan police, they had in fact "accompanied Guatemalan police on anti-hippie patrols . . . [and] in polygraph operations." The investigative team's conclusion was that "AID public safety [assistance] has cost the United States more in political terms than it has gained in improved Guatemalan police efficiency" (CFR 1971b, 6).

Clearly responding to these criticisms and the threats they posed to OPS, by mid-1971, when the Church Committee published its report on the OPS program in Brazil, OPS-Brazil had already been drastically scaled back. In fact, in 1972—claiming that it had achieved its objectives in Brazil—OPS was pulling its police training program out of Brazil altogether. However, between 1959 and 1972, OPS-Brazil had reportedly trained 100,000 Brazilian police and allocated more than $10 million—between $35 million and $45 million in 1998 U.S. dollars—toward Brazilian internal security assistance and technologies (Black 1977; Klare and Arnson 1981).[1] In its global police training program between 1962 and 1974, AID provided at least $337 million in equipment, training, and advisors to Third World police (Bruce 1988, 48). Such assistance was supposed to contribute directly to professionalizing the police; it had led in fact to internationalizing, centralizing, and authoritarianizing Brazilian and other Latin American police practices. These processes had also led to the devolution of Brazilian internal security measures. While fortifying Brazil's military government, OPS had fallen into a dialectic that contributed to the decentralization of its Brazilian recipients' operations and to OPS's own demise.

Consequently, the 1970 U.S. congressional hearings on U.S. policies and programs in Brazil held by Senator Frank Church's subcommittee turned out to be the beginning of the end, not just for the OPS-Brazil program, but for the Office of Public Safety's whole global police training initiative. In 1972 Senator J. William Fulbright offered an amendment to the 1973–1974 Senate Foreign Assistance Appropriations Bill that would cut off all funds for OPS, with the argument that,

Over the years . . . U.S. participation in the highly sensitive area of public safety and police training [has] unavoidably open[ed] the door to those who seek to identify the United States with every act of local police brutality or oppression in any country in which this program operates. (Congr. Rec. 1972, 2738)

The Fulbright amendment was killed in House and Senate appropriations debate: in 1972, the political climate was not quite ready for shutting down the OPS programs.

In fact, the final blow to the Office of Public Safety came one year later, in 1973 when newly elected Senator James Abourezk (D-N.Dak.) had OPS put on his political agenda. What had apparently sparked his interest in OPS was a visit to his office by former political prisoners from various countries; one told him "horrible stories" about police violence (Steeves 1976, 82–83). A Brazilian visitor told of brutality by police, arguing that "U.S. aid in the training of Brazilian police had caused despair among dissenters who had been jailed for political reasons." Having learned how "morally crushing [this was] for dissenters," Senator Abourezk proposed that "it might give the political prisoner some hope if someone in the Senate would speak out against . . . U.S. [police] aid" (*Washington Post* 1974).

Senator Abourezk's investigations soon disclosed to the media that OPS had provided assistance for South Vietnam's infamous "tiger cages," the brutal hanging or underground body-sized cages for holding prisoners (Excerpts [1974?]; see also *Hearings* 1973, 245–46; Exhibit D-1 [1981?]). In addition, Abourezk uncovered an OPS-CIA bomb-making school in Los Fresnos, Texas, that used International Police Academy and CIA instructors. According to Abourezk, "at least 165 foreign police officers [had] been taught the design, manufacture and potential uses of home-made bombs and incendiaries" (Abourezk 1974). The senator had also begun looking into charges that the CIA was teaching torture at the IPA (Abourezk 1974b). Armed with such information, Abourezk began his campaign to abolish all U.S. assistance to foreign police.

With pressure building to eliminate the entire OPS police program, CIA director William Colby wrote Senator Fulbright in July 1974 that Senator Abourezk's amendment "would adversely impact on the Central Intelligence Agency's relationships with foreign intelligence and internal security services and impair programs important to the [U.S.] national interest." In particular, the Abourezk amendment would "restrict activities now undertaken by the CIA . . . for the purpose of obtaining foreign intelligence information from cooperative foreign security and intelligence services" (Colby 1974, 1).

Obviously, in Colby's opinion, foreign police assistance had given the CIA an invaluable opportunity to obtain intelligence information. Indeed, by the end of 1975, the OPS program had "trained" more than one million police from all over the world and distributed more than $200 million (equivalent to between $700 million and $800 million in 1998 U.S. dollars) in arms and equipment to recipient police and paramilitary organizations (Klare and Arnson 1981). As an interesting economic sideline, OPS focused on getting foreign personnel "to need U.S. equipment by standardizing vehicles and electronic [police] gear, . . . requir[ing continued] purchases from the U.S. even after the [U.S.] Advisors leave" (Stork 1974, 68–69). In other words, one long-run consequence of technology assistance was to guarantee U.S. modes of social control and purchase of equipment from U.S. firms would operate well into the future. But Senator Abourezk's view remained that such assistance had made "repressive regimes even more repressive" (Lifschuts 1979, 121–22).

Closing the Circle

Meanwhile, the kind of devolution that OPS-Brazil was facilitating toward off-the-shelf police "extragovernality" was not taking place only in Brazil. Inside the United States, the FBI was carrying out its COINTELPRO operations—"a series of covert counterintelligence [surveillance and 'dirty tricks'] programs aimed at identifying, penetrating, and neutralizing subversive elements in the United States" (*Hearings* 1976, 676). At about the same time, the U.S. military was mounting an undercover (and on its face, illegal) domestic surveillance operation growing out of senior military officials' fears that "a true [domestic] insurgency" might emerge inside the United States if "external subversive forces develop[ed] successful control" of the antiwar and civil rights movements (*NYT* 1971). And the CIA, in clear contravention of U.S. law governing its operations, had begun assisting U.S. domestic police.

This state-run, extralegal secret intervention in politics was carried back into the international arena by President Richard M. Nixon's plans to destabilize Chile—resulting in the violent 1973 military overthrow and murder of democratically elected President Salvador Allende. According to CIA director Helms's testimony in 1975 before the U.S. House of Representatives Select Committee on Intelligence, President Nixon had told Helms—with Secretary of State Henry Kissinger and Attorney General John Mitchell present—that the CIA was to undertake the Chilean destabilization, despite what Helms claimed were the CIA's reservations about the plan's advisability. Nixon told Helms not to inform "the other members of the top-secret Forty Committee" of the Chilean destabilization plan. The 40 Committee was a select group of executive-level national security advisors above the National Security Council (NSC) who were charged with responsibility for passing on and approving not only CIA covert actions but also such undercover operations as the president himself deemed necessary—independent of any approval by Congress or the NSC (Helms 1969).[2]

As the *Village Voice* (see *Hearings* 1976) disclosed in early 1976 in its unprecedented publication of the House Select Committee's top secret intelligence hearings, leaked to the *Voice* by journalist Daniel Schorr:

Not all covert actions were generated by the CIA. In particular, paramilitary operations of the worst type seemed to come from outside the CIA. Some projects came from the President. Some projects came from his assistant for National Security Affairs, and some had their beginning in the Department of State. (*Hearings* 1976, 690)

According to former Under Secretary of State U. Alexis Johnson (1984, 347), "during the Nixon administration the President and the CIA [both] bypassed the [40] Committee on sensitive topics, notably the campaigns to 'destabilize' the regime of Chilean President Salvador Allende." The dialectic of ever more centralized yet privatized intervention, leading to secrecy and contributing to cover-ups and associated illegalities, again appeared domestically in 1972 when the "plumbers" of the Committee to Reelect President Richard M. Nixon, with White House encouragement, broke into National Democratic Party Headquarters at the Watergate Hotel.

However, such rogue quasi-government action was not without political consequences. The mounting domestic groundswell of opinion against both government intrusion into people's privacy and the illegal acts of breakaway government led to the elimination of official U.S. foreign police assistance. Indeed, congressional sentiment in favor of abolishing such foreign police assistance had become so strong by 1974 that the Office of Public Safety was the first government agency eliminated through bipartisan congressional action in the post–World War II period. OPS was dismantled in 1974 by the Gerald Ford administration, realizing that anything less than its total dismantling might lead to a full—and very embarrassing—investigation of all past OPS activities.

The elimination of OPS and its worldwide police assistance program was a by-product of devolving and privatizing internal security, a process that was occurring inside the United States itself and between the United States and recipients of OPS assistance, as well as in the countries receiving OPS assistance. The internationalizing of U.S. security through OPS police assistance, with its associated centralizing and authoritarianizing and subsequent devolution, had led to international denunciation of these visible and not so visible consequences and side effects of OPS intervention. In essence OPS-associated extralegality and violence—by generating ever broader sentiment against OPS police assistance and the necessity of covering up police atrocities—led to the OPS program's demise.

When new police assistance programs emerged again in the 1980s and 1990s under new ideological rationales—to counter terrorism and narcotics traffic—the new programs were made even more invisible than OPS operations had been by dispersing them throughout different government bureaucracies and in some cases by fully privatizing them, rather than placing them within a single special centralized bureaucratic agency. At the very least, some programs were given more covert bureaucratic auspices; even more commonly, they were contracted out to nongovernmental organizations and private individuals and groups. In the process, the new police assistance initiatives had become even less accountable to Congress—as demonstrated by U.S. negotiations with Iran in the mid-1980s and by the covert supply of arms to the Nicaraguan Contras, the breakaway off-the-shelf operations out of Colonel Oliver North's small White House office without U.S. congressional or even much executive control. Such operations brought U.S. foreign policy full circle, back to supporting with private funds a privatized militia run privately by government officials, as in the 1920s. International security operations were returning to the informal, personalistic decentralization that the whole police assistance initiative had been designed to supersede.

But were such consequences largely the unplanned and unanticipated results of U.S. training and matériel assistance to foreign police? Or were they part and parcel of the rational bureaucratizing associated with the necessary and planned devolution of authoritarian states? In his work on state building as a protection racket, Charles Tilly (1975) offers some insight on the evidence presented here, as the conclusion briefly demonstrates.

Conclusion:

Police Assistance as a "Protection Racket"

When one country trains another's police forces, some key issues are raised. First of all, the use of armed force by a modern state against any of its citizens is ordinarily defined as the legitimate and exclusive prerogative of the state. But when domestic police forces become a tool in international relations, the presumed monopoly becomes permeable. This study has focused on a situation in which police have been transformed into a security force beyond the national state's full control, in part by being used to promote the interests of another state, and partly by devolution of the state's powers of violence to extralegal forces. Can sociologists offer any understanding of this relationship?

In a discussion of the role of social control in state making, Charles Tilly suggests that the growth and elaboration of states has often involved the creation of a "protection racket": by providing protection from violence, a government builds up its capacity for control and hegemony. Going even further, Tilly declares that state makers are acting like self-seeking entrepreneurs who "create . . . a threat and then charge . . . for its reduction." A state-organized protection racket exists "to the extent that the threats against which a government protects its citizens are imaginary or are consequences of its own activities." Such "protection" often results in a consolidation of state control (Tilly 1985, 171).

Building on Tilly's argument, we can identify several steps in the creation of a state "protection racket." First, those offering protection develop a threat—whether real or constructed. In either case, the threat justifies their services. For example, Moore (1987, 110) argues that as states began to emerge in Western Europe, their rulers sought "to assert and extend their authority by creating . . . victimless crimes, offenses against abstractions such as 'the ruler,' 'the state,' 'society,' or 'morality.'" In fact, according to Moore, the transition from a traditional "segmentary society" to one governed by a state involves a shift from defining 'criminality' as an injury to specific individuals or groups to viewing it as an offense against an abstraction such as "the public interest" (Moore 1987, 110). At any rate, expanding the definition of dangers for subjects or citizens, and making it increasingly abstract, provides a justification for developing an apparatus to contain such perceived threats.

The induced need for social control thus in turn contributes to the second step in creating a protection racket—developing the machinery to control the socially constructed "evil." In the process of elaborating state repression, the "persecuting state" comes into being—legitimated by its success at protecting "good citizens" from "bad" ones. That is, successful repression is used to justify further repression, which in turn validates the state's further expanding its powers.

In any case, of course, "Governments are in the business of selling protection . . . whether people want it or not" (Tilly 1985, 175). Moore (1987, 146) explains that in Europe during the early Middle Ages, as one outcome of successful promotion of a state protection racket, "Persecution began as a weapon in the competition for political influence, and was turned by victors into an instrument for consolidating their power over society at large." Indeed, according to Frederic C. Lane, "the very activity of producing and controlling violence favor[s] monopoly. . . . The production of violence enjoy[s] large economies of scale" (Tilly 1985, 175).

In other words, organized repression increases centralization. But this has paradoxical and contrary results that can also undermine state central control and contribute to state deconstruction, as we have seen.

Police Assistance as Extortion

Among the state makers in our study of cross-national police assistance, we may count U.S. national security officials, who from the mid-1950s considered themselves as nation builders (chapters 5 and 6). These U.S. foreign policy "entrepreneurs" and associated Latin American political, diplomatic, and police officials can be thought of as part of a state-run protection racket. In offering assistance to Latin American police, the United States has been an international state-making entrepreneur promoting its interests through police training, a particular kind of protection racket that the United States sold to Latin America and other Third World client states after World War II.

We have seen that during the first three decades of the twentieth century the United States expanded the international reach of its capitalist state through "gunboat policing," using military force to promote and establish client constabularies in countries of the Caribbean and Central America crucial to U.S. political and economic interests. Gunboat diplomacy involved systematically neutralizing European competitors to U.S. hegemony in the region. In that period, U.S. armed forces often served as an occupying army, making less credible any claim of offering police assistance as protection against unacceptable change.

During the fifteen years from 1930 to the end of World War II, the United States adopted a more indirect approach to selling protection. As Latin America's Good Neighbor, the United States promoted strategies to ensure U.S. control without direct intervention, relying on contacts with indigenous police for intelligence. During this period, the United States seems to have suspended promotion of its direct control over Latin America, perhaps in part because of strongman rule in much of Latin America: national regimes were already effectively handling state-run "protection services" (see Stanley 1996). In any case, Latin American nationalists resisted overt U.S. intervention. But Shearing (1996, 287–88) explains that helping create a police intelligence apparatus, as the United States was quietly doing, makes a population more "transparent . . . [facilitating state] action at a distance," of which this was an early form for the United States.

What had been absent during the twentieth century's first four decades was an ideology justifying Latin American governments' giving over some internal security autonomy in exchange for protection by the United States. This ideology had begun to emerge just before World War II, legitimizing U.S. protection of Latin America from Nazi penetration through military assistance and FBI undercover espionage. But it took the Cold War containment ideology to effectively sell police assistance protection to Latin America. A threat to both the United States and Latin America was created out of a "deviant" political movement—"the Communist menace." This in turn justified outside expert national security assistance to combat it. In other words, the United States made a case for this specific danger and then was ready, at a price, to protect threatened countries through police as well as military assistance.

In the process, the protected became more subordinated to the protector: any country that could be convinced it was vulnerable to Communist penetration had to give up some independence in managing its own ability to protect itself in exchange for protection by its more powerful ally, the United States. As Tilly (1985, 175) has pointed out, "If a power holder . . . [is] to gain from . . . provid[ing] . . . protection, his competitors . . . [have] to yield." In this case, the assisted country's own security system and its political leaders were subordinated to U.S. political interests. But what kinds of specific arguments can be used to promote one country's subordination of another's internal security system?

We saw that the United States, in pushing its training of Latin American police to combat Communism, did so through an ideology that legitimized their loss of some autonomy over internal control in exchange for increased technical professionalism. The argument was that outside professionals know best how to help clients eliminate, stabilize, or rectify a problem or situation. As we have noted earlier (chapter 1), this helped transform the foreign-country recipients of U.S. professional police assistance into dependent clients who had to "respect the moral authority of those whose claim to power lay" in their specialized knowledge and skills; this belief, in turn, made foreign technical specialists relatively autonomous within the host country's internal security system (see Bledstein 1976, 100). Professionalism emancipated the technical expert who performed organized activities within specially delineated social spaces. Paradoxically, therefore, the ethos of professionalism had reduced the recipient government and its state to a position of vulnerability and helplessness. Such a dependent, subordinate relationship—founded as it is on a sense of emergency—elucidates one of the functions of the Cold War national security ideology: it explained the nature of the political threat and established a role for professionalized police in eliminating that threat.

Along the way, providing police assistance required the United States to build up and elaborate its own internal security machinery, as seen especially in chapters 5 and 6. Because doing so required new linkages between U.S. and recipient government security agencies, the police assistance protection racket ended up expanding and fortifying powerful elites in both protector and recipient nation states. So, as we have seen, in its relationship with these recipients of police assistance, the United States resembled a racketeer who creates a threat and then takes charge of its reduction (see Tilly 1985, 171). In effect, getting Latin American countries to accept and help finance police assistance ended up being a form of extortion: Latin American governments could either elect to accept U.S. police assistance, or else lose other forms of nonmilitary economic aid, or face much more politically and economically costly U.S. military assistance, or a U.S.-assisted military takeover (e.g., Cuba, Guatemala, Nicaragua), or even U.S. invasion (e.g., the Dominican Republic, Granada, Panama).

That police assistance was a far more invisible form of U.S. penetration into Latin American states than direct military assistance or violent intervention helped to legitimize the process. The relative invisibility of police assistance "protection" was therefore another basis for its appeal and power.

Paradoxes of Centralization: Devolving Protection

An international protection racket initially favored creating more centralized and increasingly authoritarian internal security systems in "endangered" countries. Yet over time the United States and associated recipient country elites came to see the political and economic value of mixing centralized and indirect forms of social control.

Indeed, devolution of control by centralized states has a long history in the West. According to Tilly (1985, 175), in eighteenth-century Europe, the "builders of national power all played a mixed strategy: eliminating, subjugating, dividing, conquering, cajoling, buying, as the occasions presented themselves." A ruler could not successfully control the population without assistance, even from competitors. Thus, "The managers of full-fledged [European] states often commissioned privateers, hired sometime-bandits to raid their enemies . . . , and encouraged their regular troops to take booty." When demobilized, such privateers and bandits "commonly continued the same practices, but without the same royal protection; demobilized ships became pirate vessels, demobilized troops, bandits" (Tilly 1985, 173).

In other words, the forces that had devolved from royal authority did not simply disappear once the authorities had finished with them. Of course, if the former state agents strayed too far from state control, they would undermine the state's own protection racket. Such a state would then be threatened with finding itself "the sorcerer no longer able to control the powers of the nether world he has called up by his spells" (Marx and Engels 1985, 68). Indeed, a state that covertly instigates and supports private, often vigilante, violence runs the risk of losing its claim to monopoly over the use of force (Huggins 1977) and becoming less hegemonous and legitimate in the process.

Yet organized states themselves still foster and encourage various forms of devolution from centrally controlled and legitimated violence. This use of informal vigilantism that is not state connected is not alone in spawning further devolution. Professionalization's insistence on specialized police activities seems paradoxically to lead to devolution (e.g., debureaucratization) as the activities of the professionalized, specialized, autonomous police agencies increasingly diverge from control by the centralized authorities and units that set them up (see Huggins 1977). At the very least, as the case study of Brazil has demonstrated, U.S.-assisted centralization, professionalization, and specialization of policing led to increasing conflict among the various specialized police divisions and units, and also between the new centralized authorities and the previously more localized police units and divisions. Both types of conflict certainly represent devolution from centralized control.

Indeed, Shearing (1996) has pointed out for modern social-control systems that "contemporary policing has become . . . increasingly fractured, embedded, and decentered." Such fracturing, which

applies not simply to the *mechanisms of central rule* but to the *loci of rule* itself, [results in] "subpolitical" [entities] . . . that exist within a legal and political space that is neither purely public [i.e., state] nor private. (Shearing 1996, 285–86, emphasis in original)

These "subpolitical" governing entities usually do not share a single center of control, operating through alliances that involve "state and non-state authorities [who] seek to manage each other . . . to produce effects that they regard as desirable" (Shearing 1996, 287), as with Brazil's Espirito Santo death squads.

Shearing (1996, 291) argues that for modern social-control systems:

This shift [toward decentralization] is not . . . a return to older feudal forms of rule at a distance [but is] a new formula in which governance is . . . accomplished through the operation of "loosely coupled" networks of institutions. Decentralization is rule by subcenters.

We have seen in Brazil that devolution of control, or "rule by subcenters," was easily spawned by a relatively centralized protection racket: even as the state centralizes its ability to provide protection, there necessarily is devolution toward a market of ever more distant competitors for carrying out repressive and "protective" roles. Therefore, it seems predictable that internationalizing and centralizing by U.S. police assistance would lead in the end to devolution from central control. The illusion of "action at a distance" created by such devolution— through which some kinds of social control come to be detached from direct state management—lowers the political costs of repression by refocusing national and international attention away from state violence. In Alves's words, death squads are "a less visible target for internal and international public opinion [because they] refocus . . . public attention and outrage" elsewhere (Alves 1985, 258).

Reprivatizing and Commodifying Policing

Within a devolving system, in turn, internal security and policing become perceived as commodities that "not only can be, but should be, bought and sold within a market" (Spitzer, quoted in Shearing 1996, 291). Policing becomes instrumentally defined as any activity that promotes someone's security, with "security" determined by who pays for it (Shearing 1996, 292; see also Shearing 1992). In other words, once social control becomes commodified, security and policing are transformed into customer-defined products. "Internal security" becomes a market product that requires "partial, not impartial, policing," and the objective of social control is "meeting the demands of the 'sovereign' consumer" (Shearing 1996, 292). This, in turn, helps to explain security force violence, for as Shearing (1996, 292) has pointed out:

Within the context of a mentality that sees policing as a commodity, the idea that policing should be undertaken by independent professionals answerable . . . to "the law and the law alone" makes little sense. From the standpoint of market sensibility, it is precisely this culture of independence, and the arrogance it encourages, that lies at the root of the failure of the political center and its police to provide its citizens with the security they require.

In other words, commodified security only breeds further insecurity and fosters the perceived need for an even stronger, more centralized protection racket to bring order out of internal security chaos. Thus the cycle begins again toward centralization, but with its inevitable reflex to devolution of authority.

Afterword

Rather than proposing a set of answers, this study has suggested a number of unsettling questions. Where does the dialectic of centralization and devolution end? Does the persecuting form, once institutionally in place, ever fully yield to a nonpersecuting state? Can a "protection racket state" be replaced by one based on popular political legitimacy? (see Stanley 1996, 258). Can older and emerging democratic states retain their democratic legitimacy while selling police protection? Can a world system founded on international "protection rackets" ever offer real international and internal security to citizens and nations? These pressing questions cry out for answers even as new democracies attempt to build popular legitimacy in place of authoritarian force and as old democracies come to terms with the extortion and coercion that has guided their relations with developing countries.

Appendixes

Appendix 1

Abbreviations and Acronyms: United States

AID/USAID	Agency for International Development
ATA	Anti-Terrorism Assistance Program of the United States State Department
C-I Group	Counter-Insurgency Group (JFK's cabinet-level Special Group for Counter Insurgency)
CIA	Central Intelligence Agency
COIAA	See IAA
COINTELPRO	Covert Counter-Intelligence Program of the FBI
DEA	United States Drug Enforcement Administration
FBI	Federal Bureau of Investigation
IACP	International Association of Chiefs of Police
IAPA	Inter-American Police Academy
ICA	International Cooperation Administration (predecessor to AID)
ICITAP	International Criminal Investigative Training Assistance Program of the United States Justice Department
IDA	Institute for Defense Analysis
IAA/IIAA/COIAA	Office of the Coordinator of Inter-American Affairs
INPOLSE	International Police Services, Inc.
IPA	International Police Academy
NSC	National Security Council
OCB	Operations Coordinating Board of the National Security Council
OIDP	Overseas Internal Defense Policy
OISP	Overseas Internal Security Program
OPS	Office of Public Safety
SIS	Special Intelligence Service of the FBI
USAID	See AID
USIA	United States Information Agency
USIS	United States Information Service (of USIA)

Appendix 2

Abbreviations and Acronyms: Brazil

ALN(ANL)	Aliança de Libertação Nacional (National Liberation Alliance)
ARENA	Aliança de Renovação Nacional (Alliance for National Renovation)
CBC	Cruzada Brasileira Anti-Communista
CENIMAR	Centro de Informações de Marinha (Naval Intelligence Center)
CIEX	Centro de Informações do Exército (Army Intelligence Center)
CODI	Centro de Defeza Interna (Internal Defense Operations Command Center)
DEIC	Departamento Estadual de Investigações Criminais (São Paulo Civil Police Criminal Investigations Division)
DFSP	Departamento Federal de Segurança Pública (Federal Department of Public Safety)
DOI	Departamento de Ordem Interna (Department of Internal Order)
DOPS	Departamento de Ordem Política e Social (Political and Social Police)
FEB	Força Expedicionária Brasileira (World War II Brazilian Expeditionary Forces)
GOE	Grupo de Operações Especiais (Special Operations Squad of the Rio de Janeiro Militarized Police)
IA	Ato Institucional (Institutional Act)
INI	Instituto Nacional de Identificação (National Institute of Identification)
IPM	Inquérito Polícial Militar (Militarized Police Inquiry)
MDB	Movimento Democrático Brasileiro (Brazilian Democratic Movement Party)
MNR	Movimento Nacionalista Revolucionário (Nationalist Revolutionary Movement Party)
MR-8	Movimento Revolucionário–8
OBAN	Operação Bandeirantes (Operation Bandeirantes)
RONE	Rondas Noturnas Especiais de Polícia Civil (São Paulo Civil Police Roving Night Patrols)
ROSA	Rondas do Setor de Assaltos (São Paulo Civil Police Roving Patrol Against Assaults)

RUDI	Rondas Unificadas do Departamento de Investigações (São Paulo Civil Police Night Rounds of the Criminal Investigations Department)
SESI	Serviço Social de Indústria (Industrial Social Service Organization)
SNI	Serviço Nacional de Informação (National Information Service)

Appendix 3

Some Predecessor Agencies to USAID

Institute of Inter-American Affairs (IIAA), 1942–1950
Economic Cooperation Administration (ECA), 4/3/48–10/31/51
Technical Cooperation Administration (TCA), 6/1/50–7/31/53
Mutual Security Agency (MSA), 11/1/51–7/31/53
Foreign Operations Administration (FOA), 8/1/53–6/30/55
International Cooperation Administration (ICA), 7/1/55–11/3/61
Agency for International Development (AID/USAID), 11/4/61

Source: Smith, 1997

Notes

Preface

1. These interviews were part of a study with Mika Haritos-Fatouros on Brazilian police torturers (see Huggins 1997, Huggins and Haritos-Fatouros 1996a, 1996b).

Chapter 1   Policing International Politics: Theory and Practice

1. I am indebted to Charles Call for suggesting from his own work on ICITAP how best to write about this new foreign police assistance initiative.

2. Of course, U.S. training of Latin American militaries themselves also contributed to the development of Latin American authoritarian states, as research by Stepan (1973), Black (1977), Lernoux (1980), and Crahan (1982) clearly demonstrates. U.S.-sponsored legal reform, underwritten in the 1960s by USAID, also helped restructure Latin American legal systems in various ways that supported authoritarian states (see Gardner 1980).

Chapter 2   "Gunboat" Policing: The First Twenty-five Years

1. Under "valorization," the Brazilian government was to guarantee São Paulo coffee export prices by using foreign loans to purchase surplus coffee from São Paulo planters. The coffee purchased in surplus years would be stockpiled and sold at higher prices abroad when coffee harvests were low. The taxes levied on coffee exports would be used to repay the foreign loans. Valorization could work only if the federal government was willing to manipulate the exchange rate for Brazilian currency to favor the state price for the coffee growers' surplus (Love 1980, 217).

Chapter 4   From Policing Espionage to Suppressing "Communism": World War II and Its Aftermath

1. Unable to pronounce or spell his Eastern European name, a U.S. immigration official had said, "make it Mills," recorded as "Make Mills" (Donner 1990, 49).

Chapter 5   Policing Containment

1. The Operations Coordinating Board (OCB) was established by Presidential Executive Order 10483 on September 2, 1953. As part of the National Security

Council structure, with membership at the under-Secretary level, OCB was charged with "coordination and development . . . of detailed operational plans to carry out [U.S.] national security policies" that had been approved by the president or by his National Security Council. OCB was also empowered under certain circumstances to "develop additional [national security] projects of its own . . . within the existing framework of national security policies" (Lay and Johnson 1960, 47–48).

Chapter 6   Counterinsurgency Policing: Internationalization and Professionalization

1. In a memorandum, McGeorge Bundy stated that a five-week course was to be repeated throughout the year in order to reach all middle- and senior-grade U.S. government civilian and military officers (U. A. Johnson, 1984).

2. OPS presumably justified training this military official at its police academy because, at the time, Brazil's police were subordinated to the military.

Chapter 7   Policing Brazil's "Cleanup"

1. In the late 1960s, São Paulo Civil Police had a number of divisions, including the Departamento Estadual de Investigações Criminais (DEIC).

2. While my interviewee from Brazil's SNI claims that Dan Mitrione was "with the CIA," Langguth's careful research (1978), including his interviews with several former CIA agents, suggests that Mitrione was not a CIA agent. Moreover, Philip Agee (1997) maintains that "Mitrione was definitely not CIA." It is very possible that, as Langguth argues, Mitrione was merely a "useful tool" for the CIA (Langguth 1997). The distinction between being an instrument of the CIA and a CIA agent could easily be overlooked by many Brazilians, who might consider Mitrione's informal affiliation with the CIA sufficient evidence of his being a CIA agent.

Chapter 9   Fortifying Security and Privatizing Repression: Torture and Death Squads in Authoritarian Devolution

1. On the original typed testimony obtained through FOIA, authorship is "sanitized" (i.e., blacked out) but is clearly three letters long. At other similarly sanitized locations in Helms's testimony, it is very clear that Helms is referring to his own agency, the CIA.

2. DOI/CODI is the acronym for Departamento de Ordem Interna/Centro de Defeza Interna (Information Operations Detachment/Center for Internal Defense Operations).

3. In the research for this book the AID Freedom of Information Act officer was asked to indicate, from a moderately long list of known and indicted Brazilian members of police death squads, any who the records revealed had received OPS training: the only person so identified was José Dias Lopes.

Chapter 10   Closing the Circle: Devolution Abroad and at Home

1. Brazil itself budgeted at least three times this amount to supplement OPS internal security assistance.

2. The top secret "40 Committee" had its origins in the Eisenhower-era "54-12 Committee," established by National Security Council Action Memorandum no. 12 in 1954. The 54-12 Committee was reconstituted in mid-1964 during the Lyndon Johnson administration and renamed the "303 Committee," referring to National Security Action Memorandum no. 303, which had created the commit-tee (NSAM 1964). This 303 Committee, also known as the "Special Group," had come into existence after the 54-12 Committee had been exposed in Daniel Wise and Thomas B. Ross's *The Invisible Government* (1964). The 54-12 and 303 Commit-tees were charged with "passing on or approving . . . the covert action operations of [the CIA], and beginning in 1961, approving reconnaissance activities . . . whoever might be conducting them" (Helms 1969, 20; see also U. A. Johnson 1984, 346). Such operations included the Pueblo Mission in North Korea (Helms 1969, 20), CIA training of Meo tribespeople in the mountains of Vietnam, and campaign contributions to anti-Communists in Italy (U. A. Johnson 1984, 347).

References

Abourezk, James. 1974a. Letter to J. William Fulbright, 29 July. James Abourezk Papers, Richardson Archives. I. D. Weeks Library. University of South Dakota, Vermilion.

——. 1974b. Notes on International Police Academy, 26 July. James Abourezk Papers, Richardson Archives. I. D. Weeks Library. University of South Dakota, Vermilion.

——. [1974?]a. Draft of letter to Senators John Stennis, John Sparkman, and Lucien Nedzi. Joseph Spear Files. Jack Anderson Organization, Washington, D.C.

——. [1974?]b. Draft of letter to President Richard Nixon. James Abourezk Papers, Richardson Archives. I. D. Weeks Library. University of South Dakota, Vermilion.

——. [1974?]c. Notes on U.S. Training of Foreign Police. James Abourezk Papers, Richard Archives. I. D. Weeks Library. University of South Dakota, Vermilion.

——. 1975. Letter to John Sparkman, chair, Senate Foreign Relations Committee, 8 January. James Abourezk Papers, Richardson Archives. I. D. Weeks Library. University of South Dakota, Vermilion.

——. 1986. Telephone interview by author, ca. October.

Agee, Philip. 1974. Interview by Joseph Spear. December. Joseph Spear Research Files, Jack Anderson Organization. Washington, D.C.

——. 1975. *Inside the Company: CIA Diary.* London: Penguin.

——. 1997. Fax to author. 7 October.

AID Assistance. 1969. AID Assistance to Civil Security Forces, 20 February. James Abourezk Papers, Richardson Archives. I. D. Weeks Library. University of South Dakota, Vermilion.

AID-PIOP. 1965. VIP Observation Tour, AID Police Training Requisition, 17 June. National Archives, PIOP, 512-070-50342/7-65. National Archives Branch Depository, Suitland, Md.

Alencar, Frei Tito de. 1969. Letter from a Brazilian Jail, March. James Abourezk Papers, Richardson Archives. I. D. Weeks Library. University of South Dakota, Vermilion.

Alves, Maria Helena Moreira. 1985. *State and Opposition in Military Brazil.* Austin: University of Texas Press.

American Embassy. 1951. Request for Police "Fellowships." Airgram from American Embassy, Rio de Janeiro, to Secretary of State, 23 October. National Archives, Washington, D.C.

American Intelligence Service Report. 1943, 1 August. National Archives, State Department Division, 832.105/75. Washington, D.C.

Americas Watch. 1988. Closing the Space: Human Rights in Guatemala. *Americas Watch Report.* New York: Americas Watch.

Amory, Robert. 1966. Interview by Joseph E. O'Connor, 9 and 17 February. Oral History, John F. Kennedy Library. Boston, Mass.

Andersen, Martin Edwin. 1993. International Administration of Justice: The New American Security Frontier. *SAIS Review* 13 (winter/spring).

Aranha, Oswaldo. 1938. Letter to Cordell Hull, 3 November. Fundação Getúlio Vargas Archives, OA, 38.11.03/11. Rio de Janeiro, Brazil.

Arendt, Hannah. 1951. *The Origins of Totalitarianism*. New York: Harcourt Brace.

Arévalo, Juan José. 1961. *The Shark and the Sardines*. New York: Lyle Stuart.

Army Special Warfare. 1962. Observations and Suggestions Bearing upon Improvement of Counter-Insurgency Capability. U.S. Army Special Warfare Center, Fort Bragg, N.C., 26 February. John F. Kennedy Library, NSF 211-220. Boston, Mass.

Arnold, Edwin H. 1958. World View Review of Public Safety Programs (FY 59-60). Confidential Memorandum to Mr. J. H. Smith Jr., 12 November. FOIA: USAID, AID/OPA.

Asbury, Herbert. 1990. *The Gangs of New York*. New York: Paragon House.

Barr, Richard M. 1951. Memorandum to Herbert Cerwin, 20 August. National Archives, State Department Division, Mandatory Review NND832414. Washington, D.C.

Bayley, David M. 1990. *Patterns of Policing: A Comparative International Analysis*. New Brunswick, N.J.: Rutgers University Press.

——. 1991. *Forces of Order: Policing Modern Japan*. Berkeley and Los Angeles: University of California Press.

——. 1993. What's in a Uniform? A Comparative View of Police-Military Relations in Latin America. Unpublished paper.

——, ed. 1977. *Police and Society*. Beverly Hills, Calif.: Sage.

Beck, L. C. 1942. Memorandum for Mr. Holloman, 21 April. FOIA: BUFILE 67-159998, sec. 1. FBI, Washington, D.C.

Bell, David. 1964. The Role of AID in Development and Internal Defense. Speech, 4 March. David Bell Papers, Box 25, John F. Kennedy Library. Boston, Mass.

Berle, A. A. 1939. Letter to Sumner Welles, 18 October. National Archives, Old State Department Division, 821-105/73. Washington, D.C.

——. 1945. Memorandum no. 2832 from U.S. Embassy, Rio de Janeiro, to Secretary of State, 17 September. Franklin D. Roosevelt Library. Hyde Park, N.Y.

(BIB) *Brazilian Information Bulletin*. 1971. American Friends of Brazil, February. Berkeley, Calif.

Bird, Don C. 1943. Possibility of Placing an Agent in the Police Department at Pôrto Alegre, Brazil. Memorandum for Mr. Carson, 10 April. FOIA: BUFILE 64-29833-205-8. FBI, Washington, D.C.

Birr, Kendall, and Merle E. Curti. 1954. *Prelude to Point Four: American Technical Missions Overseas*. Madison: University of Wisconsin Press.

Black, Jan Knippers. 1977. *United States Penetration of Brazil*. Philadelphia: University of Pennsylvania Press.

Bledstein, Burton J. 1976. *The Culture of Professionalism: The Middle Class and the Development of Higher Education in America.* New York: Norton.

(BNM) Archdiocese of São Paulo. 1986. *Torture in Brazil.* New York: Vintage.

Bourdieu, Pierre. 1977. *Outline of a Theory of Practice.* New York: Cambridge University Press.

Bowles, Chester. 1961a. Counter-Subversion Training for Latin American Police Forces. Memorandum for President John F. Kennedy. John F. Kennedy Library, NSAM File 333. Boston, Mass.

———. 1961b. Letter to President John F. Kennedy, 30 September. John F. Kennedy Library, National Security File 328. Boston, Mass.

Braddock, Daniel M. 1943. Establishing of Federal Political Police. Political Report no. 70, from American Consul in Pôrto Alegre to Jefferson Caffrey, U.S. Ambassador, Rio de Janeiro, 6 May. National Archives, State Department Division, 832-105/72. Washington, D.C.

Braden, Spruille. 1939a. Confidential letter from American ambassador, Bogotá, Colombia, to Secretary of State, no. 123, 22 May. National Archives, Old State Department Division. Washington, D.C.

———. 1939b. American ambassador, Bogotá, Colombia, to Secretary of State, 25 July. National Archives, Old State Department Division, 821.105/61 LDG. Washington, D.C.

———. 1939c. Telegram from U.S. ambassador, Bogotá, Colombia, to Secretary of State, 3 August. National Archives, Old State Department Division. Washington, D.C.

Bradley, W. J. 1943a. Police Liaison Work in Brazil. Bradley to FBI, 11 December. FOIA: BUFILE 64-29833-205-62. FBI, Washington, D.C.

———. 1943b. Re: Police School Liaison, Rio de Janeiro. Bradley to FBI, 14 December. FOIA: BUFILE 64-29833-205-63. FBI, Washington, D.C.

Branch, Taylor. 1988. *Parting the Waters: America in the King Years, 1954–1963.* New York: Simon and Schuster.

Branch, Taylor, and John Marks. 1975. "Tracking the CIA: Training the World's Police. Acting on INPOLSE, Your Intrepid Reporters Stalk the CIA and Hit Paydirt," *Harpers' Weekly* 64, no. 3109 (24 January): 144–45.

Brown, H. W. 1920. Telegram to director of U.S. Military Intelligence, Washington, D.C., 1 March. National Archives, Old State Department Division. Washington, D.C.

Bruce, Robert H. 1988. Human Rights and U.S. Training of Third World Police. *Conflict Quarterly* 8, no. 1: 48–60.

Bundy, McGeorge. 1962. Training Objectives for Counter-Insurgency, 14 June. National Archives, State Department Division. Washington, D.C.

Caffrey, Jefferson. 1942. Telegram to Secretary of State, 25 July. National Archives, State Department Division, 832.105/46. Washington, D.C.

Cain, Maureen. 1979. Trends in the Sociology of Police Work. *International Journal of the Sociology of Law* 7:143–67.

Call, Charles. 1997. Police Aid and the New World Disorder: Institutional Learning within the U.S. International Criminal Investigative Training Assistance Program (ICITAP). In *Policing the New World Disorder: Peace Operations and the Public Security Function,* edited by Robert Oakley and Michael Dziedzic. Washington, D.C.: National Defense University.

Cancelli, Elizabeth. 1993. *O Mundo da Violência: A Polícia da Era Vargas.* Brasília, D.F.: Editora Universidade de Brasília.

Capanema, G. 1933. Letter to Marc Bischoff, 15 August. Fundação Getúlio Vargas Archives, GC, 30.11.26, eII-38. Rio de Janeiro, Brazil.

Cardoso, Fernando Henrique. 1978. On the Characterisation of Authoritarian Regimes in Latin America. Working Papers, Series no. 30, Centre of Latin American Studies, Cambridge University, U.K.

Carson, C. H. 1945. Police Liaison, Rio de Janeiro, Brazil. Memorandum to D. M. Ladd, FBI, 24 May. FOIA: BUFILE 64-29833-205258. FBI, Washington, D.C.

Carter, Calvin B. 1927. The Kentucky Feud in Nicaragua: Why Civil War Has Become Her National Sport. *World's Work* 54 (July): 312–21.

Cava, Ralph della. 1970. Torture in Brazil. *Commonwealth,* 24 April. 135–41.

(CCAA1). 1922–1923. Conference on Central American Affairs. General Treaty of Peace and Amity Approved by the Conference on Central American Affairs. Washington, D.C.: Pan American Union Treaty Series.

(CCAA2). 1922–1923. Conference on Central American Affairs. The Conference on Central American Affairs held in Washington, D.C., from December 4, 1923 to February 7, 1923. New York: American Association for International Conciliation.

Cerwin, Herbert. 1952. Anti-Communist Activity in Brazil. Memorandum no. 1614 from counselor of U.S. Embassy, Rio de Janeiro, to State Department, 28 March. Franklin D. Roosevelt Library, no. 832414-7. Hyde Park, N.Y.

(CFA) Committee on Foreign Affairs. 1963. Castro-Communist Subversion in the Western Hemisphere. Hearings before Subcommittee on Inter-American Affairs of U.S. House of Representatives, 88th Congress, 18–28 February and 4, 5, 6 March. Washington, D.C.: U.S. Government Printing Office.

———. 1964. U.S. House of Representatives, Hearings on Foreign Assistance Appropriations, HR 118:2. Washington, D.C.: U.S. Government Printing Office.

(CFR) Committee on Foreign Relations. 1964. Individual Views of Senator Wayne Morse. U.S. Senate, Foreign Assistance Act of 1964. Washington, D.C.: U.S. Government Printing Office.

———. 1971a. United States Policies and Programs in Brazil. Hearings before the U.S. Senate Subcommittee on Western Hemisphere Affairs, 5 May. Washington, D.C.: U.S. Government Printing Office.

———. 1971b. Guatemala and the Dominican Republic, 30 December. Washington, D.C.: U.S. Government Printing Office.

Chase, Gordon. 1964. Deterrence of Latin American Dictators. Memorandum to McGeorge Bundy, 19 March. Lyndon Baines Johnson Library, NSF, Latin Agency Box 1. Austin, Texas.

Chevigny, Paul. 1995. *Edge of the Knife: Police Violence in the Americas*. New York: New Press.

Christian Century. 1976. Tyranny in Uruguay, May 12.

(CI-AA) Coordinator of Inter-American Affairs. 1947. History of the Office of the Coordinator of Inter-American Affairs. Historical Records on War Administration. Washington, D.C.: U.S. Government Printing Office.

Clegg, Heber M. 1945. Police Liaison: Foreign Miscellaneous, Police Matters. Memorandum to FBI, 12 July. FOIA: BUFILE 64-29833-205276. FBI, Washington, D.C.

Colby, W. E. 1974. Letter to Senator J. William Fulbright, 31 July. James Abourezk Papers, Richardson Archives. I. D. Weeks Library. University of South Dakota, Vermilion.

Collier, David. 1979. *The New Authoritarianism in Latin America*. Princeton, N.J.: Princeton University Press.

Colligan, D. 1976. The New Science of Torture. *Science Digest,* July.

Congressional Record. 1972. U.S. Senate, 92nd Congress. *Congressional Record Proceedings,* 118.

Crahan, Margaret E., ed. 1982. *Human Rights and Basic Needs in the Americas*. Washington, D.C.: Georgetown University Press.

Crenshaw, R. P. [1955?]. U.S. Internal Security Activities in Honduras and El Salvador. OCB Memorandum to Mr. Dearborn. Dwight D. Eisenhower Library, OSANSA, OCB, Box 3. Abilene, Kans.

Daland, Robert T. 1971. Letter to Senator Frank Church, 19 March. Frank Church Archives. Idaho State University, Boise, Idaho.

Dallari, Dalmo de Abreu. 1976. The *Força Pública* of São Paulo in State and National Politics. In *Perspectives on Armed Politics in Brazil*, edited by Henry H. Keith and Robert A. Hayes. Tempe, Ariz.: Center for Latin American Studies, Arizona State University.

(DAR) Division of American Republics. 1944. Information concerning Revolutionary Movements in Brazil. Division of American Republics—Analyses and Liaison, 22 August. National Archives, State Department Division 832.00/8/22/44/ Washington, D.C.

Darvall, Frank O. 1969. *Popular Disturbances and Public Order in Regency England*. New York: Augustus M. Kelley Publishers.

Dassen, Joan. 1986. The Culture of Fear. *Social Science Research Council Items* 40, no. 1 (March).

Davidson, C. R. 1945. SA Rolf L. Larson. Secret FBI Memorandum to Mr. Callahan, 12 August. FOIA: BUFILE 67-159998, sec. 5. FBI, Washington, D.C.

Dawson, William. 1936. Report to Under Secretary of State Sumner Welles from U.S. Legation, Bogotá, Colombia, 24 February. National Archives, Old State Department. Washington, D.C.

Diederich, Bernard, and Al Burt. 1969. *Papa Doc: The Truth about Haiti Today*. New York: Avon.

Dixon, Marlene, and Susanne Jonas. 1983. *Revolution and Intervention in Central America*. San Francisco: Synthesis.

Donner, Frank. 1990. *Protectors of Privilege: Red Squads and Police Repression in Urban America*. Berkeley and Los Angeles: University of California Press.

DOPS Record. 1941. 00001. Serviço Secreto Americano, 19 February. Records of the Departamento de Ordem Político e Social (DOPS) of the Civil Police of Rio de Janeiro, Arquivo Público do Rio de Janeiro, Niterói, Rio de Janeiro.

———. 1969a. 30-Z-1602294. Internal Memorandum, 6 October. Records of the Departamento de Ordem Político e Social (DOPS) of the Civil Police of São Paulo. Arquivo Público de São Paulo, Brazil.

———. 1969b. 30-Z-1606246. Frente Brasileira de Informações Pública (account of prisoner's testimony). Records of the Departamento de Ordem Político e Social (DOPS) of the Civil Police of São Paulo. Arquivo Público de São Paulo, Brazil.

———. 1969c. 50-Z-910210. São Paulo: Operação Bandeirantes, Central de Difusão. Contra Propaganda Anti-Terrorista. Proposta Para Ação Psychológica, September. Records of the Departamento de Ordem Político e Social (DOPS) of the Civil Police of São Paulo. Arquivo Público de São Paulo, Brazil.

———. 1974. 50-D-19280. Operação Bandeirante, Organização do CODI/II Ex. Memorandum by José Canavarro Pereira, 17 June. Records of the Departamento de Ordem Político e Social (DOPS) of the Civil Police of São Paulo. Arquivo Público de São Paulo, Brazil.

———. 1977. 50-K-6263. Depoimento de Aldo Avantes, 16 December. Records of the Departamento de Ordem Político e Social (DOPS) of the Civil Police of São Paulo. Arquivo Público de São Paulo, Brazil.

Draper Commission. 1959. Supplement to the Composite Report of the President's Committee to Study MAP (Annex), 17 August. Dwight D. Eisenhower Library. Abilene, Kans.

Duggan, Lawrence. 1936. Air mail letter to U.S. Ambassador Hugh Gibson, 6 March. National Archives, Old State Department Division. Washington, D.C.

Dulles, Allen. [1958?]. Pertinent Paragraphs from Letter to James Smith Concerning OISP Policy. [30 November?]. Dwight D. Eisenhower Library, 01412. Abilene, Kans.

Dulles, John W. 1978. *Castello Branco: The Making of a Brazilian President*. College Station: Texas A&M University Press.

Echandia, Alfonso Reyes. 1991. Legislation and National Security in Latin America. In *Vigilantism and the State in Modern Latin America: Essays on Extra-Legal Violence*, edited by Martha K. Huggins. New York: Praeger.

Embassy La Paz. 1964. Telegram from U.S. Embassy, La Paz, to Secretary of State, 24 February. John F. Kennedy Library. Boston, Mass.

Engelberg, Stephen. 1994. A Haitian Leader of Paramilitaries Was Paid by CIA. *New York Times*, 8 October, 1.

Engle, Byron. 1972. A.I.D. Assistance to Civil Security: The Office of Public Safety. *Police Chief*, May, 24–29.

———. 1985. Interview by author. Bethesda, Md. 15 September.

Enloe, Cynthia. 1975. Ethnicity and Militarization Factors Shaping the Roles of Police in Third World Nations. In *The Military, The Police, and Domestic Order: British and Third World Experiences,* edited by Cynthia H. Enloe and Ursula Semin-Panzer. London: Richardson Institute for Conflict and Peace Research.

(Estado) O Estado de São Paulo. 1968. Polícia Já Não Oculta Crise, 26 July. *O Estado de São Paulo* Archives, São Paulo.

———. 1969. RUDI Não Moudou na Volta, 27 March. *O Estado de São Paulo* Archives, São Paulo.

———. 1977. Documentos Denunciam Esquadrão, 14 January. *O Estado de São Paulo* Archives, Pasta no. 51659. São Paulo.

Excerpts. [1974?]. Excerpts from Term Papers Written by Students at the International Police Academy. James Abourezk Papers, Richardson Archives. I. D. Weeks Library. University of South Dakota, Vermilion.

Exhibit D-1. [1981?]. *Saenz, Adolph, v.* Playboy *Enterprises, Inc., and Roger Morris.* United States District Court for the Northern District of Illinois Eastern Division. Records of Roger Morris, Document no. 81, C5723. Albuquerque, N.Mex.

Expedito Filho. 1992. A Lei da Barbárie. *Veja* (18 November).

F. 1993. Interview by author. Rio de Janeiro, 18 August.

(FAA) Foreign Assistance Appropriations. 1964. U.S. Senate Hearings on Foreign Assistance, 21 April. Washington, D.C.: U.S. Government Printing Office.

———. 1965. U.S. House of Representatives, HR 11812. Bell Papers, John F. Kennedy Library. Boston, Mass.

FBI. 1941. Coverage by the Special Intelligence Section of the FBI in the Western Hemisphere (Map), 12 November. National Archives, Washington, D.C.

Fenwick, Charles G. 1952. *International Law.* 4th ed. New York: Appleton-Century-Croft.

Ferdinand, Theodore N. 1967. The Criminal Patterns of Boston since 1849. *American Journal of Sociology* 73, no. 1 (July):84–99.

———. 1972. Politics, the Police, and Arresting Policies in Salem, Massachusetts since the Civil War. *Social Problems* 19, no. 4 (spring):572–88.

Ferguson, Kathy. 1984. *The Feminist Case against Bureaucracy.* Philadelphia: Temple University Press.

Fernandes, Heloisa Rodrigues. 1974. *Política e Segurança.* São Paulo: Editora Alfa-Omega.

Fishman, Mark. 1977. Crime Waves as Ideology. *Social Problems* 25:531–43.

Fleming, E. C. 1931. Reorganizing and Improvement of Police Forces of the Capital. U.S. military attaché (G-2) in Brazil to U.S. State Department, 2 December. National Archives, Old State Department Branch, 2001-178. Washington, D.C.

Flynn, Peter. 1978. *Brazil: A Political Analysis.* Boulder, Colo.: Westview Press.

(FOA/IIAA) Foreign Operations Administration/Institute of Inter-American Affairs. 1954. Confidential Report, U.S. Operations Mission, Brazil, 4 January. Minutes of the 25th Meeting of the Technical Cooperation Program, 21 December 1953. National Archives, 361.3 FOA/IIAA, Box 16. Washington, D.C.

Fogelson, Robert M. 1977. *Big-City Police.* Cambridge, Mass.: Harvard University Press.

(*Folha*) *Folha de São Paulo.* 1979. Os desaparecidos, uma questão que vai persistir, 28 January, 1st Caderno.

Fon, Antonio Carlos. 1986. *A Tortura: A História da Repressão Política no Brasil.* São Paulo: Editora Global.

Fontoura, João Neves da. [1938?]. Memorandum. 1938–1939 Series. Fundação Getúlio Vargas Archives, OA-38/08/25/3. Rio de Janeiro, Brazil.

Foxworth, P. E. 1941. Re: Rolf Lamport Larson, Special Agent. Memorandum for FBI Director, 10 September. FOIA: BUFILE 67-159998, sec. 1. FBI, Washington, D.C.

(FRUS) 1923. *Papers Relating to the Foreign Relations of the United States.* Vol. II. Washington, D.C.: U.S. Government Printing Office.

———. 1925. *Papers Relating to the Foreign Relations of the United States.* Vol. II. Washington, D.C.: U.S. Government Printing Office.

G. 1993. Interview by author. Rio de Janeiro, 20 August.

G-2 Report. 1933. Status of Minas Gerais State Military Police. Memorandum from William Sackville, U.S. military attaché in Brazil, 6 October. National Archives, Old State Department Division, 832.105/7. Washington, D.C.

———. 1936a. Brazil—Popular and Social Conditions, Subject: Police System; Brazil's First Police Convention, Report no. 1725. Lawrence C. Mitchell, U.S. military attaché in Brazil, 22 October. National Archives, Old State Department Division, 832-105/19LH. Washington, D.C.

———. 1936b. Military Missions: Italian Mission to Bolivia and Ecuador, 2257-E-65. G. H. Paine, U.S. military attaché in Rome, 2 December. National Archives, Old State Department Division. Washington, D.C.

———. 1940. Brazilian Secret Police. Report no. 2501 from Edwin L. Sibert, U.S. military attaché in Rio de Janeiro, 11 November. National Archives, Military Affairs Division, 2006-102-10. Washington, D.C.

———. 1941. Report from Lt. Col. Gilbert Procter, U.S. military attaché in Ecuador, 20 June. National Archives, State Department Division. Washington, D.C.

Gannon, C. A. 1943. Possibility of Liaison with São Paulo Police. Memorandum for Mr. Carson, FBI, 2 April. FOIA: BUFILE 64-29833-205-7. FBI, Washington, D.C.

(GAO) U.S. Government Accounting Office. 1976. Stopping U.S. Assistance to Foreign Police and Prisons. Comptroller General's Report to the Congress. Washington, D.C.: U.S. Government Printing Office.

———. 1992. Foreign Aid: Police Training and Assistance. Report to Congressional Requestors, March. Washington, D.C.: U.S. Government Printing Office.

Gardner, James A. 1980. *Legal Imperialism: American Lawyers and Foreign Aid in Latin America.* Madison: University of Wisconsin Press.

Gibson, Hugh. 1935. Telegram from U.S. ambassador, Rio de Janeiro, to U.S. State Department, 28 December. National Archives, Old State Department Division. Washington, D.C.

———. 1936a. Telegram from U.S. ambassador, Rio de Janeiro to Secretary of State, 15 January. National Archives, Old State Department Division. Washington, D.C.

———. 1936b. Letter from U.S. ambassador, Rio de Janeiro, to Secretary of State, 23 January. National Archives, Old State Department Division. Washington, D.C.

———. 1936c. Letter from U.S. ambassador, Rio de Janeiro, to Lawrence Duggan, Department of State, 30 January. National Archives, Old State Department Division. Washington, D.C.

Gilderhus, Mark T. 1980. Pan-American Initiatives: The Wilson Presidency and Regional Integration, 1914–17. *Diplomatic History* 4, no. 4:409–23.

Gill, Peter. 1994. *Policing Politics: Security Intelligence and the Liberal Democratic State.* London: Frank Cass.

Gilpatric, Roswell. 1970. Oral History, 27 March. John F. Kennedy Library, Boston, Mass.

Goin, Lauren ("Jack"). 1985. Interview by author. North Arlington, Va., 7 August.

Goldstein, Robert J. 1978. *Political Repression in America: From 1870 to the Present.* New York: Schenkman.

Goldwert, Marvin. 1962. *The Constabulary in the Dominican Republic and Nicaragua.* Gainesville: University Press of Florida.

Gordon, George A. 1942. Personal and Confidential. Acting Chief of Foreign Activity Correlation to J. E. Hoover, FBI, 31 July. National Archives, State Department Division, 832.105/47. Washington, D.C.

Gordon, Lincoln. 1964a. Telegram from American embassy, Rio de Janeiro, to Secretary of State, 8 April. Lyndon Baines Johnson Library, Austin, Tex.

———. 1964b. Telegram from U.S. Ambassador, Rio de Janeiro, to Secretary of State, 9 April. Lyndon Baines Johnson Library, Austin, Tex.

———. 1964c. Telegram from American embassy, Rio de Janeiro, to Secretary of State, 10 April. Lyndon Baines Johnson Library, Austin, Tex.

———. 1964d. Telegram from American embassy, Rio de Janeiro, to Secretary of State, 19 April. Lyndon Baines Johnson Library, Austin, Tex.

———. 1964e. Telegram from American embassy, Rio de Janeiro, to Secretary of State, 6 July. Lyndon Baines Johnson Library, Austin, Tex.

———. 1964f. Telegram from American embassy, Rio de Janeiro, to Secretary of State, 22 July. Lyndon Baines Johnson Library, Austin, Tex.

———. 1965. Telegram from American embassy, Rio de Janeiro, to Secretary of State, 27 October. Lyndon Baines Johnson Library, Austin, Tex.

Greene, Winthrop S. 1936. Legation of the United States Communiqué no. 925. Chargé d'Affairs to U.S. State Department, 12 August. National Archives, Old State Department Branch. Washington, D.C.

Gross, Leonard. 1970. Brazil: Government by Torture. *Look*, 14 July, 70–71.

Gruson, Lindsey. 1989. Political Violence Sweeping Once Quiet Honduras. *New York Times*, 27 August, 14.

Guimarães, Ewerton Montenegro. 1978. *A Chancela do Crime.* Rio de Janeiro: Âmbito Cultural.

Gutman, Herbert G. 1961. Trouble on the Railroads in 1873–1874. *Labor History* 2, no. 2 (spring):215–35.

——. 1962. Reconstruction in Ohio: Negroes in the Hocking Valley Coal Mines in 1873–1874. *Labor History* 3, no. 3 (fall): 243–64.

——. 1968. Class, Status, and Community Power in Nineteenth-Century American Industrial Cities—Paterson, New Jersey. A Case Study. In *The Age of Industrialism in America: Essays in Social Studies and Cultural Values,* edited by F. Jaher. New York: Free Press.

Haines, Gerald. 1977. Under the Eagle's Wing: The Franklin Roosevelt Administration Forges an American Hemisphere. *Diplomatic History* 1, no. 4:373–88.

Haller, Mark H. 1976. Historical Roots of Police Behavior: Chicago, 1890–1925. *Law and Society Review* 10, no. 2:303–23.

Hamburger, Joseph. 1963. *James Mill and the Art of Revolution.* New Haven, Conn.: Yale University Press.

Harring, Sidney L. 1983. *Policing a Class Society: The Experience of American Cities, 1865–1915.* New Brunswick, N.J.: Rutgers University Press.

Harris, Richard N. 1961. *The Police Academy: An Inside View.* New York: Wiley.

Harrison, Mr. 1956. Implementation of 1290d Program—Bolivia. NSC letter from U/OP to Mr. King (ARA), 16 August. Dwight D. Eisenhower Library, Abilene, Kans.

Harvey, Matthew. 1974. Letter to Senator James Abourezk AID Assistant Administrator for Legal Affairs, 4 June. James Abourezk Papers, Richardson Archives. I. D. Weeks Library. University of South Dakota, Vermilion.

Hays, Samuel P. 1964. The Politics of Reform in Municipal Government in the Progressive Era. *Pacific Northwest Quarterly* 55, no. 4 (October):157–69.

——. 1965. The Social Analysis of American Political History, 1880–1920. *Political Science Quarterly* 80, no. 3 (September):373–94.

Hearings. 1973. *Hearings before the Committee on Foreign Relations,* U.S. Senate, 93d Congress, 1st Session. Foreign Economic Assistance, June. Washington, D.C.: U.S. Government Printing Office.

——. 1976. *Hearings before the Committee on Standards of Official Conduct,* House of Representatives, 94th Congress, 2d Session, July–September. Washington, D.C.: U.S. Government Printing Office.

Helms, Richard. 1969. Interview by Ted Gittinger, 4 April. Oral History, no. 2. Lyndon Baines Johnson Library, Austin, Tex.

——. 1971. Testimony to the Committee on Foreign Relations of the U.S. Senate. *U.S. Policies and Programs in Brazil,* 5 May. FOIA: Helms's testimony.

Herring, George. 1979. *America's Longest War.* New York: Knopf.

Hinckle, Warren. 1966. The University on the Make. *Ramparts Magazine* 4, no. 12 (April), 11–22.

Holdaway, Simon. 1977. Changes in Urban Policing. *British Journal of Sociology* 28, no. 2 (June):119–37.

Holloman, F. C. 1942. Memorandum for Mr. Ladd, re Rolf L. Larson, 6 April. FOIA: BUFILE 67-159998, sec. 1. FBI, Washington, D.C.

Holloway, Thomas H. 1993. *Policing Rio de Janerio: Repression and Resistance in a 19th-Century City.* Stanford, Calif.: Stanford University Press.

Hoover, Mr. 1952. Relative Size of Point 4 Country Programs. Handwritten supplement from ARA to Mr. Cook (IIAA), 28 April. National Archives, 720-5 MSP/4-2852. Washington, D.C.

Huggins, Martha. 1987. U.S. Training of Foreign Police Backfires. *Los Angeles Times,* 25 March, sec. 2, p. 5.

———. 1991. *Vigilantism and the State in Modern Latin America: Essays on Extra-legal Violence.* Westport, Conn.: Praeger.

———. 1992. Violência Institucionalizada e Democracia: Ligações Perigosas. Lecture at the Núcleo de Estudos da Violência, University of São Paulo, 21 November.

———. 1997. From Bureaucratic Consolidation to Structural Devolution: Police Death Squads in Brazil. *Policing and Society* 7, no. 4.

Huggins, Martha, and Myriam Mesquita. 1996a. Scapegoating Outsiders: The Murders of Street Youth in Modern Brazil. *Policing and Society* 5, no. 4:265–80.

———. 1996b. Exclusion, Civic Invisibility, and Impunity as Explanations for Youth Murders in Brazil. *Childhood: A Global Journal of Child Research* 3, no. 1 (February).

Huggins, Martha, and Mika Haritos-Fatouros. 1996a. Conciencia Torturada: Secretos e Moralidad en La Violencia Policial Brasileña. In *Justicia en La Calle: Ensayos Sobre la Policía en América Latina,* edited by Peter Waldmann. Medellín Colombia: Konrade Adenauer Stiftung, CIEDLA, ISLA, Biblioteca Juridica Diké.

———. 1996b. Tortured Consciousness: Secrets and Moralities in Brazilian Police Violence. Unpublished.

———. 1996c. Training Brazilian Police for Torture: A Study in Torture Moralities. Unpublished.

Hull, Cordell. 1939. Special Agent Edgar K. Thompson Sailing on 14 January. Telegram from Secretary of State to American ambassador, Rio de Janerio, 12 January. National Archives, State Department Division. Washington, D.C.

(IC) Intelligence Conference. 1940. Federal Bureau of Investigation Secret Memorandum, 3 June. National Archives, 9794-186, A-3. Washington, D.C.

ICA Report. 1957. Annual Status Report on Operations Pursuant to NSC Action 1290-d. International Cooperation Administration Report, 15 January. Dwight D. Eisenhower Library. Abilene, Kans.

IDA. 1959a. Studies for the President's Committee to Study the U.S. Military Assistance Program, Institute for Defense Analysis, 31 March. Dwight D. Eisenhower Library, President's Committee to Study MAP, Draper Commission, Box 11. Abilene, Kans.

———. 1959b. A Study of U.S. Military Assistance Programs in the Underdeveloped Areas, Final Report. Institute for Defense Analysis, 3 March. Dwight D. Eisenhower Library, President's Committee to Study MAP, Draper Commission, Box 11. Abilene, Kans.

(IPA) International Police Academy. [1974?]. Psychological Operations Course

Summary, Attachment 2. United States Army Institute for Military Assistance, Fort Bragg, N.C. James Abourezk Papers. Richardson Archives, I. D. Weeks Library. University of South Dakota, Vermilion.

(ISLE) Institute for the Study of Labor and Economic Crisis. 1975. *The Iron Fist and the Velvet Glove.* San Francisco: Crime and Social Justice Associates.

Isto É. 1978. Dossiê da Repressão, 27 September.

J. 1993. Interview by author. Brasília, 23 October.

(*JB*) *Jornal do Brasil.* 1974. Novo Diretor de DPF Vem da Escola de Informações e Já Esteve com Bandeira, 13 March, 1st Caderno. *Jornal do Brasil* Archives, Rio de Janerio.

———. 1985. Sargento do DOI Matou Colega antes de Desaparecer, 3 November, 1st Caderno. *Jornal do Brasil* Archives, Rio de Janerio.

Johnson, Bruce C. 1976. Taking Care of Labor: The Police in American Politics. *Theory and Society* 3, no. 1 (spring):89–117.

Johnson, Rhea. 1988. AID Freedom of Information Act officer. Telephone interview by author. 20 February.

Johnson, U. Alexis. 1984. *The Right Hand of Power.* Englewood Cliffs, N.J.: Prentice-Hall.

(*JT*) *Jornal da Tarde.* 1968a. 20 June. *Estado de São Paulo* Archives, No. 51654. São Paulo.

———. 1968b. 22 June. *Estado de São Paulo* Archives, São Paulo.

———. 1968c. Esquadrão da Morte Já Saiu para Matar, 12 July. *Estado de São Paulo* Archives, São Paulo.

———. 1968d. Polícia Pode Parar a Qualquer Momento, 15 July. *Estado de São Paulo* Archives, São Paulo.

———. 1968e. As Causas de Uma Velha Rivalidade, 22 July. *Estado de São Paulo* Archives, São Paulo.

———. 1968f. Os Federais Contra o Esquadrão, 9 December. *Estado de São Paulo* Archives, São Paulo.

K. 1993. Interview by author. Brasília, 22 October.

Kalmanowiecki, Laura. 1994. Military Power and Policing during the Justo Administration, 1932–1938. Paper presented at Latin American Studies Association Congress, Atlanta, Ga.

Kennan, George F. 1967. *Memoirs.* Boston, Mass.: Little, Brown.

Kennedy, Robert F. 1964. Speech to Graduates at the International Police Academy, Washington, D.C., 28 February. James Abourezk Papers. Richardson Archives, I. D. Weeks Library. University of South Dakota, Vermilion.

Klare, Michael T., and Cynthia Arnson. 1981. *Supplying Repression: U.S. Support for Authoritarian Regimes Abroad.* Washington, D.C.: Institute for Policy Studies.

Klare, Michael T., and Daniel Schechter. 1974. International Police Academy: The "State of Siege" Besieged. *The Real Paper,* 26 June.

Koifman, Henrique. 1986. Documento: Eu, ZuZu Angel, Procuro Meu Filho. *Manchete,* 8 November.

Komer, Robert. 1962a. Should Police Programs Be Transferred to DOD? Memorandum for McGeorge Bundy and General Taylor, 18 April. John F. Kennedy Library, NSF: Carl Kaysen, Box 37. Boston, Mass.

——. 1962b. Memorandum for the Record. Conversation on police programs with General Taylor, 23 April. John F. Kennedy Library, Boston, Mass.

Krajick, Kevin. 1981. Policing Dissent: The New Limits on Surveillance. *Police Magazine* 4 (September):6–11.

Ladd, D. M. 1942. Memorandum for the Director, 26 February. FOIA: BUFILE 67-159998, sec. 1. FBI, Washington, D.C.

LaFeber, Walter. 1983. *Inevitable Revolutions: The United States in Central America.* New York: Norton.

Lago, Henrique, and Ana Lagoa. 1979. A Repressão á Guerrilha Urbana no Brasil. *Folha de São Paulo,* 28 January, 1st Caderno, Nacional, 6.

Langguth, A. J. 1978. *Hidden Terrors.* New York: Pantheon.

——. 1997. Fax to Martha Huggins. 23 September.

Larson, R. L. 1941. Confidential letter, Com No. 2A, Rio de Janerio, to FBI, 18 November. FOIA: BUFILE 67-159998, sec. 1. FBI, Washington, D.C.

Lay, James, and Robert H. Johnson. 1960. An Organizational History of the National Security Council, 30 June. Dwight D. Eisenhower Library, White House Office of Special Assistant to National Security, Box 5. Abilene, Kans.

LeFever, Ernest. 1973. U.S. Public Safety Assistance: An Assessment, December. Prepared for U.S. Agency for International Development under contract CDS-3361. Washington, D.C.: Brookings Institution.

LeMoyne, James. 1986. Latin American Police Get Some Pointers from Washington. *New York Times,* 16 February, sec. 4.

Lernoux, Penny. 1980. *Cry of the People.* Garden City, N.Y.: Doubleday.

Levine, Robert M. 1970. *The Vargas Regime: The Critical Years, 1934–1938.* New York: Columbia University Press.

Lifschuts, Lawrence. 1979. *Bangladesh: The Unfinished Revolution.* London: Zed Press.

LO. 1993. Interview by author. Brasília, 11 and 17 October.

Lobe, Thomas David. 1975. U.S. Police Assistance for the Third World. Ph.D. diss., University of Michigan–Ann Arbor.

Love, Joseph L. 1980. *São Paulo in the Brazilian Federation: 1889–1937.* Stanford, Calif.: Stanford University Press.

Lugar, Richard. 1985. Securing Democracy in Central America. *New York Times,* Letter to the Editor, 25 December.

M. 1993. Interview by author. São Paulo, 5 and 11 August.

Madar, Julius. 1968. *Who's Who in the CIA.* Berlin: Julius Madar.

Maechling, Charles, Jr. 1986. Letter to Martha Huggins, 8 April.

——. 1988. Counter Insurgency: The First Ordeal by Fire. In *Low Intensity Warfare,* edited by Michael T. Klare and Peter Kornbluh. New York: Pantheon.

Malloy, James. 1977. *Authoritarianism and Corporatism in Latin America.* Pittsburgh, Pa.: University of Pittsburgh Press.

Malloy, James, and Mitchell A. Seligson, eds. 1987. *Authoritarians and Democrats: Regime Transition in Latin America.* Pittsburgh, Pa.: University of Pittsburgh Press.

Marchetti, Victor, and John D. Marks. 1974. *The CIA and the Cult of Intelligence.* New York: Knopf.

Marcondes, Julio Salgado (Cel). 1932. Letter to São Paulo Força Pública, 18 July. Fundação Getúlio Vargas Archives, GC/32.07.08, c, I-71. Rio de Janerio, Brazil.

Marks, John. 1976. The CIA's Corporate Shell Game. July. Washington, D.C. Center for National Security Studies.

Marx, Gary. 1988. *Undercover: Police Surveillance in America.* Berkeley and Los Angeles: University of California Press.

Marx, Karl, and Fredrich Engels. 1985. *The Communist Manifesto.* Bergenfield, N.J.: Penguin.

McCain, William D. 1937. *The United States and the Republic of Panama.* Durham, N.C.: Duke University Press.

McCann, Frank D., Jr. 1973. *The Brazilian-American Alliance.* Princeton, N.J.: Princeton University Press.

———. 1977. The Nation in Arms: Obligatory Military Service during the Old Republic. In *Essays Concerning the Socioeconomic History of Brazil and Portuguese India,* edited by D. Alden and W. Dean. Gainesville: University Press of Florida.

MEMCON. 1939. Loan of Special Agent of Federal Bureau of Investigation to Assist the Colombian Government. Memorandum of Conversation, FBI, 16 August. National Archives, Old State Department Division. Washington, D.C.

MEMCON. 1945. Reported Secret Agreement between Gestapo and Brazilian Police Authorities. Memorandum of Conversation, U.S. State Department, 11 September. National Archives, Old State Department Division. Washington, D.C.

Memo. 1957. Further Applications of the "New Look" to U.S. Defense Effort Overseas. Memorandum for the President, 19 June. Dwight D. Eisenhower Library, OSANSA, Special Assistant, Box 5. Abilene, Kans.

Miller, Wilbur R. 1975. Police Authority in London and New York City, 1830– 1870. *Journal of Social History* 11 (winter):81–101.

———. 1977. *Cops and Bobbies: Police Authority in New York and London, 1830–1870.* Chicago: University of Chicago Press.

Millett, Richard 1977. *Guardians of the Dynasty.* Maryknoll, N.Y.: Orbis.

Mingardi, Guaracy. 1991. *Tiras, Gansos, e Trutas: Cotidiano e Reforma na Polícia Civil.* São Paulo: Editora Scritta.

Monkkonen, Eric H. 1981. *Police in Urban America, 1860–1920.* Cambridge, U.K.: Cambridge University Press.

Moore, R. I. 1987. *The Formation of a Persecuting Society.* Oxford: Blackwell.

Morais, Fernando. 1985. *Olga.* São Paulo: Editora Alfa-Omega.

Morgan, Edwin. 1931. Brazilian Ambassador's Request for New York City Police Training. Foreign Service Dispatch no. 3593 from American Ambassador to State Department, 11 May. National Archives, Old State Department Division 832.105/7. Washington, D.C.

Morse, Wayne. 1964. Individual Views of Senator Wayne Morse. U.S. Senate, Committee on Foreign Relations, Foreign Assistance Act of 1964. Washington, D.C.: U.S. Government Printing Office.

Mosse, George L., ed. 1975. *Police Forces in History.* Beverly Hills, Calif.: Sage.

Munro, Dana G. 1964. *Intervention and Dollar Diplomacy in the Caribbean, 1900–1921.* Princeton, N.J.: Princeton University Press.

Nadelmann, Ethan Orram. 1993. *Cops Across Borders: The Internationalization of U.S. Criminal Law Enforcement.* University Park: Pennsylvania State University Press.

Nairn, Alan. 1994. Behind Haiti's Paramilitaries. *The Nation,* 24 October.

Nash. 1945. Subject: Felinto Muller. Attachment to Department of State Memorandum of 22 December. Cultural Affairs Officer to U.S. ambassador to Brazil, 1 October. National Archives, State Department Division. Washington, D.C.

Natal Consul. 1942. Cable to the State Department, 14 January. National Archives, Old State Department Division, 800.20232/118. Washington, D.C.

Neumann, William, Jr. 1947. *Recognition of Governments in the America.* Washington, D.C.: Foundation for Foreign Affairs.

New Yorker. 1988. The Talk of the Town, 4 April, 24–25.

NSAM. 1964. National Security Action Memorandum 303. National Security Council, 2 June. Dwight D. Eisenhower Library, NSC Files. Abilene, Kans.

NSC. 1954a. United States Objectives and Courses of Action with Respect to Southeast Asia. Special Annex to NSC 177 on National Security Council Debate, 1954. Dwight D. Eisenhower Library, National Security Paper. Abilene, Kans.

——. 1954b. Record of Actions by the National Security Council at Its 229th Meeting, December 21. Dwight D. Eisenhower Library, NSC Actions 1289-1292. Abilene, Kans.

NSCPP. 1955a. *National Security Council Policy Papers,* 3 February. Dwight D. Eisenhower Library, OSANSA, NSC, Policy Papers, Box 13. Abilene, Kans.

——. 1955b. *National Security Council Policy Papers,* 10 August. Dwight D. Eisenhower Library, OSANSA, NSC, Policy Papers, Box 13. Abilene, Kans.

(NYT) *New York Times.* 1971. Army in '68 Feared Civil Insurgency, 28 February, 1.

——. 1988a. America Shadowed by Death Squads, 22 January.

——. 1988b. Terrorism's Toll Rises in El Salvador, 20 December.

(OCB) Operations Coordinating Board. 1954. Project Report on U.S. Policy Toward the Philippines, 12 August. Dwight D. Eisenhower Library, OSANSA, NSC, Policy Papers. Abilene, Kans.

——. 1955a. Minutes of the Operations Coordinating Board, 6 June. Herbert Hoover Jr., chair. Dwight D. Eisenhower Library, WHO, NSC Staff, OCB Secretariat, Box 12. Abilene, Kans.

——. 1955b. Outline Plan of Operations for Brazil, 20 June. Dwight D. Eisenhower Library, Abilene, Kans.

——. 1955c. Report to the National Security Council Pursuant to NSC Action 1290-D, 23 November. Dwight D. Eisenhower Library, Abilene, Kansas.

——. 1957. U.S. Policies toward Latin America. *OCB Progress Report,* 11 September. Dwight D. Eisenhower Library, OSANSA, NSC Policy Papers, Box 12. Abilene, Kans.

——. [1957?]. Summary. Dwight D. Eisenhower Library, Abilene, Kans.

——. 1958a. Status of Mutual Security Programs as of June 30, 1958. *Report to the NSC,* 30 June. Dwight D. Eisenhower Library, WHO, Office of Special Assistant to National Security Affairs, NSC, Box 8. Abilene, Kans.

——. 1958b. Report to the NSC Pursuant to NSC Action 1290d, 23 November. Dwight D. Eisenhower Library, Abilene, Kans.

——. 1958c. U.S. Policy Toward Latin America (for the period 22 May 1958–26 November 1958), 26 November. Dwight D. Eisenhower Library, Abilene, Kans.

——. 1959a. Statement of U.S. Policy Toward Latin America, 16 February, NSC 5902. Dwight D. Eisenhower Library, WHO, Office of Special Assistant to National Security Affairs, NSC, 5902, Latin America, Box 8. Abilene, Kans.

——. 1959b. Report of the Ad Hoc Working Group in Connection with the Overseas Internal Security Program, 10 March. Dwight D. Eisenhower Library, Mandatory Review. Abilene, Kans.

——. 1959c. Memorandum for the Board Assistants, 25 March. Dwight D. Eisenhower Library, Abilene, Kans.

——. 1959d. Report of the Ad Hoc Working Group in Connection with the Overseas Internal Security Program, 27 March. Dwight D. Eisenhower Library, Mandatory Review. Abilene, Kans.

——. 1959e. Report in Connection with the Overseas Internal Security Program, 1 April. Dwight D. Eisenhower Library, Abilene, Kans.

——. 1959f. Public Safety Program for Brazil, 19 August. Dwight D. Eisenhower Library, Abilene, Kans.

O'Donnell, Guillermo. 1988. *Bureaucratic Authoritarianism: Argentina, 1966–1973.* Berkeley and Los Angeles: University of California Press.

Oniz, Juan de. 1971. 70 Prisoners Released by Brazilians Charge Torture, *New York Times* 16 January, sec. 1, 3.

(ONR) Office of Naval Research. 1969. Constabulary Capabilities for Low-Level Conflict. Report Prepared for the Office of Naval Research by M. Dean Havron, et al., April. Archives of the U.S. Naval War College.

PA. 1993. Pôrto Alegre Police Archivist. Civil Police Academy. Interview by author. Pôrto Alegre, Brazil, 6 November.

Packenham, Robert A. 1973. *Liberal America and the Third World.* Princeton, N.J.: Princeton University Press.

(PAP) Pôrto Alegre Police Archives. 1993. Site visit to Historical Archives of Pôrto Alegre Civil Police, Pôrto Alegre, Brazil, 6 November.

Parker, Phyllis R. 1979. *Brazil and the Quiet Intervention, 1964.* Austin: University of Texas Press.

Pauker, Guy J. 1959. Southeast Asia as a Problem Area in the Next Decade. *World Politics* 11, no. 3 (April).

Pieper, N. S. L. 1940. Report of an Interview with Applicant Rolf Lamport Larson, 5 August. FOIA: BUFILE 67-159998, sec. 1. FBI, Washington, D.C.

Pincus, Walter. 1994. FBI Expands Training of Police from Abroad. *Washington Post*, 14 December.

Pinheiro, Paulo Sergio. 1991. *Estratégias da Ilusão*. São Paulo: Companhia das Letras.

Platt, Anthony, and Lynn Cooper. 1974. *Policing America*. Englewood Cliffs, N.J.: Prentice-Hall.

Police Chief. 1955. Picture of Castillo Armas receiving IACP Award. *Police Chief* 21, no. 3 (March).

Police School. 1943. Re: Police School, Rio de Janerio, 16 April. FOIA: BUFILE 64-29833-205-16. FBI, Washington, D.C.

Raab, Selwyn. 1986. CIA Is Recruiting New York Police. *New York Times*, 27 October, A-1.

Rabe, Stephen G. 1988. *Eisenhower and Latin America: The Foreign Policy of Anti-Communism*. Chapel Hill: University of North Carolina Press.

Ranelagh, John. 1986. *The Agency: The Rise and Decline of the CIA*. New York: Simon and Schuster.

Reiss, Albert J., Jr. 1971. *The Police and the Public*. New Haven, Conn.: Yale University Press.

Rejali, Darius M. 1994. *Torture and Modernity: Self, Society, and State in Modern Iran*. Boulder, Colo.: Westview Press.

Richardson, James F. 1970. *The New York Police: Colonial Times to 1901*. New York: Oxford University Press.

———. 1974. *Urban Police in the United States*. Port Washington, N.Y.: Kennikat Press.

Rio de Janerio. 1951. Request for Police "Fellowships." Airgram from American Embassy, Rio de Janerio, to Secretary of State, 23 October. National Archives, Washington, D.C.

Robinson, Cyril D. 1978. The Deradicalization of the Policeman: A Historical Analysis. *Crime and Delinquency* 24, no. 2 (April):129–51.

Rockefeller, Nelson A. 1969. *The Rockefeller Report on the Americas: The Official Report of a Presidential Mission for the Western Hemisphere*. Chicago: Quadrangle Books.

Rodriguez, Enrique. 1981. Quatro Cientos Años de Policía en Buenos Aires. Buenos Aires: Political Biblioteca.

Rostow, W. W. 1960. *The Stages of Economic Growth*. New York: Cambridge University Press.

———. 1964. Interview by Richard Neustadt, 11 April. Oral History. John F. Kennedy Library, Boston, Mass.

———. 1965. Brazilian Politics, 1965–1966. Memorandum to Lyndon Baines Johnson, 30 November. Lyndon Baines Johnson Library, White House Executive file, FG 105, Box 133. Austin, Tex.

Rouquié, Alain. 1987. *The Military and the State in Latin America*. Los Angeles: University of California Press.

Rout, Leslie B., and John F. Bratzel. 1986. *The Shadow War*. Frederick, Md.: University Publications of America.

S. 1993. Interview by author. São Paulo, 5 August.

Saenz, Adolph. [1981?]. *Adolph Saenz, Plaintiff, v. Playboy Enterprises, Inc., and Roger*

Morris, Defendant. United States District Court for the Northern District of Illinois Eastern Division. Document No. 81, C5723. Personal records of Roger Morris, Albuquerque, N.Mex.

Saxe-Fernandez, Ivan. 1972. The Vietnamization of Latin America. *North American Congress on Latin America and Empire Report* 7, no. 5 (May–June).

Schmitter, Philippe. 1973. The "Portugalization" of Brazil. In *Authoritarian Brazil,* edited by Albert Stepan. New Haven, Conn.: Yale University Press.

Schurmann, Franz. 1974. *The Logic of World Power.* New York: Pantheon.

Scotten, R. 1938. Letter to Under Secretary of State Sumner Welles, 4 November. National Archives, Old State Department Division. Washington, D.C.

Shearing, Clifford. 1992. The Relation between Public and Private Policing. In *Modern Policing* 15, edited by Michael Tonry and Norvil Morris. Chicago: University of Chicago Press.

———. 1996. Reinventing Policing: Policing as Governance. In *Policing Change, Changing Police: International Perspectives,* edited by Otwin Marenin. New York: Garland.

Sheldon, Stan. [1979?]. Ambassador's Job. No Bed of Roses. Draft of an article. Personal records of Stan Sheldon, former OPS Advisor.

Silver, Allen. 1967. The Demand for Order in Civil Society: A Review of Some Themes in the History of Urban Crime, Police, and Riot. In *The Police: Six Sociological Essays,* edited by David J. Bordua. New York: Wiley.

Sixty-Ninth Congress. 1926. 69th Congress, 1st session. *U.S. Statutes at Large* 44, no. 2, chaps. 334–36:565.

Skolnick, Jerome H., and James J. Fyfe. 1993. *Above the Law.* New York: Free Press.

Skolnick, Jerome H., and Thomas C. Gray, eds. 1975. *Police in America.* Boston: Educational Associates.

Smith, J. H. 1958. Memorandum for the Honorable Allen Dulles, Director, Central Intelligence Agency, 28 November. Dwight D. Eisenhower Library, Abilene, Kans.

Smith, Willette L. 1997. Personal correspondence from acting chief, Office of Information Support Services, USAID, 3 March.

Snook, T. D. 1961. Report on IACP Police Assistance, January, 1955–August 31, 1962. Report dated January–September. International Association of Chiefs of Police Archives, Gaithersburg, Md.

Spear Files. [1974?]. Research notes of Joseph Spear, journalist, Jack Anderson Organization. Washington, D.C.

Spear, Joseph. 1987. Interview by author. Offices of Jack Anderson Organization, Washington, D.C., c. 15 February.

Spitzer, Steven, and Andrew T. Scull. 1977. Social Control in Historical Perspective: From Private to Public Responses to Crime. *Correction and Punishment,* edited by David F. Greenberg. Beverly Hills, Calif.: Sage.

Stanley, William. 1996. *The Protection Racket State.* Philadelphia: Temple University Press.

State Department Memorandum. 1931. Re: Brazilian Police Organization,

24 February. National Archives, Old State Department Division 832.105/6. Washington, D.C.

Statistical Abstract of the United States. 1943. Washington, D.C.: U.S. Government Printing Office.

Steeves, William D., Jr. 1976. The U.S. Public Safety Program: Its Evolution and Demise. M.A. thesis, George Washington University, Washington, D.C.

Stepan, Albert. 1973a. The New Professionalism of Internal Warfare and Military Role Expansion. In *Authoritarian Brazil.* New Haven, Conn.: Yale University Press.

———. 1973b. *Authoritarian Brazil.* New Haven, Conn.: Yale University Press.

Stork, Joe. 1974. World Cop: How America Builds the Global Police State. In *Policing America,* edited by A. Platt and L. Cooper. Englewood Cliffs, N.J.: Prentice-Hall.

Sugai, Shuichi. 1957. The Japanese Police Systems. In *Five Studies in Japanese Politics,* edited by Robert W. Ward. Occasional Papers, no. 7, Center for Japanese Studies, University of Michigan, Ann Arbor.

Szulc, Tad. 1964. U.S. Denies Switch in Its Latin Policy. *New York Times,* 20 March, 1, 4.

Taylor, Maxwell D. 1965. Address at International Police Academy Graduation, 17 December. USAID Press Release, 17 December.

Thompson, Edgar K. 1939a. Memorandum to J. Edgar Hoover, 29 January. FOIA: BUFILE 61-7588-2, sec. 1. FBI, Washington, D.C.

———. 1939b. Memorandum to J. Edgar Hoover, 15 February. FOIA: BUFILE 61-7588-6, sec. 1. FBI, Washington, D.C.

———. 1939c. Memorandum to J. Edgar Hoover, 22 March. FOIA: BUFILE 62-7588-10. FBI, Washington, D.C.

———. 1939d. Memorandum to J. Edgar Hoover, 5 June. FOIA: BUFILE 61-7588-30, sec. 1. FBI, Washington, D.C.

Tilly, Charles, ed. 1975. *The Formation of National States in Western Europe.* Princeton, N.J.: Princeton University Press.

———. 1985. War Making and State Making as Organized Crime. In *Bringing the State Back In,* edited by Peter Evans, Dietrich Rueschemeyer, and Theda Skocpol. New York: Cambridge University Press.

Time. 1964. Brazil: Toward Profound Change. *Time,* 17 April, 49–50.

———. 1969. The Death Squads of Rio, 25 April.

TOAID. 1964a. A-1551. Agency for International Development, Public Safety Report for March, 24 April. OPS-Brazil. FOIA: Agency for International Development. Washington, D.C.

———. 1964b. A-1679. Agency for International Development, Public Safety Report for April, 22 May. OPS-Brazil, FOIA: Agency for International Development. Washington, D.C.

———. 1965a. A-1003. Agency for International Development, Public Safety Report for January, 15 February. OPS-Brazil. FOIA: Agency for International Development. Washington, D.C.

——. 1965b. A-1486. Agency for International Development, Public Safety Report for April, 25 May. OPS-Brazil. FOIA: Agency for International Development. Washington, D.C.

——. 1965c. A-1553. Agency for International Development, Public Safety Report for May, 4 June. OPS-Brazil. FOIA: Agency for International Development. Washington, D.C.

——. 1965d. A-76. Agency for International Development, Public Safety Report for June, 13 July. OPS-Brazil. FOIA: Agency for International Development. Washington, D.C.

——. 1965e. A-242. Agency for International Development, Public Safety Report for July, 6 August. OPS-Brazil. FOIA: Agency for International Development. Washington, D.C.

——. 1965f. A-576. Agency for International Development, Public Safety Report for August, 24 September. OPS-Brazil. FOIA: Agency for International Development. Washington, D.C.

——. 1965g. A-846. Agency for International Development, Public Safety Report for November, 15 December. OPS-Brazil. FOIA: Agency for International Development. Washington, D.C.

——. 1966a. A-113. Agency for International Development, Public Safety Report for June, 18 July. OPS-Brazil. FOIA: Agency for International Development. Washington, D.C.

——. 1966b. A-667. Agency for International Development, Public Safety Report for September, 19 October. OPS-Brazil. FOIA: Agency for International Development. Washington, D.C.

——. 1966c. A-824. Agency for International Development, Public Safety Report for October, 21 November. OPS-Brazil. FOIA: Agency for International Development. Washington, D.C.

——. 1967. A-2068. Agency for International Development, Public Safety Report for May, 23 June. OPS-Brazil. FOIA: Agency for International Development. Washington, D.C.

——. 1968a. A-1215. Agency for International Development, Public Safety Report for January, 14 February. OPS-Brazil. FOIA: Agency for International Development. Washington, D.C.

——. 1968b. XA-2532. Agency for International Development, Public Safety Report for February, 7 March. OPS-Brazil. FOIA: Agency for International Development. Washington, D.C.

——. 1968c. A-1489. Agency for International Development, Public Safety Report for March, 23 April. OPS-Brazil. FOIA: Agency for International Development. Washington, D.C.

——. 1968d. A-1620. Agency for International Development, Public Safety Report for April, 21 May. OPS-Brazil. FOIA: Agency for International Development. Washington, D.C.

——. 1968e. A-1971. Agency for International Development, Public Safety Report for May–June, 26 July. OPS-Brazil. FOIA: Agency for International Development. Washington, D.C.

———. 1968f. A-2079. Agency for International Development, Public Safety Report for July, 20 August. OPS-Brazil. FOIA: Agency for International Development. Washington, D.C.

———. 1968g. A-2437. Agency for International Development, Public Safety Report for September, 14 November. OPS-Brazil. FOIA: Agency for International Development. Washington, D.C.

———. 1968h. A-2537. Agency for International Development, Public Safety Report for October, 13 December. OPS-Brazil. FOIA: Agency for International Development. Washington, D.C.

———. 1968i. A-2562. Agency for International Development, Public Safety Report for November, 20 December. OPS-Brazil. FOIA: Agency for International Development. Washington, D.C.

———. 1969a. A-86. Agency for International Development, Public Safety Report for December 1968, 28 January. OPS-Brazil. FOIA: Agency for International Development. Washington, D.C.

———. 1969b. A-322. Agency for International Development, Public Safety Report for December 1968, 12 February. OPS-Brazil. FOIA: Agency for International Development. Washington, D.C.

———. 1969c. A-165. Agency for International Development, Public Safety Report for January, 25 February. OPS-Brazil. FOIA: Agency for International Development. Washington, D.C.

———. 1969d. A-234. Agency for International Development, Public Safety Report for February, 18 March. OPS-Brazil. FOIA: Agency for International Development. Washington, D.C.

———. 1969e. A-361. Agency for International Development, Public Safety Report for March, 18 April. OPS-Brazil. FOIA: Agency for International Development. Washington, D.C.

———. 1969f. A-428. Agency for International Development, Public Safety Report for April, 13 May. OPS-Brazil. FOIA: Agency for International Development. Washington, D.C.

———. 1969g. A-688. Agency for International Development, Public Safety Report for June, 15 July. OPS-Brazil. FOIA: Agency for International Development. Washington, D.C.

———. 1969h. A-845. Agency for International Development, Public Safety Report for July, 26 August. OPS-Brazil. FOIA: Agency for International Development. Washington, D.C.

———. 1969i. A-916. Agency for International Development, Public Safety Report for August, 12 September. OPS-Brazil. FOIA: Agency for International Development. Washington, D.C.

———1969j. A-1059. Agency for International Development, Public Safety Report for September, 21 October. OPS-Brazil. FOIA: Agency for International Development. Washington, D.C.

———. 1969k. A-2043. Agency for International Development, Public Safety Report for October, 14 November. OPS-Brazil. FOIA: Agency for International Development. Washington, D.C.

———. 1969l. A-1259. Agency for International Development, Public Safety Report for November, 23 December. OPS-Brazil. FOIA: Agency for International Development. Washington, D.C.

———. 1970a. A-112. Agency for International Development, Public Safety Report for December, 30 January. OPS-Brazil. FOIA: Agency for International Development. Washington, D.C.

———. 1970b. A-134. Agency for International Development, Public Safety Report for January, 6 February. OPS-Brazil. FOIA: Agency for International Development. Washington, D.C.

———. 1970c. A-264. Agency for International Development, Public Safety Report for February, 20 March. OPS-Brazil. FOIA: Agency for International Development. Washington, D.C.

———. 1970d. A-785. Agency for International Development, Public Safety Report for July, 14 August. OPS-Brazil. FOIA: Agency for International Development. Washington, D.C.

———. 1970e. A-986. Agency for International Development, Public Safety Report for September, 16 October. OPS-Brazil. FOIA: Agency for International Development. Washington, D.C.

———. 1970f. A-1151. Agency for International Development, Public Safety Report for November, 23 December. OPS-Brazil. FOIA: Agency for International Development. Washington, D.C.

———. 1971a. A-232. Agency for International Development, Public Safety Report for March, 7 April. OPS-Brazil. FOIA: Agency for International Development. Washington, D.C.

———. 1971b. A-323. Agency for International Development, Public Safety Report for April, 14 May. OPS-Brazil. FOIA: Agency for International Development. Washington, D.C.

Treaster, Joseph B. 1985. Caribbean War Games: Not Everyone Is Delighted. *New York Times*, 16 September, A2.

Troy, Thomas. 1981. *Donovan and the CIA: A History of the Establishment of the Central Intelligence Agency.* Frederick, Md.: University Publishers of America.

UN. 1993. *U.N. Truth Commission Report on El Salvador.* Report prepared for the Committee on Foreign Affairs, U.S. House of Representatives, Congressional Research Service. Washington, D.C.: U.S. Government Printing Office.

(USDC) U.S. Department of Commerce. 1989. *Historical Statistics of the United States: Colonial Times to 1970.* White Plains, N.Y.: Kraus International Publications.

U.S. Embassy. 1953. Point IV Training, U.S. Embassy to State Department, 20 May. National Archives, 832.50115-2053 XR 522.323. Washington, D.C.

U.S. Embassy. 1964. Telegram from U.S. Embassy, La Paz, to Secretary of State, 24 February. John F. Kennedy Library, Boston, Mass.

(USIA) United States Information Agency. 1955. USIA Propaganda File, CBC, C, 26 August. USIA Archives, Washington, D.C.

———. [1955?]. Juizes Comunistas Solapando a Justica Brasileira. USIA Propaganda File. USIA Historical Archives, Washington, D.C.

U.S. Senate. 1974. 20 June.

Ustra, Carlos Alberto Brilharte. 1987. *Rompendo o Silencio*. Brasília: Editora Editorial.

Valli, Virginia. 1986. *Eu, ZuZu Angel, Procuro Meu Filho*. Rio de Janeiro: Philobiblion.

Veja. 1970. Justiça é Feita, 29 July.

———. 1983. 23 November. *Veja* Archives, São Paulo.

———. 1992. A Lei da Barbárie, 18 November.

———. 1997. Memórias do SNI. 9 July.

Walmsley, Walter N. 1953. "Gradual Reorganization and Consequent Weakening of Anti-Communist Division of Federal [DOPS] Police. Foreign Service dispatch to State Department, 29 October. National Archives, 832.501/10-2953, XR 732.001. Washington, D.C.

Washington Post. 1970. Oppression in Brazil. Editorial, 28 February.

———. 1974. Abourezk Fights to End Aid to Foreign Police, 22 September.

Weber, Max. 1978. *Economy and Society* 1. Edited by Guenther Roth and Claus Wittich. Berkeley and Los Angeles: University of California Press.

Welles, Sumner. 1938. Letter to U.S. attorney general, 14 December. National Archives, State Department Division. Washington, D.C.

———. 1939a. Letter to Attorney General Murphy, 17 May. National Archives, State Department Division, 821/105/57. Washington, D.C.

———. 1939b. Confidential letter to Franklin D. Roosevelt, 29 May. National Archives, Old State Department Division. Washington, D.C.

Weschler, Lawrence. 1987. A Reporter at Large: A Miracle, A Universe, II. *New Yorker*, 1 June.

Wickersham, George W. 1931. Report on Lawlessness in Law Enforcement, 25 June. National Commission on Law Observance and Enforcement.

Wise, Daniel, and Thomas B. Ross. 1964. *The Invisible Government*. New York: Random House.

Wright, Jaime. 1987. Interview by author. São Paulo, Brazil, 20 November.

Index

Abourezk, James, xv, 4, 109, 115, 192
Above the Law, 7
Ação Popular, 129
Agee, Philip, 89, 107, 124
Agency for International Development (AID), xiv, ix, 88–90, 100, 102–8, 115, 124–25
Agripino, João, 148
Aleixo, Pedro, 156
Alencar, Frei Tito: *Look* (magazine) article, 187; Operação Bandeirantes (OBAN) torture of, 153–54
Aliança de Renovação Nacional (ARENA), 128–29
Aliança Libertação Nacional (ALN), 152, 156
Allende, Salvador, 194
Alliance for Progress, 102
Allport, Gordon, 151
Alves, Francisco Rodrigues, 36
Alves, Helena, 158
Alves, Márcio Moreira, 146
Amado, Jorge, 83
American Civil Liberties Union, 51
Amnesty International, 152
Amory, Robert, xvii, 88, 101
Anderson, Jack, 187
Angel, ZuZu, 189–90
Anti-Americanism, 29
Anti-Terrorist Assistance Program (ATA), 1–2
Appropriations Committee (U.S. Senate), 188–89
Aranha, Oswaldo, 48–49, 52, 54
Argentina: intelligence network in, 43; and Point Four Program, 76; Special Intelligence Service in, 60; strongman president in, 42
Aristide, Jean Bertrand, 6
Armas, Castillo, 86–87

Army (U.S.), 103, 108, 111
Arraes, Miguel, 121
Arrests, 46, 51, 121, 147, 158
Asia, 75–76, 85
Authoritarianization, 20, 23–24, 79, 115, 117–18, 123

Ball, John O., 116
Bandits (bandilleros), 96, 111–12
Barros, Ademar de, 139
Battalion 316, 5
The Battle of Algiers (film), 110, 113–14
Bay of Pigs, 99
Bell, David, 115, 188–89
Benário, Olga Gutman (Maria Prestes), 48–49
Berger, Harry (Arthur Ernst Ewert), 46–47, 52
Berle, A. A., 62, 64–65
Bernardes, Artur, 37
Betancourt, Romulu, 112
Bethlem, Hugo, 67
Black budgets, 90
Black propaganda, 114
Bloody June, 143
Boilessen, Hennig Albert, 152
Bolivia, 66, 85, 92
Bomb-making school, 110, 192
Bowles, Chester, 104, 116
Braden, Spruille, 54–56
Bradley, William, 61
Braggio, Major, 125
Branch, Taylor, 190
Branco, Humberto de Alencar Castelo, 120–22, 128
Brasília Police Academy, 124
Brazil, xii–xiii, 159–60, 162, 178; anti-communism in, 83, 86; communist threat, 85; and Estrada Doctrine, 119; Institutional Acts, 120,

Brazil (*cont.*)
128–29, 155, 158, 174; military re-
volts, 45, 119; Operação Limpeza,
120–21; and Point Four Program,
76; Special Intelligence Service in,
60. *See also* Office of Public Safety
(OPS)
Brazilian: Air Force, 143; Army, 136,
145; Congress, 129, 146; Human
Rights Commission, 188; Justice
Department, 47; Secret Service, 52
Brazilian Communist Party, 45, 83, 96
Brigada Militar, 131
British Secret Service, 48
Brizola, Lionel, 120
Brown, Theodore, 151–52, 154, 188
Buzaid, Alfredo, 162, 175

Caco units, 29
Caffrey, Jefferson, 62
Cancelli, Elizabeth, x
Capanema, Gustavo, 44
Carabineros, 56
Caracas Resolution, 86
Carceral systems, 159
Carter, Calvin Boone, 32, 33
Cassação, 128–29, 146–47
Castro, Fidel, 99
CENIMAR, 156
Censorship, 147–48, 175–76
Central American Treaty of Peace and
Amity, 30
Central Intelligence Agency (CIA),
xi–xvi, 75, 87–88, 90, 107–9, 124,
127, 162–63, 185, 192; and 1290d
Police Program, 88, 91; assistance
to U.S. domestic police, 193; classi-
fied documents, ix, xv; and coun-
terinsurgency, 105; Counterintelli-
gence Division, 107; creation, 74;
and Forty Committee, 194; and establishment of FRAPH in Haiti, 6;
in Guatemala, 81; knowledge of
torture in Brazil, 154; and Nixon

administration, 194; and Phoenix
Program, 151; and U.S. military in
Haiti, 1; U.S. Senate hearings, xv,
4, 187–88, 191; and U.S. university
foreign police training, 88; views
on Brazilian government repression, 176; wanted lists, 146; war
against terrorism, 5
Centralization, 19–20, 23, 40, 42, 46,
111, 117–18, 180; in Argentina, 43;
of Brazil's internal security organizations, 127; of foreign police
training, 104, 105; in Haiti, 39–40;
of Latin American police, 191; in
Nicaragua, 34, 39, 40; and orga-
nized repression, 198; of police sys-
tem during Brazilian military
period, 130, 162–63; student dem-
onstrations as rational for, 140;
Vietnam-era, 79
Centralization proposition, 18–19,
23–24
Centro de Defeza Interna. *See*
DOI/CODI
Centro de Informações de Marinha,
156
Chamorro, Emiliano, 31–33
Chandler, Charles, 157
Chase, Gordon, 116
Chevigny, Paul, 7–8, 15
Chicago police, 50
Chile, 85–86; destabilization of, 194;
Special Intelligence Service in, 60
China, 25, 77, 99
Church, Frank, xv, 4, 187–88
Church Committee report, 191
C-1 Bible, 100
Civil Police, 133–34; Criminal Inves-
tigations Division (DEIC), 150; and
death squads in São Paulo, 139;
Delegados, 127, 132–33; and Law
317, 130–31; recruitment of mem-
bers, 164; targets of military revolu-
tion, 178

Civil rights, 178, 193
Class-neutral policing, 9, 11
CODI. *See* DOI/CODI
Coelho, Moacir, 109
Coffee, 36, 209 chap. 2 n.1
COINTELPRO, 193
Colby, William, 90, 192–93
Cold War, 71, 76, 96; containment
    doctrine, 2; national security ideol-
    ogy, 8, 18, 23, 200
Colombia, 1, 34, 42, 56, 60, 111–12
Colombian National Police, 34, 42
Comintern, 46, 48, 52
Commission on Human Rights, 175
Committee on Foreign Relations (U.S.
    Senate), 187
Communism, 20, 58, 66, 68–86, 108,
    199; insurgency, 99–101; and
    Movimiento Nacionalista Revolu-
    cionario (MNR), 85. *See also* Con-
    tainment
Communist Party, 75, 83. *See also*
    Comintern
Communist propaganda, 111
Communists, 47; arrests during Ope-
    ração Limpeza, 122; insurgency,
    99–101; investigation by FBI of, 51
Constabulary forces, 26–30, 38–39
Constant, Emmanuel "Toto," 6
Constitutionalists, 44
Constitution (Brazilian), 147
Containment, 2, 74, 85; economic ap-
    proaches to, 74; and Eisenhower
    administration, 79; globalizing of,
    75; ideology, 71; and Marshall Plan,
    75; militarization of, 78; and Soviet
    Union, 70; support for military ap-
    proaches, 77
Conze, Jean, 29
Cops Across Borders, x
Correia, Henrique de Miranda, 47, 49
Corvée law, 29
Counterinsurgency, 99–101; chal-
    lenges to, 102; concerns, 106; ide-
    ology, 102; and military, 104, 127;
    models, 136; in Venezuela, 112
Counter-Insurgency Group (C-1
    Group), 101–4
Counterintelligence Office, 91
Counterterrorism training, 5–6
Criminal Investigations Division
    (DEIC), 150
Criminalistics, 16
Cuba, 3; Bay of Pigs, 99; Castro, Fidel,
    99; constabulary forces in, 26–27;
    Kennedy, John F. and, 99; Special
    Intelligence Service in, 60
Cupertino, José Bretas, 150

Daland, Robert, 134–35
Death flights, 143
Death squads, 5, 21–22, 96, 98, 136–
    40, 175, 181, 203; drug use by
    members, 139; in Espírito Santo
    state, 180, 202; and Law 317, 132;
    of Operação Bandeirantes, 150;
    proliferation of, 97, 134, 140; in
    São Paulo, 137–39, 172; ties to for-
    mal police system, 97
de Barros, João Alberto Lins, 65
de Cavalo, Cara, 97
Defense Department (U.S.), ix,
    104–5
Defense Program to Assist National
    Police Forces, 1
Denys, Major, 62
Departamento de Ordem Interna. *See*
    DOI/CODI
Departamento de Ordem Político e
    Social (DOPS), xvi, 46, 52, 67, 149;
    raid on by DOI/CODI team, 178;
    in Rio de Janeiro, 62; U.S. relation-
    ship with, 172
Departamento Federal de Segurança
    Pública. *See* Federal Department of
    Public Safety (DFSP)
Department of Internal Order (DOI).
    See DOI/CODI

Desaparecido, 4
Devolution, 18, 20–24, 40, 96, 139–40, 201–2; of Brazil's internal security, 77, 98, 191; and Brazil's national security legislation, 159; of Brazil's police system, 98; in São Paulo, 39; Vietnam-era, 79
Diaz, Adolfo, 33
Dictatorship by consent, 161
Dictatorships: U.S. attitude about, 115–16
Dies, Martin, 58
Dies Committee, 58
Disappearances, 4, 159, 181, 189
DOI/CODI, 149, 162–63, 169; agent work schedules, 167; Amazon region mission, 165; anonymity of agents, 168–70; CIA view of, 163; conflict and competition, 177; cooperative effort, 165–66; internal security zones, 171, jurisdictions, 177; pressure to make arrests, 177; purpose, 163; raids, 178; repression, 176; secrecy, 164, 168, 170; specialization of operations, 164–65; specialized torture centers, 171; squad composition, 163–64; stress, 168
Dominican Republic, 26–27, 41, 190–91
Donovan, William S. ("Wild Bill"), 69
Dória, Seixas, 121
Draper Commission, 93–94
DTBAIL operation, 107–8
Dulles, John Foster, 82, 92
Durkheim, Émile, 165
Dutra, Enrico Gaspar, 48
Duvalier, François "Papa Doc," 41

Economic development, 94, 100, 118, 200
Ecuador, 56
Edge of the Knife: Police Violence in the Americas, 7–8, 15
Eisenhower, Dwight D., 93; and communism, 79–80, 101; and foreign police assistance, 78–80; and New Look, 79
Elbrick, C. Burke, 156–57
Elections, 125, 128–29
Electric shock, 167, 172
El Salvador, 5, 91
Enforced silence, 175
Engle, Byron, xvii, 73, 107
Ernesto, Geisel, 122
Espirito Santo state, 180–83, 202
Esquadrão de Morte, 97
Esquadrão Motorizado (E.M.), 97, 136
Estado de São Paulo, xvi
Estado Novo, 45–46
Estensoro, Paz, 85
Estrada Doctrine, 119
Etchegoyan, Alcides, 62
Europe, 9, 11, 197, 201
European Recovery Plan, 74–75
Ewert, Arthur Ernst (Harry Berger), 46–47, 52

Favelas (slums), 134, 136
Federal Bureau of Investigations (FBI), xiv–xv, 41, 54–57, 65, 124; and COINTELPRO, 193; in Brazil, 52–54; classified documents, ix; in Colombia, 52; domestic surveillance, 58; in Ecuador, 56; espionage, 199; and foreign police assistance, 1, 58; and Franklin D. Roosevelt, 51; intelligence gathering in Latin America, 59; investigation of communist and nazi groups, 51; in Rio de Janeiro, 64; in Rio Grande do Sul, 63; Special Intelligence Service of, 59, 65–66; wiretaps, 59
Federal Department of Public Safety (DFSP), 123–26
Federal Police (Brazil), 149
Fifth Column, 64

Fifth Institutional Act (IA-5), 146–49, 174, 180
First Institutional Act (IA-1), 120
Fleury, Sérgio Parahos, 138, 140, 178
Flying squads, 15, 42–43
Força Expedicionária Brasileira, 96
Força Pública, 35–39, 43, 133
Ford, Gerald, 195
Foreign police assistance, ix–x, 5, 19–20, 23, 75, 95, 155, 191, 195–96; and Cold War national security ideology, 3, 200; consequences of, 4–5, 22, 39, 190, 195–96; and Eisenhower administration, 78–80; empirical theses, 18–19; methodology in study of, xiii, xiv; and military training, 116–17; and nation builders, 94–95; privatization of, 195; rationale, x–xi, 2, 8, 199–200; Senate hearings on, 4–5, 187–88, 191; theory and practice, 16–17; and Truman administration, 67, 73
Foreign police training, xvi: centralization of, 104–5; counterinsurgency, 101; effects of, 6–8; and rule of law, 5
Forty Committee, 194, 211 n.2
Foucault, Michel, 159
FRAPH, 6
Freedom of Information Act (FOIA), xii, xiii, xiv, 88–89
Fulbright, J. William, xv, 90, 161, 192
Furtado, Celso, 120
Fyfe, James, 7

Garde d'Haiti, 28–29
Geladeira, 166–67, 171
Germany, 52; Communist Party of, 46; and foreign police assistance, 73; Gestapo, 48
Getúlio Vargas Foundation, xvi
Gibson, Hugh, 46, 48
Gill, Peter, x
Gilpatric, Roswell, 102

Goin, Loren "Jack," xvi–xvii, 174
Golpe (military), 45, 119–22, 126–28, 140, 146, 156, 170
Good Neighbor policy, 41–42, 51
Gordon, Lincoln, 119–21, 128
Goulart, João, 86, 119–20
Greece, 85
Grenada, 5
Grunnewald, Augusto Rademacker, 119
Grupo de Operações Especiais. *See* Special Operations Squad
Guanabara state, 143–44
Guarda Civil, 132
Guatemala: communist threat in, 85–86; consequences of police assistance, 190–91; overthrow of Jacobo Arbenz Guzmán, 4, 81; and Point Four Program, 76; torture and killings in, 86; U.S. intervention, 99
Guerrilla groups, 156, 178
Gunboat policing, 25–39, 198–99
Guzmán, Jacobo Arbenz, 4, 86

Haiti: constabulary forces in, 26–29, 38, 41; FRAPH, 6; Jean Bertrand Aristide, 6; U.S. occupation, 28
Haritos-Fatouros, Mika, xviii
Hazen, David, 123
Helms, Richard, 154, 158, 161–63, 186–88, 194
Heneken, Herman, 29
Himmler, Heinrich, 49
Homens corajosos (motorized squad), 96
Honduran Special Investigators Directorate, 5
Honduras, 5, 91
Hoover, Charles S., 37
Hoover, Herbert (U.S. President), 50
Hoover, Herbert C., 101
Hoover, J. Edgar, 51, 53, 55–56, 60, 62
Hoover, Orton, 37

Hoover Commission, 101
House Committee on Un-American Activities (Dies Committee), 58
Hughes, Charles Evans, 31
Human rights, 114, 134, 189

Indigenous militaries, 83
Indigenous police, 1, 83, 199
Inquérito Policial Militar (IPM), 122–23
Institute for Defense Analysis (IDA), 94
Institute for Inter-American Affairs, 94
Institutional Acts, 128–29, 155
Institutionalized torture, 171, 175
Instituto Nacional de Identificação. *See* National Institute of Identification (INI)
Instrumentalism, 173–74, 177
Intelligence. *See* National Institute of Identification (INI), National Information Service (SNI)
Intelligence training, 109–10
Inter-American Police Academy (IAPA), 108, 126
Internal Defense Operations Command Center (CODI). *See* DOI/CODI
Internal defense zones, 163
Internal security, 84, 162–63, 165, 191
International Association of Chiefs of Police (IACP), xv, xvi, 77, 86–88
International Business Machines (IBM), 125
International Commission of Jurists, 122, 187
International Cooperation Administration (ICA), 87–88, 91, 105–6
International Criminal Investigative Training Program (ICITAP), 2
Internationalization, 26–27, 40–41: of foreign police assistance, 74, 78–79; ideology, 74; of Latin American

police practices, 191; proposition, 18–19, 23–24; of U.S. security, 67, 88, 118
International Police Academy (IPA): bomb-making school, 110, 192; criticism of, 190; curriculum, 110–15; purpose, 109; recruitment methods, 108
International Police Service, Inc. (INPOLSE), 87–90
International Telephone and Telegraph (ITT), 43
Iran, 99, 195
Irish Republican Army, 136
Italy, 52, 55

Japa, Mário (Shizuo Ozawa), 178
Japan, 52, 72–73, 79
Javits, Jacob, 161
Jeffers, William, 65
Johnson, Lyndon B., 119
Johnson, U. Alexis, xvii, 104, 106, 194
Jornal do Brasil, 186
Jornal do Comércio, 36
Julião, Francisco, 121
Jullien, Francisco, 47–49
Justiceiro (lone-wolf killers), 21
Justo, Agustin P., 43

Kai-shek, Chiang, 77
Kalmanowiecki, Laura Fleischman, x, 43
Kelly, Raymond W., 1
Kenman, George, 70, 72, 74, 77–78
Kennedy, John F.: Bay of Pigs, 99; and Central Intelligence Agency (CIA), 88; counterinsurgency, 101–2; and foreign police assistance, 100, 112; U.S. State Department policy under, 88
Kennedy, Robert, 101, 108
Kidnappings, 174
Killings, 4, 86

Komer, Robert, xvii, 105–6
Korea, 73
Kruel, Amaury, 95–96, 136–37
Kruel, Riograndinho, 124–25
Kubitschek, Juscelino, 81–82, 86, 120

Labor unions, 12–13, 129, 151
Landsdale, Edward, 82
Langguth, A. J., 135, 142–43
Larson, Rolf, 62–64, 66
Law 317, 130–33, 149
Law 667, 181
Lebanon, 99
Le Cocq, Milton, 97, 136
Lei Monstro, 46
Lenczyki, Machla (Elise Saborowski),
    46–47, 52
Leoni, Raul, 113
Liberal Alliance, 44
Lightning demonstrations, 141–42
London Financial Times (editorial), 176
Lopes Filho, Cristiano Dias, 181–82
Lopes, José Dias, 181–83
Look (magazine): account of Frei Tito
    Alencar's torture, 187
Los Angeles Times, 113
Luis, Edison, 141

MacArthur, Douglas, 72–73
Madar, Julius, 124
Maechling, Charles, Jr., 88, 102, 107,
    116
Mandatory Review, xiii, xiv
Mann, Thomas, 115
Marighella, Carlos, 153
Marines, U.S., 26–29, 31–32, 34, 41
Marks, John, 190
Marshall Plan (European Recovery
    Plan), 74–75
Marx, Gary, x
Mattos, Carlos de Meira, 150
Mazzilli, Paschoal Ranieri, 119
Médici, Emílio Garrastazu, 161–62,
    175

Melo, Francisco de Assis Correia, 119
Mena, Luis, 33
Mesa de operação, 171
Mexico, 60
Michigan State University, xvi, 87–
    88, 183
Middle East, 75–76, 85
Milano, Plinio Brasil, 63–66
Militarized Police, 130–31, 141–45,
    150, 162, 168–69, 177
Military coup (golpe), 45, 119–22,
    126–28, 140, 146, 156, 170
Militias, 12, 21, 29
Mills, Make, 58
Minas Gerais state, 42, 44, 132;
    DOPS, 149; Operação Limpeza,
    123; shock troops, 134; torture, 170
Mitrione, Dan, 134–36, 190, 210
    chap. 7 n.2
Modernization theory, 100
Molina, Rafael Leonidas Trujillo, 41
Monteiro, Gois, 48
Morgan, Edwin W., 45
Mormon missionaries, 62–63
Morris, Fred, 166
Morse, Wayne, 92
Motorized patrols, 15, 96, 136
Movimento Democrático Brasileiro
    (MDB), 128, 146
Movimento Revolucionário (MR), 152
Movimento Revolucionário-8 (MR-8),
    156
Movimiento Nacionalista Revolu-
    cionário (MNR), 85
Müller, Felinto, 47–48, 52, 62
Munro, Dana, 28–30
Murder, 165, 176
Mutual Security Act, 92–93

Nadelman, Ethan, x
National Archives, xiii–xiv
National Commission for the Repres-
    sion of Communism, 46
National Guards, 39, 41

National Information Service (SNI), 123, 126–27, 161
National Institute for Identification (INI), 123–25, 131–32
National Liberation Alliance (ANL), 45
National Security Council (NSC), xiv, xv, 74–75, 194: 1290d Program, 80; militarization of containment, 78; and New Look, 79; Overseas International Security Program, 92
National Security Law (Brazilian), 148–49
National security zones, 129
Nation builders: in Europe, 201; military as, 117; theses, 94–95, 103
Navy (U.S.), 27
Nazism, 14, 51–52, 58–60, 62–63, 199
New Look, 79
News suppression. *See* Censorship
New York Bar Association, 50
New York City police, 1, 10, 26, 45, 50
New York Times: report on condition of released prisoners, 189
New York Trade Bureau, 190
Nicaragua, 31–34, 39; constabulary forces in, 26–30, 38; police training, 30–32; and United States Legation Guard, 31; U.S. State Department in, 32
Niemeyer, Oscar, 120
Nixon, Richard M., 155, 194
North, Oliver, 196
Northwestern University Traffic School, 87
Nunca Mais, 137

Office of Public Safety (OPS), xiv, 107, 111, 122–26, 132, 141, 143, 150, 152–53, 161, 172–74; Congressional hearings, 190–91; criticism of, 187; and death squads, 137, 175;

183–84; in Guatemala, 191; and Institutional Acts, 131, 147–48, 173–74; and Law 317, 130–31; and military triumvirate, 156; mission, 173; motorized patrols, 134; and Peasant League, 128; reorganization, 133; Senate investigation of, 192; training, 88, 109, 127, 134, 182, 186, 191–92; in Venezuela, 113; weapons, 182, 192–93
Office of Strategic Services, 69, 74
O Estada de São Paulo, 133
O Globo, xvi
Oliveira, Luis de França, 137, 145
Open Door policy, 25
Operação Bandeirantes (OBAN), 149, 151–54, 157, 161
Operação Limpeza, 120–21
Operação Lysistrata, 146
Operation Cleanup. *See* Operação Limpeza
Operation Pan America, 82
Operation San Martin, 110–11, 144
Operations Coordinating Board (OCB), 80–88, 91–92, 95–96, 209–10 chap. 5 n.1
Otero, Alejandro, 89
Overseas Internal Defense Policy (OIDP), 80–81, 84–85, 92–93, 100–101
Ozawa, Shizuo (Mario Japa), 178

Palmatória, 153
Panama, 3, 26, 30–31, 108
Pan American Airways, 61
Paramilitary, 21–22
Paraná state, 127, 132–34
Parker, David, 114
Parrot's perch, 49–50, 153–54
Pauker, Guy, 94
Paulista Railway Company, 36
Peasant League, 128
Pentagon, 102–3
Peralte, Charlemagne, 29

Pereiro, José Canavarro, 150
Pernambuco state, 128, 134
Philippines, 82
Phoenix Program, 151
Pinto, Costa, 156–57
Poderosos, 26
Point Four Program, 75–76, 96
Poland, 52
Police, 9–13, 177
Police Advisory Committee, 104–6
Police assistance. *See* Foreign Police
Assistance
Police constabularies. *See* Constabulary forces
Police matériel, 15, 90, 124, 137, 196.
See also Weapons
Police Organic Law, 33, 130, 149
Police tax, 183
Polícia Federal (Brazil), 109
Policing Politics: Security Intelligence and the Liberal Democratic State, x
Polish Corridor, 153
Political prisoners, 187–89, 192
Pôrto Alegre, 63, 149
Presidential libraries, xiv
Prestes Column, 37
Prestes, Luis Carlos, 37, 45, 48
Prestes, Maria (Olga Gutman Benário), 48
Preventive Penal Law, 86
Privateers, 201
Privatization, 118
Privatized justice, 22, 24
Proctor, Gilbert, 56
Professionalization, 180, 200–201:
consequences of, xi, 13–18; in foreign police training, 7, 109–11; as government-organized protection racket, 14
Propaganda, 80–83, 85, 111, 151
Protection racket (state), 14, 199; as cause of devolution, 202; and economic aid, 200; steps in creation of, 197

Protests. *See* Student demonstrations
Prussian Army, 14
Psychological training, 109–10

Quandros, Jânio, 119

Radford, Arthur, 79
Raposo Filho, Amerino, 124–25
Red squads, 15–16, 50–51, 58
Regional Security System, 5
Rejali, Darias, 159
Repression, 146, 155, 193, 202–3; and Brazilian National Security Law, 148; and DOI/CODI, 176; resulting from Institutional Acts, 128; legitimization of, 118, 143, 173; and National Information Service (SNI), 127; and Operação Bandeirantes (OBAN), 151; and state protection rackets, 198; in U.S., 50
Rio de Janeiro: arrests, 122, 149, 163; Bernardes, Artur, 37; death squads, 136, 185; militarization of police in, 134, 141–44; Tenente rebellion, 37–38; torture, 96, 134, 170
Rio de Janeiro Cruzada Brasileira Anti-Comunista (CBC), 83
Rio Grande do Sul, 134
Rio Squad, 185
Riot control, 16, 42, 109–10
Rockefeller, Nelson A., 94, 155
Rondas do Setor de Assaltos (ROSA), 137
Rondas Noturnas Especiais da Polícia Civil (RONE), 137–40, 164
Rondas Unificadas de Departamento de Investigações (RUDI), 137
Roosevelt, Franklin, 56, 59
Root, Elihu, 25
Rostow, Walt W., 100, 120
Rubber Development Program (U.S.), 65
Rule of law, 2, 5, 13

Saborowski, Elise (Machla Lenczyki), 46–47, 52
Sam, Guillaume, 27
São Paulo, 95, 149, 163–64, 170–72; death squads, 137, 184; labor unrest, 35–36; police conflict, 132–33; police training by France, 30, 39; professionalization of police, 35, 38
Scuderie Le Cocq Club, 97
Servicio (Serviço), 76
Serviço de Diligéncia Especial ("E.M."), 96
Serviço Nacional da Informação (SNI), 109
Serviço Nacional de Informação. *See* National Information Service (SNI)
Serviço Social da Indústria (SESI), 68
Shock troops, 134
Silva, Arthur Da Costa e, 119, 129, 146, 155–56
Silva, Golbery do Couto e, 126
Silveira, Badger, 120
Skolnick, Jerome, 7
Social control, 198, 203. *See also* foreign police assistance rationale
Solórzano, Carlos, 33–34, 39
Somoza, Anastasio, 41
Spear, Joseph, 187
Special Group for Counter-Insurgency, 88
Special Intelligence Service (SIS), 59–66
Specialization, 177–80
Special Operations Squad (GOE), 145
Stages of Economic Growth, 100
Star-chamber proceedings, 46
State builders, 19, 145, 196–97. *See also* nation builders
State Department (U.S.), 46–58, 70, 87, 90, 102–3, 116, 194; and communism, 51, 69; and Federal Bureau of Investigations, 69; and foreign

police assistance, 30–31, 87; and International Association of Chiefs of Police, 77
State makers, 198. *See also* nation builders, state builders
State of Seige (film), 135, 190
State protection racket. *See* protection racket
Strikes, 12–13, 148, 174
Strongman rule, 42, 117, 199
Student demonstrations, 129, 140, 146; Office of Public Safety and, 145; in Rio de Janeiro, 141–42; in Rio Grande do Sul, 134; University of Brasília, 125
Subversion, 76, 109, 162, 193
Suez Canal, 99
Sugar crops, 36, 128

Taiwan, 87
Taylor, Maxwell, 103–4
Telephone torture, 167
Tenente Rebellion, 37–39
Teuto-Brazilians, 63
Third Institutional Act (IA-3), 128
Third World: counterinsurgency training, 103–4; police, 79
Thompson, Edgar K., 53–56
Tibiriçá, Jorge, 35–36
Tiger cages, 192
Tilly, Charles, 196–97
Tiradentes groups, 152
Torture, 47, 61, 96, 134, 170, 188; attitudes about, 4, 114–15; by death squads, 177; diplomatic silence about, 47, 175, 188; disclosure of, 187, 189–90; and DOI/CODI, 165–66, 171, 176; drug use by torturers, 179; and Fifth Institutional Act (IA-5), 147; in Guatemala, 4, 86; in Honduras, 6; methods of, 47, 49–50, 153, 166–67, 171–72; Michel Foucault on, 159; and Operação Bandeirantes (OBAN), 152–

53; during Operação Limpeza, 122;
training to withstand, 135
Truman, Harry S., 69, 74, 77, 94
Truman Doctrine, 72, 75
Tse-tung, Mao, 77
Tupamaro urban guerrillas, 135, 190
Turma de Pesada, 97

Ubico, Jorge, 57
Union Telefonica, 43
United States Information Agency
(USIA), 80–83, 85
United States: domestic security, 58;
foreign policy, 25; law enforcement
methods of, 50–51; monitoring of
Latin America, 57–58; occupation
of Haiti, 28; training of Latin Amer-
ican military in, 58
United States Legation Guard, 31
University of Brasília, 146
University of Southern California,
87–88
Uriburu, José, 42
U.S. Drug Enforcement Administra-
tion (DEA), 2
U.S. economic aid, 74
U.S.-Japan peace treaty, 72
U.S. military, xi; and Central Intel-
ligence Agency, 1; domestic sur-
veillance operations of, 193;
indigenous defense system, 79; oc-
cupation forces, 72; with United
Nations forces, 1; post–World
War II intelligence role, 69
U.S. Military Assistance Program, 93
U.S. Standard Electric Company, 43
Ustra, Carlos Brilhante, 158, 163,
166

Valentine, Lewis J., 72
Valorization, 209 chap. 2 n.1
Vanguarda Popular Revolucionária
(VPR), 178
Vargas, Getúlio, 42–45, 52, 57, 67
Venezuela, 112–13
Vietnam, 79, 88, 104, 127, 151
Vigilantism, 21–22, 98
Village Voice, 194
Volta Redondo steel complex, 143
Voluntary Public Defenders Commit-
tee, 50
Voto Nulo, 129

Wanted lists, 145–46
War Department (U.S.), ix, 26, 31
Washington Post (newspaper): article
about torture of subversives, 187
Watergate, 194
Weapons, 90; for Nicaraguan contras,
195–96; training in IPA schools,
110; U.S. expenditures on OPS
training programs, 193. *See also* In-
ternational Police Services, Inc.
(INPOLSE); Operations Coordi-
nating Board; Police matériel
Weatherwax, Phillip, 124
Weber, Max, 173
Welles, Sumner, 56, 62
White slavery, 55
Who's Who in the CIA, 124
Wickersham Commission, 50
Wilson, Woodrow, 25
Wiretaps, 89
World War II, 3, 23–24, 57–58
Wright, Jaime, 166

Xanthaky, Theodore, 46

Martha K. Huggins is Roger Thayer Stone Professor
of Sociology at Union College and author of *Vigilantism
and the State in Modern Latin America* and *From Slavery
to Vagrancy in Brazil*.

Library of Congress Cataloging-in-Publication Data

Huggins, Martha.
Political policing : the United States and Latin America / Martha K. Huggins.
p. cm.
Includes bibliographical references (p.   ) and index.
ISBN 0-8223-2159-9 (cloth : alk. paper).
ISBN 0-8223-2172-6 (pbk. : alk. paper)
    1. Police—Latin America—International cooperation.   2. Police training—Latin
America—International cooperation.   3. Technical assistance, American—Latin
America.   4. United States—Foreign relations—Latin America.   5. Latin America—
Foreign relations—United States.   I. Title.
HV8160.A2I I84 998
363.2'0973—dc21   97-52378